# The Emerging Professional Counselor

## Student Dreams to Professional Realities

Second Edition

by
Richard J. Hazler
Jeffrey A. Kottler

AMERICAN COUNSELING ASSOCIATION
5999 Stevenson Avenue
Alexandria, VA 22304
www.counseling.org

The
# Emerging
# Professional Counselor

## Student Dreams
## to Professional Realities

Second Edition

10   9   8   7   6   5   4   3   2   1

**American Counseling Association**
5999 Stevenson Avenue
Alexandria, VA 22304

**Director of Publications**
Carolyn C. Baker

**Production Manager**
Bonny E. Gaston

**Copy Editor**
Lucy Blanton

**Type and cover design** by Bonny E. Gaston

**Library of Congress Cataloging-in-Publication Data**
Hazler, Richard J.
    The emerging professional counselor : student dreams to professional realities, second edition / by Richard J. Hazler, Jeffrey A. Kottler.—2nd ed.
        p.    cm.
    1. Counseling—Vocational guidance.  2. Counselors—Training of.
I. Kottler, Jeffrey A.   II. Title.

BF637.C6H368 2005
361'.06'02373—dc22        2004025401

# Dedication

- To counseling students who are seeking growth

- To counselor educators who treat their students as human beings first and as students a distant second

# Table of Contents

# About the Authors

Richard J. Hazler is a professor of counselor education at Pennsylvania State University in University Park. He did counseling graduate work at Trenton State College (now the College of New Jersey), and earned his doctorate at the University of Idaho. Richard has been a counselor educator for 25 years and previously worked as a sixth-grade school teacher and as a counselor in the Army, a prison, private practice, and all levels of the public schools. He has developed a variety of programs, including ones for gifted children, at-risk college students, and graduate students.

Richard has spent a large part of his counselor educator career working to support the needs and encourage the efforts of graduate students. He has chaired the ACA Graduate Student Committee for several years, done research on graduate students, and initiated and continues to edit the *Counseling Today* column "Student Focus" and the *EXEMPLAR* column "Student Insights." Richard is also the author of numerous professional articles and books, and has been an editor of the *Journal of Humanistic Education and Development*. His active involvement in the profession has included service as president of state counseling associations in Kentucky and Ohio, national president of the Association for Humanistic Education and Development, president of Chi Sigma Iota, and chair of numerous state and national committees.

❖ ❖ ❖

Jeffrey A. Kottler is professor and chair of the Counseling Department at California State University, Fullerton. He received his master's degree from Wayne State University and his doctorate from the University of Virginia. Jeffrey has worked as a counselor in a variety of settings, including schools, hospitals, mental health centers, clinics, universities, and corporations, and in private practice. He has been a Fulbright Scholar in Peru and Iceland, and has taught counseling in many parts of the world including Australia, Nepal, New Zealand, Singapore, Thailand, and Venezuela.

Jeffrey is the author or coauthor of over 55 books, some of which have been translated into over a dozen languages. His most recent works include *Making Changes Last, Doing Good, Doing Better, On Being a Therapist, The Mummy at the Dining Room Table, American Shaman, Bad Therapy*, and *Counselors Finding Their Way*.

# Acknowledgments

Yvonnea (Vonnie) Bittikofer played an important part when she volunteered to draft focus activities for the first edition of this book and was continually ready to offer quality opinions on our ideas. She did that as a graduate student while carrying an associateship, taking on extra teaching opportunities, carrying a full doctoral course load, developing a dissertation proposal, being a wife, and preparing for a move to a new job in a new area. This would have overwhelmed most people; not Vonnie. She found time in her schedule simply because she believed the book was a good thing. Many of these same qualities and abilities make her the outstanding practitioner and supervisor she is today.

Thanks go to the many students who provided the content and emotional support that pushed us to write the first edition of this book. Dianne Albright, Ruth Barry, Yvonnea (Vonnie) Bittikofer, Betsy Bryan, Linda Carter, Dr. Brenda Fling, Bob Long, and Dr. Barbara Smith deserve special mention because they were the students at Ohio University who helped write the ACA pamphlet *A Guide for Your Journey Through Graduate School*, which was a forerunner to this book.

Nearing graduation in 1979, Brent Snow and Richard Hazler agreed to develop a program for a national convention simply for graduate students and about the graduate student experience. The idea did not sound professional enough to be accepted, but the two new graduates felt sure it was necessary, based on their experiences. Brent Snow, Richard Hazler, and Jeffrey Kottler have put on that program and others like it many times since. The emphasis is always on the human dimensions of students, counselors, and clients. Brent Snow deserves special recognition for his role in the inception of these ideas and for his continuous personalized work with students.

# Preface:
# Making This Book Work for You

*I want to be a counselor and I'm willing to work hard to get there . . . But . . . Can I learn all that I need to learn in the ways I am asked to do it? Can I financially, emotionally, and socially afford to get through graduate school? Have I got what it takes to help others in need? Will I like the work once I finally graduate from a counselor education program? Will my career be personally, professionally, and financially rewarding? Will I be able to put aside the problems of my clients at the end of the day so that my work doesn't consume my personal life?*

❊ ❊ ❊

These questions or related ones are at one time or other on the minds of most counselors-to-be. Unfortunately, crystal balls are not yet part of counselor education training programs, and the emerging professional counselor's view of the future remains more a series of changing questions than of clear-cut answers. This book is designed to provide information on and insight into the process and problems associated with development as a professional counselor. It is designed for those thinking about entering a counselor training program, students in training, and professionals who deal with the instruction or supervision of counselors. It provides information, focus, and support for members of each of these groups as they deal with the myriad technical, ethical, practical, professional, and personal issues that surround the development of effective professional counselors.

This book is based on the studies and personal experiences of the authors and our continuing interactions with clients, students, peers, friends, and family. We emphasize the concept that counselors and counselor trainees are people first and students and professionals second. We recognize that there is no magic, overnight metamorphosis from nonstudent to student to professional. Events like receiving an A or graduating do not cause your anxieties to disappear, allow you to wake up one morning with a full set of perfect skills, or relieve you of such human reactions as jealousy, self-doubt, fallibility, or the need for love and appreciation. All of us, including competent professionals, have weaknesses, problems, strengths, and accomplishments that cause us to experience successes, failures, highs, and lows nearly every day. This book emphasizes these human, student, and professional commonalties. Many others have traveled the road you have chosen. This book offers a map of the development of a counselor and describes the mile markers of the journey.

Information is presented directly and personally—which is the way we believe you must approach many of the key decisions you must make. The chapters lead you from selection of a program to successful transition through the program and then to beginning your first professional counseling position. The information comes straight from our experiences as students, counselors, faculty, and readers, and perhaps most of all, as people who have been close observers of ourselves and others. Each chapter looks at specific issues important in your transition to a professional counselor and offers focus activities to help you continue your growth beyond the text.

The process of becoming a professional counselor generally starts with the recognition of a personal desire to help others struggling through personal or social difficulties. Many times this desire to help is accomplished through marriage, friendship, or volunteer work, but a few people decide they are interested in and committed enough to the helping process that they want to do it professionally. It is at this time that selecting a graduate program leading to professional counselor status becomes the major decision.

## What Each Chapter Offers

Chapter 1 examines the motivations behind the decisions that must be made around attending a graduate program in counseling. It explores the factors involved in choosing a program or, if you are already in a program, the factors that will influence the quality of your experience. Comparing the information to your personal life experiences and individual preferences will help you judge what aspects of a program will facilitate your experience and which ones may produce more problems than benefits.

Once you know what kind of program you want to enter and perhaps what specific schools match you best, the next task is gaining entry into a program. It has been our experience over decades of being counselor educators that most applicants do not show off their qualities and speak to their weaknesses effectively in the admission process. Those who do put their best foot forward in the process often gain admission over others who might be stronger but do not demonstrate it effectively. Chapter 2 provides guidance on understanding the admission process and the ways to go about applying that will increase your chances of acceptance.

Chapter 3 describes the essentials of a quality counselor education program, how it will influence your experience, and the impact on your professional future. Programs differ in many respects, but accrediting bodies and hiring agencies have identified and recognized commonalties. The chapter includes information on these groups, which set licensure and certification requirements, as well as the program ingredients they support. Core content areas and experiential components that are available in the best quality programs are identified and explained. Also discussed are the types of required culminating experiences, such as comprehensive exams and theses.

One of the major decisions once you have begun a counseling program is evaluating what specializations are best for you. The basics of counseling are included in every quality program, but developing a specialization is more the responsibility of the student. Taking actions to identify your specialization early in your program will give you the time you need to set up necessary courses and select the unique experiences that will make you stand out from the crowd as a professional. Chapter 4 identifies the key early specialization decisions that need to be made, and Chapter 5 provides more specifics on how to turn those decisions into positive realities.

You need the support of others close to you in order to get the most out of your program. All too often students perceive that individual energy and concentration are all that is needed to achieve success in a counseling program. Certainly these are essential, but they will not ensure success by themselves. Counseling and counselor training create social and emotional pressures that need to be given immediate attention for the benefit of yourself and those close to you. Chapter 6 offers guidelines on how to get off to a positive physical, social, and emotional start in your program.

People entering counselor education programs have already demonstrated academic skills as undergraduates, but the skills demanded of graduate students are different and produce new challenges. Chapter 7 provides information on the specific strategies that will lead to academic success in a counselor education program.

One set of challenges faced by people in their development as professional counselors is related to the personal development and changes experienced by students. Chapter 8 highlights a number of personal challenges that emerging professionals might like to ignore, but which must be faced if they are to become holistic, effective counselors and persons. Counselors in training often recognize their own problems, but choose to put them aside or hide them while simultaneously learning to help clients bring their problems out into the open for examination and development. Personal issues, a need for approval by others, a tendency toward perfectionism, and recognition of strengths and weaknesses are common problems for clients and the emerging professional alike. These problems often lead to conflicts and burnout that can disrupt both learning and life in potentially disastrous ways. This chapter clarifies how to recognize these problems in yourself and others, and offers methods for approaching the problems in ways that are meaningful and productive for all concerned.

No matter how great the quality of your instructors, texts, and attention to class work, there are always other valuable professional growth experiences available in your counselor training beyond the classroom. These opportunities often make the difference between getting just the required basics and getting an outstanding education supported by your own initiative. The choices of where, when, and how much to supplement formal education must, however, remain primarily with the individual student. Suggestions may be offered by faculty, but supplements to training generally remain voluntary, and their inclusion should be based on the individual student's motivation, needs, and abilities. Chapter 9 surveys a number of the opportunities that successful emerging professionals can use to supplement their formal training and other developmental activities, such as volunteering to help other professionals in their research and service projects, finding and using a mentor, and getting involved in professional organizations. More personalized actions to strengthen and broaden your professional development are also discussed, such as being a client, keeping a journal, reading novels, and exploring different cultures.

A counselor education training program emphasizes growth, skill development, and learning, all of which are designed to prepare you for finding appropriate work once you leave school. Counseling students must first clarify what work settings they are specifically seeking and identify professional opportunities that match their needs. Chapter 10 provides strategies for successfully initiating and accomplishing these tasks, such as interviewing people in your ideal job, attending conferences, networking, subscribing to professional publications, being geographically mobile, volunteering, and reframing rejection. This chapter also offers suggestions on how to present your best professional self on paper and in person so that you have the best possible chance for eventual satisfactory employment.

The master's degree is generally considered the entry-level professional degree for professional counselors, and therefore, most discussion of training programs centers on this level. However, all counselors either before, during, or after their master's degree work ask themselves what the advantages of a doctoral degree might be and whether it is a viable option in their specific situations. There are a variety of well-founded and also unfounded anxieties that people have about such a step. Chapter 11 calls attention to both types of anxieties, shows the reader how to tell the difference between them, and offers methods for dealing with them productively. This chapter also discusses the advantages and disadvantages of such a step and outlines the general process and requirements of the doctoral program. Particular attention is paid to some of the most anxiety-producing aspects of doctoral programs, including how to select a program, get admitted, find success in statistics, and complete a dissertation.

Emerging professional counselors in training hold tightly to their dreams of eventually graduating and being employed, professionally stable, and successful. These dreams can certainly become realities, but around the time of graduation the realities of making the transition to professional counselor become more pressing and bring new sets of concerns. Chapter 12 explores these concerns that are manageable if recognized early and dealt with realistically and professionally. The chapter helps you prepare for meeting your personal and professional needs, including what differences and self-directive actions you need to consider, how to recruit a new mentor, and how to adjust to the realities of everyday practice as well as deal with organizational politics and with a new level of immediacy in legal and ethical concerns.

Reading this preface and considering the topics in the table of contents may well lead you to feelings that combine both excitement and anxiety about the process of becoming a counseling professional. That is probably as it should be because those things that are most exciting generally come with a significant degree of risk. Certainly that has been our experience as we have traveled the road from low-average students, to counselors, to faculty and writers. We have had and continue to have the feelings of boredom, fear, and anxiety about our potential failures. However, the feelings of excitement, hope, expectation, satisfaction, and just plain joy at doing things that are useful to ourselves and others keep us moving forward. Our emergence as professionals has not been smooth, and we have paid close attention to the bumps experienced by ourselves and others along the way. It is our hope that you will be able to identify with our feelings and the common ups and downs of the process. The information offered here should help you to better understand and deal with these ups and downs in your own development as a professional.

## Getting Focused

This book was written to assist you in planning and exploring issues at each stage of your journey. We hope you are as excited about reading this text as we were writing it. Your excitement, however, may be coupled with anxiety as you explore the numerous issues we discuss in this book. Keep in mind that you will not deal with these issues simultaneously but experience them at different stages throughout your career as a graduate student and professional counselor. You may read it in its entirety prior to making your decision to become a counselor, or you may want to use it as a frequent reference to assist you in your progress through the counseling field.

Note that each chapter addresses a unique theme and the many issues surrounding it. Also note that specific activities and suggestions are offered at the conclusion of each chapter to help you focus on the specific issues, facilitate understanding of the material, and direct you in ways to help make your own decisions about how to best use the information. We suggest purchasing a notebook to record what you learn about the issues involved and about yourself and your development. This way you will have a record of your development that will help you in making the best possible professional decisions and in planning for the future.

# 1

# The Graduate Program That Fits You

It was not all high-quality planning and foresight that got us through our training as counselors. Happenstance, luck, and blundering played significant roles. Even the decision to begin graduate school was less intentional than we might prefer to admit. Like so many important transitions in life, our emergence as professional counselors became a series of serendipitous events. People influenced us often in contradictory ways. We selected courses because of scheduling conveniences, and sometimes simply took the path of least resistance.

Our training came before accreditation, before standardized programs, even before comprehensive curricula. Yours doesn't. You cannot count on serendipity. Today we know from our experiences and studies as counseling professionals and counselor educators that you, as a newcomer, will make more effective choices and be better off professionally if you can develop honest answers to the questions that are the focus of this chapter:

1. Will the counseling profession make a good fit with you and your lifestyle?
2. What factors ought to be considered when choosing a graduate program?
3. What type of graduate training is most likely to meet your needs?
4. What will help you get into the program you choose?

Perhaps you are already in a program, and the issues of choosing one seems to come a little late in your progression toward being a professional counselor. Well, there is more to this selection process than you might imagine. The more you know about yourself, and the program you select, the better you will be able to adjust to the inevitable challenges you will face. Remember that you are a *developing* professional. You have not reached your zenith yet, and when you think you have gotten there, some additional growth spurt frequently seems to pop up.

## Personal Motives and Professional Aspirations

You are considering counseling as a career for a number of reasons, some of which are universal and others are perhaps unique to your life situation. You are aware of many of these as a part of your personal agenda, but others are hidden from view and may only emerge years in the future. Among the most common reasons given by professionals in the field for entering the profession are the following:

- "I believe we all have a moral obligation to help others less fortunate than ourselves in any way we can. Being a counselor is a way that I can be useful to people."
- "I was helped by a counselor once. I really admired her and the work she was doing. I wanted to be just like her."
- "I was tired of being in the classroom, and I did not want to be a principal."
- "I couldn't get into medical school. This represented another way that I could help people."
- "I'm kind of nosy, I guess. I like learning about other people's lives and having access to a world that is hidden from everyone else."
- "It's an honorable profession. For thousands of years certain elders or healers have been sanctioned by their societies to provide comfort, support, and advice. I like the idea of that kind of role."
- "I have had my own troubles over the years. Learning to be a counselor was one way I tried to keep a lid on my own sense of powerlessness. In a way, I have a better perspective on myself when I see the problems of other people."
- "I enjoy close relationships and working with people. Counseling provides a kind of controlled intimacy. I feel close to my clients, and I like knowing that I have a positive impact on their lives."
- "People have always come to me for help. I thought that I might as well get paid for it. Sometimes I can't believe this is a job since I get so much from it."

Evident in these disclosures is that altruism is tempered with intensely personal motives in choosing counseling as a career. The feelings of power and control, as well as the opportunities to work through one's own issues, are among the most frequently cited reasons. These underlying reasons mean that the counseling professional can be a source of tremendous satisfaction; but they can also become major blocks to professional effectiveness. You can even do great harm to others if you meet your own needs, or act out your own unresolved issues, during sessions. It is for this reason that quality counselor training programs offer components that emphasize personal development as well as skill and knowledge acquisition.

## Program Factors to Consider

Accountability movements within the profession, and an increasing consensus among researchers and practitioners regarding appropriate standards of behavior, have led to greater commonality in programs. However, there is still considerable variation among graduate programs as to their faculty, philosophy, student and idea diversity, and specialty areas. These factors, as well as training levels, accreditation, and location and class times (both of which reflect focus on full-time versus part-time students), need to be considered.

## *Faculty*

You may find significant differences between publicly espoused objectives and actual policies as they are implemented daily within programs. Two of the best ways to uncover these differences are to look at how well faculty work together as a unit and as colleagues, and at their time availability. Another is to look at racial, gender, and ethnic diversity reflected in their cultural backgrounds and the gender balance of the faculty. Yet another is to look at their diversity in approach and style that you can find in their theoretical orientations, clinical experiences, teaching methods, and personalities.

### *How Faculty Work Together*

Some programs have faculty who are cooperative, supportive, and respectful of one another, making it safe for students to find their own paths to learning. Other programs can have faculty who are unduly competitive, threatened, or constantly perturbed by each other or the system. Students can sometimes get caught in the middle of these struggles. This is, of course, not a phenomenon unique to academia: all human organizations spark similar political struggles for power and control as individuals and groups try to promote the goals and methods they believe are the best.

Remember that faculty are human beings like you before they are professionals. They have self-doubts and anxieties, and get angry just like any other person. They work hard to live up to the professional status they are accorded based on their accomplishments, but even that carries personal baggage. Making mistakes and learning from them is expected when, as students, you are new and relatively unaccomplished in a field. Faculty members, as well, struggle to maintain success in the face of pressures from multiple sources. It is like getting all A's in your first semester of courses and then feeling the need to continuously live up to, or surpass, those accomplishments. We are not making excuses for particular instructors who may appear unjust or insensitive; we just wish you to understand the context for their behavior.

The issue is not whether conflict and competition exist in a particular department, which in itself may be quite constructive. Rather, it is a question of the ways faculty disagree with one another. Are they respectful toward each other? What have you heard about the ways instructors support or sabotage one another? Do they avoid embroiling students in their skirmishes? Does there seem to be a general feeling of cooperation and consensus in the department regarding the primary mission of training students? Are they forgiving of other faculty and student misjudgments, mistakes, and threat-promoted behaviors?

The answers to these questions can be found by speaking to other students about how well they perceive faculty are getting along, how disagreements are handled, and how conflicts are managed. Expect a reasonable amount of intellectual strife. Professors are, by their nature and training, an argumentative lot who enjoy a certain degree of debate and controversy. That is, after all, one way that growth and change take place. By arguing our positions, lobbying for what we believe in, and standing up for our ideals and standards, we are able to continuously refine and evolve our ideas. This can produce a vigorous program that is on the cutting edge of the profession. The unhappy alternative, however, takes place when professionals become rigid and intolerant of those different from themselves. Those are the conditions most likely to lead to ongoing petty skirmishes and outright war that can impact students as well as faculty.

The strength of a faculty is based on much more than how well they get along, however. Other things to look for, as described in the following sections, include time availability; racial, gender, and ethnic diversity; and approach and style diversity.

### Time Availability

Walk down the hall during several afternoons (graduate classes are often offered in the evenings). Who is available? Are students around who are interested in talking to, and working with, their instructors? Are faculty around who are interested in talking to their students?

Different expectations are placed on faculty, depending on the norms and mission of their institutions. Some programs find faculty constantly in their offices working on their research projects, advising students, serving on committee assignments, and generally available and interested in talking with students. Other norms exist, however, in which some professors may often not be around because of other professional commitments. Who is available when needed is one barometer for assessing the commitment of faculty to students.

You are not an undergraduate any more. Just going to classes and doing the assignments will no longer get you all the results you want from this degree. Classes are smaller so that you can enjoy more individual attention, both in class and more informal settings. The more time faculty have available for you, and the more use you make of that time, the better will be your experience.

### Racial, Gender, and Ethnic Diversity

Does there seem to be a mix of instructors who exhibit, by their cultural differences, a priority to infuse multicultural awareness and sensitivity into the program? The mandate of our profession is to reach out to those who need our services the most: the disadvantaged and those who are not part of the power base that controls things. One of the ways we help prepare counselors to work with people of diverse cultures, religions, and ethnic and racial backgrounds is to provide models of successful professionals representing diverse cultures.

Seeing faculty members who are mixed in gender and color is a visible sign that diversity is present and appreciated, but it does not tell the whole story. Gender preferences, cultural heritages, religious convictions, and significant experiences with a variety of diverse populations have great importance, but are much less easily recognized. This mixture serves to promote actions that encourage maximum growth and development in the widest variety of people. Such an environment is good for challenging students, bringing out their best, and maximizing their multicultural counseling potentials.

You will notice that in almost every text you read, every ethical code, and almost every issue of a journal or professional newsletter, there is a strong statement somewhere about the commitment made to diversity issues. If this is not just lip service given to a politically correct position, then you will see this important value manifested not only in talk but also in action. Although you cannot tell from the color of people's skin, their accent, or other such obvious features, whether they have a commitment to counteracting racism, discrimination, and marginalization of oppressed people, at least some diversity in backgrounds is important to demonstrate followthrough on espoused values.

*Approach and Style Diversity*
The best way to do counseling, and the best way to develop counselors, has been endlessly and heatedly debated. It is generally agreed, however, that it is advisable to be exposed to many theoretical approaches and teaching styles during your tenure as a student. By learning in a variety of educational settings such as content focused, experientially based, interactive, introspective, supportive, controversial, informal, and highly structured, you can select those features that best fit your personality, career goals, and preferences. Such a variety will also help you see your strengths and weaknesses, and how you are different from others. No two students or clients are the same, and the more you understand the differences among people, and between others and yourself, the better able you will be to help people. This exposure to many different models also better prepares you for the wide variety of employment, organization, and peer styles that will present themselves after graduation.

Exposure to academic diversity can also be quite confusing and stressful if faculty attempt to recruit you to their camp while demeaning what others are doing. You must not only be exposed to differences in helping approaches, but also be helped to reconcile discrepancies and integrate aspects of the many features into your own style. There are, thus, two features of diversity as applied to your learning environment. First, it is interesting to be introduced to many different viewpoints in the journey to find your own way. Second, it is confusing to be offered so many apparent differences of opinion. For this reason, it is critical that faculty value one another's differences and engage in respectful dialogue with one another, and with you, in sorting out such differences.

Faculty diversities include those in

- **pedagogical methods:** lectures, discussions, work groups, field studies;

- **evaluation criteria and course requirements:** papers, take-home exams, objective exams, group presentations;
- **class atmosphere:** formal, relaxed, permissive, structured;
- **program tracks:** rehabilitation, school, mental health, community agency, marriage and family;
- **specialty areas:** appraisal, group work, computer-assisted guidance, early childhood intervention, substance abuse, older persons;
- **theoretical orientations:** existential, behavioral, cognitive, gestalt, psychodynamic, constructivist; and
- **personality:** intense, gregarious, demanding, flexible.

Each of these dimensions rarely occurs in pure form in any one faculty member because most of us make attempts to adapt what we do according to the situation. Nevertheless, most counselor educators can, and should, articulate a set of beliefs about which they feel most passionate. Likewise, with some systematic observation, you should also be able to identify a consistent style with which each faculty member prefers to operate. It is through this observation and interaction that you will find yourself being more comfortable with certain faculty and less comfortable with others. Just don't get too comfortable! Remember you are in the program to better understand yourself and diversities in people, and to be productively flexible with that increased knowledge. You need to seek and accept the challenges of working with faculty who are different than yourself in order to maximize your growth.

### *Philosophy*

Training programs were once easily identifiable as subscribing to the tenets of a single theoretical base such as psychoanalytic, humanistic, or behavioral. It is now rare to find allegiance among all staff members to a particular counseling approach; but even when there is a consensus, methods of instruction among faculty are likely to be more different than similar. One of the joys of the profession is that each of us is permitted to discover ways of helping others that also fit us best, as long as we maintain ethical and competence standards established by our peers—and remain responsive to client needs.

In spite of the variations in methods of instruction, approaches to counseling, and even personality styles of faculty, many departments do espouse a particular philosophy of counselor education. This mission statement may be simply the requirement of an accreditation standard, or in many cases, it represents a well-thought-out summary of what the program intends to do and how these goals are to be carried out.

The best way to quickly explore the philosophy of a program and its faculty is to look up the stated philosophy and goals on printed materials or the Web, get a sense of what they mean to you, and then discuss them with faculty. Questions for you to consider include

- How well does the stated mission match with your own goals?

- What do you know about your learning style?
- Do faculty comments on the philosophy and goals clarify how you would see them applied as a student?

Consider, for example, two distinctly different program types as outlined in Table 1. Both are legitimate ways of training counselors. In fact, research suggests variables included in each of these programs are important in learning to be a counselor.

Few programs are as pure as those described in the table, however. The emphasis today is on integration and synthesis of theories and practice. The best features of competency- and experience-based approaches are combined into programs that include

- content and information acquisition;
- skill development through systematic modeling and supervision;
- process interaction in small groups;
- emotional/personal development through group and self-reflective assignments;
- evolution of a personal style of practice through supervised experience; and
- refinement of counseling interventions through feedback on videotapes.

Every program emphasizes some of these ingredients over others. Decide which ones are most appealing to you or, better yet, which ones are likely to be most helpful to you in your emergence as a professional counselor. Your learning style, values, experiences, goals, personal needs, and levels of development all affect how well a given model will work for you.

### Diversity of Students and Ideas

Training to be a counselor involves more than learning a new set of skills and knowledge. You will also be asked to explore your personal thoughts, feelings, and behaviors at the same time that you are learning how important it is to recognize these in the people you are helping. Your ability to recognize, understand, and effectively utilize the interaction between the client's uniqueness and your own is a critical factor in becoming a success-

• Table 1 •
#### Polarities in Counselor Training

| Competency Based | Experience Based |
| --- | --- |
| • Emphasis on courses | • Emphasis on learning experiences |
| • Emphasis on content and skill development | • Emphasis on process and on moral and emotional development |
| • Lecture and discussion | • Interaction and group experience, and self-reflective activities |
| • Evaluation by examination | |
| • Reliance on the technology of systematic instruction | • Self-evaluation and by writing papers |
| | • Reliance on the human dimension |

ful counselor. For this reason, it is important to have diversity not only among your faculty but also among your fellow students.

Consider the development of Derrick Paladino (2002) and his description of how his experiences in a counselor training program changed his perceptions of himself as a biracial person.

> My relation to and concept of my ethnicity and identify development is currently a strong one, but through most of my graduate studies, it was vague and got little attention. I had tunnel vision. But things changed as the training and experiences with other people began calling attention to my ethnic identity development and the impact of ethnicity as I grew through new experiences. (p. 26)
>
> I revisited moments from my past, entered discussions with peers, and brought up my new topical interest to my professor. A growing awareness began extending to other areas of my life including clinical work. . . . I broached the subject in my supervisor's office one day. I told her, "I just realized I'm biracial." This was the first time I said it to someone other than the safe relationship of a peer, but certainly not the last, nor the most powerful. She offered support and understanding as we discussed her personal experience with a family member growing up biracial. (p. 30)

Derrick was fortunate in finding a program in which he could test his developing racial identity out with others. It is not an easy road to travel, but it is one that can bring critically productive growth to developing counselors.

Diversity of people in programs does not just relate to race or ethnicity. It can include mixtures of genders, sexual orientation, and even religion. Jake Protivnak (2003) told of how his program had promoted his growth in the ability to challenge his long-held beliefs.

> My background was similar to that of most kids, except for being raised in a family that belonged to a separatist religious sect. Conformity was the key to being a good member and receiving the positive rewards of membership in the organization.
>
> Reflecting on the religious beliefs that my family provided for me as a child, I recognized the need to change my world view and personal beliefs. Questioning the dogmatic beliefs of my religion brought me to the conclusion that my life was incongruent with other information I was acquiring. Being curious helped me develop as a person, and I believe the same curiosity can help students become better counselors. (p. 33)

It is not just information and skills that you need to become an effective professional counselor. You need to learn and explore yourself just as you will ask clients to do. The program of choice should be one that offers enough diversity of people, ideas, and experiences to give you multiple views of the world and how you can and do relate to them.

### Specialty Areas

One of the keys to securing employment is developing an area of expertise that is both interesting to you and in demand by others. Depending on the needs in your area, there may, for example, be a scarcity of elementary school counselors, certified rehabilitation counselors, substance abuse specialists, student personnel professionals, or marriage and family counselors. There are many other specialties as well, each of which shares common elements yet also has focused expertise to help specific client populations deal with particular issues.

The function of program specialization is to compensate for the increasingly complex circumstances in which counselors are asked to work. Like professionals in medicine or law, counseling professionals are presented with requests for services that require a high degree of competence or expertise in a particular area, whether that is a tropical disease, partnership law, or career decision making. Having specialized training in a given area increases the likelihood that the counselor is sensitive to unique client needs and aware of the most current thinking on dealing with those issues.

All counselors receive exposure to the core knowledge base of our profession, including developmental theory, career development, assessment, multicultural understanding, and individual and group interventions as well as training in the skills of helping. However, most practitioners also choose to concentrate in a particular professional area that requires specialized training.

This choice of a specialty may be based on a deliberate personal decision, for example, on a love of working with young children or older adults. Such a decision may also be based on expediency, such as a surplus of specialized jobs in a given geographic area. Even though you may choose to concentrate in a relatively narrow aspect of helping, you will still be able to market yourself in a number of ways. For example, a student who receives her degree in secondary school counseling while also satisfying the requirements for licensure in her state is not only qualified to work in schools but also to be employed as an expert in adolescent development in community agencies, substance abuse facilities, or private practice.

Most counseling programs emphasize several distinct specialties rather than one general program. Typically, all students take together a core set of courses. These include foundation classes in human development, research methods, assessment techniques, counseling theory, multicultural issues, career development, and other subjects considered to be part of the necessary training for all practitioners, regardless of specialty. Then, depending on such factors as faculty interests and qualifications, program accreditations, the institution's historical precedents, and the area's political climate, particular specialty areas may be developed. Table 2 provides a sample of those specialties and subspecialties, along with their associated employment opportunities.

The specialties are not quite as discrete as they may at first appear. Although it is a good idea to think in terms of one area in which you want to specialize, the different concentrations share a basic set of principles, a common base of knowledge, and a similar collection of skills and interventions. Sometimes the differences between two specialty areas may only be a few courses. Other specialties such as mental health or marriage and family are likely to require additional training beyond the basic degree. For

• Table 2 •

## Sample Program Specialties and Employment Opportunities

| | | |
|---|---|---|
| • School counseling | • Elementary<br>• Secondary | • School counselor<br>• Child intervention specialist<br>• Youth work in residential facility<br>• Parent education<br>• Drug education |
| • Student personnel | • Academic affairs | • College administration<br>• College residential life |
| • College counseling | • Student counseling | • College counseling center |
| • Rehabilitation | • Vocational rehabilitation<br>• Substance abuse | • Private rehabilitation agency<br>• Rehabilitation hospital<br>• Substance abuse clinics<br>• Department of social services |
| • Mental health<br>• Community agency | • Outpatient<br>• Inpatient<br>• Consultation<br>• Supervision<br>• Probation | • Department of mental health<br>• Department of social services<br>• Department of corrections<br>• Employment assistance programs<br>• Private practice group |
| • Marriage and family | • Marriage<br>• Family<br>• Sex counseling | • Private practice<br>• Community agencies<br>• Child abuse<br>• Divorce mediation<br>• Sex education |
| • Pastoral | • Ministerial | • Spiritual and religious organizations<br>• Community agencies<br>• Hospitals |
| • Gerontological | • Grief<br>• Retirement<br>• Hospice | • Hospitals<br>• Community agencies<br>• Hospice homes |
| • Career | • Employment<br>• Career development | • Employment agencies<br>• College career centers |

example, accredited marriage and family counselors in most programs may take a basic 48-semester-hour graduate program and then additional course work in family dynamics, family systems, family interventions, marriage counseling, and sex counseling. Many state counseling licensure programs will require a 60-semester-hour program that includes additional courses emphasizing psychopathology, diagnosis, and other information needed for employment in the community. A similar model holds true for other specialties.

How can you choose the best specialty for you? Several factors should be considered when making a tentative specialty choice:

- additional qualifications (e.g., some states require a teaching certificate for school counseling);
- the population you prefer to work with (young children, adolescents, adults, older adults);
- the job opportunities available in your preferred geographic region;
- the drive and passion you feel toward a particular kind of professional identity;
- the relative strength of the faculty, resources, and support within the various specialties available; and
- the match between your personal strengths and weaknesses and those of a particular specialty (e.g., crisis intervention versus longer term counseling relationships).

One of the best ways to find out what you most enjoy is to talk to as many counselors in the field as possible. Visit as many different settings as you can. This should include those related to your anticipated specialty and also others that may help you to explore additional options.

### Training Levels: Master's and Doctoral

The master's degree in counselor education is now considered the entry-level preparation for qualification as a professional practitioner. There was a time when a bachelor's degree in social work, psychology, or human services was considered sufficient to secure a job in the field (and still is in some rural areas), but today most professional positions in schools and agencies require a master's degree as a minimal credential. The master's degree is, in fact, the foundation for national certification or state licensure as a counselor.

Master's-level training is essentially a counseling practitioner's degree that qualifies you to apply the skills of assessment and clinical intervention in various settings (schools, agencies, universities, private practice) and with different modalities (individual, group, and family counseling). It is the degree that allows you to perform these services under supervision in nearly all states. Once you have gained the 2 to 3 years of post-master's-degree experience required by most states, you are then allowed to practice without supervision and usually also carry the qualification to supervise others.

The past 30 years have seen the importance of the master's degree in counseling grow tremendously in terms of public and legislative acceptance of what graduates can be expected to do professionally. Schools, agencies, and private practices recognize the importance of this degree, and what professional counselors can do, so that both responsibilities and pay for services have increased substantially. Another result for the master's degree student is that course work to meet these heightened expectations and rewards has also grown substantially. Programs that were once a year in length now require a minimum of 2 years of full-time study (48 to 60 semester hours) or its equivalent (3 to 5 years part time).

Because the master's degree in counselor education produces practicing professional counselors who can also go on to be supervisors, the doctoral degree emphasizes other knowledge and skills. The result is that doctoral training in counselor education places as much or more emphasis on research, supervision, and teaching as it does practice. This degree is intended to prepare professionals to function independently as scholars, educators, and consultants as well as to develop advanced practitioner and supervisor skills. The additional 3 to 5 years spent in school are intended to help students master the knowledge, research, and skill base of the field so that they can go beyond being good counselors by adding new knowledge to the field of counseling and expanding the skills of other counselors. Doctoral specialty areas are generally designed to meet individual student career aspirations that may include being a consultant, administrator, supervisor, researcher, or counselor educator.

Because of the variety of specific doctoral degrees in the counselor education and counseling psychology fields, choosing to go for a doctorate is not as simple a decision as it sounds. There are different degree areas (such as counselor education, counseling psychology, clinical psychology), specializations (such as mental health, school, business and industry, rehabilitation), and degree designations (such as PhD, EdD, PsyD) that each serve to confuse the issues. However, these differences also serve the purpose of helping you select the program and career path that best matches you. Chapter 11 provides more specific information on these issues, the decisions involved, and the potential outcomes.

### Accreditation

The program selection factors described in the preceding section are also the foundation of the program accreditation movement in counseling. Program accreditation, which is discussed more thoroughly in chapter 3, is a means of assuring students, potential students, consumers, and clients of students that programs meet professionally accepted minimum standards of training. For example, accreditation standards emphasize maximum student-to-faculty ratios so that students will get a reasonable degree of personalized attention. They also identify critical content and experiential components that must be in place to ensure the knowledge base and competencies of graduates.

The Council for Accreditation of Counseling and Related Educational Programs (CACREP) is the primary accrediting body designed specifically for counseling programs. Similar recognized bodies are the American Psychological Association (APA) for psychologists, the American Association for Marriage and Family Therapy (AAMFT) for family counselors, and the Council on Rehabilitation Education (CORE) for rehabilitation counselors. Graduating from an appropriately accredited program assures employers and students that both the university's standards and the reputation of the associated national organization are fully supportive of the quality of the graduates' educational experience.

Earning accreditation, and maintaining it, is expensive and time consuming for programs, so institutions take this process very seriously. Accreditation is regularly publicized in fliers and handouts. Knowledgeable and committed applicants are the ones who understand enough about the program they are considering to be able to recognize the importance of accreditation in discussions with faculty. Nonaccredited programs are likely to have given extensive consideration to becoming accredited, but for a number of reasons (e.g., unable or unwilling to meet the standards, preference to function independently), they have elected not to follow through with the process. These institutions, as well, appreciate the prospective student who knows enough about the issues to be able to ask intelligent questions about why accreditation was not pursued.

## Location

It is perhaps unfortunate that the single most important reason considered by prospective students in choosing a graduate program is the pragmatic issue of geographical proximity of the institution. We do not wish to demean the practical realities that are involved in attending graduate school. Many counseling students must juggle families, employment, leisure pursuits, and friends with their education. They make significant financial sacrifices and major time commitments. Obviously, it is often easier to attend a school that is closer to home. But the program may not fit your needs or style, and you can end up with preparation that does not equip you with the necessary skills, expertise, and job opportunities that you want. Attending a particular institution simply because it is nearby should not be the only consideration.

## Class Times

When classes are offered may not sound like much of an issue, but it can have a significant effect on how much you can make of your program. Will you want to work full time or part time while attending the program you choose? Do you have children that you need to care for during the day or in the evenings? Your answers to questions like these can make a big difference in how or even whether you can attend a particular program.

The majority of master's degree programs arrange courses in the late afternoon and evening for a couple of reasons. Most of these programs offer relatively few scholarships or student work opportunities, and so the majority of students need employment to support their education. These programs attract people like teachers, social workers, and case managers who are seeking to improve their professional positions as well as students who can find day jobs to support themselves. Schools serving these types of individuals most often provide courses in the late afternoon and evening when the potential for students to attend is greatly increased. Other programs go a step further and offer some courses on weekends or on-line to help people fit the program into busy lives.

Doctoral programs and master's degree programs at large universities are the most likely to offer more traditional day classes. These types of programs are seeking people who can work on the program full time, and they generally have more sources of funding available for students in the way of scholarships and graduate student work. They tend to be less accessible to part-time students or those with full-time day employment, but are more appropriate for the students who are able to give all their energies to their training.

## Focus Activities: Making Personal Use of This Chapter

This chapter focuses on choosing a graduate program. Several key factors are mentioned as considerations in selecting a good match for your needs. They include exploring your personal motives and professional aspirations as well as considering faculty and program characteristics. The following questions and activities should help you to relate the issues in this chapter to your personal interests and unique situation. They should also help you in deciding whether counseling is truly for you and in narrowing your choice of counselor education programs.

### *Exploring Your Personal Motives and Professional Aspirations*

1. **List your personal motives for becoming a counselor.** Which of these intentions seem productive and which might be inappropriate or possibly detrimental to future clients or to your ability to function as a counselor? A good way to judge them is to think about which ones you would be willing to share with faculty at an interview and which ones you would want no one to know.
2. **List your ideas of your personal strengths and weaknesses related to becoming a counselor.** How could they help or hinder your ability to complete a counselor training program and perform effectively as a counselor? Which ones will you need to work on more and which ones less?
3. **List the personal and professional goals you have set for yourself.** Is completion of a graduate program necessary for attainment of these goals? What factors do you feel are necessary in achieving your goals?
4. **List your interests in specific kinds of counseling or working with a specific population** (e.g., chemical dependency counseling, counseling children). How might these relate to your choice of program? As you think about possible specializations consider

- **your qualifications:** What are you qualified for now and what do you need to do in order to become qualified for your desired position?
- **job opportunities:** Are there options available where you live or where you would like to live?
- **your strengths and weaknesses:** Are your strengths and weaknesses positive or negative factors that could impact treating a specific population?
- **your reasoning:** What are the personal and practical considerations (e.g., money, location) that most impact your decisions? Reevaluate your reasoning to ensure that you are specializing in something for the right reasons.

5. **Contact three or more counselors in your area and interview them.** Ask about qualifications, responsibilities, and pros and cons of their work. This will enable you to get more information about different areas of counseling and help you pinpoint your interests. Get the phone book, look under counseling or social/human service agencies, and call and ask for an interview. Most agencies are very receptive and enjoy sharing about themselves, their work, and their experiences on the job.
6. **When you contact agencies, ask about opportunities for doing volunteer work.** This will allow you to get experience necessary for admission into many graduate programs while further helping you to clarify those areas that interest you and those that do not.
7. **List your personal and professional needs and expectations.** These must be kept in mind so that the choices you make can be measured against your hopes and plans for yourself.

## Considerations of Faculty and Program Characteristics

1. **What are your personal and professional needs and expectations of a graduate program** (e.g., program curriculum, program orientation and philosophy, faculty interests and composition, financial resources, time commitments, opportunities for professional leadership)?
2. **Identify programs that appear to match your needs and expectations.** Go to the Internet, library, or career placement center at a nearby college. Locate graduate college catalogs, and choose those universities that appear to meet your needs. Write or contact each program for additional information, brochures, and applications.
3. **Contact the handful of departments that interest you most.** Request the following if they are not on the program's Web site:

    - *statement of program policies and procedures,*
    - *statement of program orientation and philosophy,* and
    - *information on faculty* (so that you may choose those programs that have faculty who may best meet your needs and interests).

4. **Consider your learning style.** Do you prefer more didactic training or experiential learning? Although most programs integrate the two, check to see whether they are more knowledge based or more experientially based. Try to find out which programs might best match your learning style.

5. **Speak with a faculty member and student from the programs that interest you most.** Ask each about the program, courses offered, philosophy, policies and procedures, how faculty and students get along, professional leadership activities available, and the area and what it offers in terms of social activities. This will allow you to get several human responses to your questions and a more personal feel for the program and whether or not it is right for you.

# 2

# Getting Accepted Into a Program

The process of deciding (or redeciding) what program feels like the right one for you can be exciting and encouraging as you realize the possibilities for your future. Then comes the unpleasant task of putting your personal reputation on the line by actually applying for a program. This stage of asking people to make judgments on your worthiness is one in which many people drop out of the process as their fears get the worst of them. It is an anxiety-provoking professional development stage, but then who ever said that making major professional steps forward were relaxing?

The doubts these students describe may perhaps seem a familiar to you:

- "For years I dreamed about being a counselor, but the programs and requirements always scared me away. I was sure I wasn't smart enough to measure up."
- "What if I don't score well on the admissions tests? How will I ever face my husband, children, or myself? I'm doing all right the way I am, so why should I put myself through that?"
- "I had a master's degree, good job as a counselor, and was respected by clients and colleagues. The thought of trying to get into a doctoral program and maybe getting rejected was not one I wanted others to know. So I put it off for years, saw others go on to do it, and finally decided I'd had enough. If people could do it who didn't know as much as me, had less experience, and were not respected like I was, then surely these programs would want a person like me!"
- "I only had a bachelor's degree, but I worked in children's services where people would give me good recommendations. But my writing wasn't great and I never was a good test taker. I worried and worried about whether my success at working with kids would be something the admission committee thought was important enough to balance some other weaknesses. And then I worried they might accept me and whether I really could do the work. My self-doubt was running all over the place through the whole process."

There is no getting over the anxiety around applying to a master's or doctoral program in counseling. The answer is not to look for ways to avoid the anxiety, but instead to gain enough information and take the appropriate actions that will get you through the anxiety to explore the realities of gaining entrance. In some cases it is a matter of persistence. Even more important is to select a program that best matches your particular qualifications.

## In Competition With Others

Admission to most quality counseling programs is competitive because spaces are limited by the number of faculty in the department. This is most true for those programs accredited by organizations like CACREP and more true for doctoral programs than for master's programs. More information about accredited programs can be found in chapter 3 and at the Web sites listed in Appendix A.

Master's programs are supposed to give more individual attention to students than undergraduate programs, so classes will generally be smaller. In order to accomplish this, fewer students can be admitted. Competition is even more of an issue for doctoral programs for the simple reason that even fewer spaces are available. At this level, students should be expecting to see even smaller classes and work directly on projects with individual faculty. The more individualized attention programs plan to give to students, the fewer students they can admit and the more people will gain nonacceptance notices.

Although the competition for gaining entry into counseling programs is a fact, it is certainly not the whole story. There is a continually growing demand for counselors, particularly at the master's level, which pushes programs to hire more faculty so they can train more students. Some programs fill their spaces quickly, but many others continually have openings. The more openings that are available, the less competition there is for those slots, so the chances for gaining admission have been and probably will continue to increase.

Another factor increasing opportunities for admission is that programs emphasize different things. Regional institutions tend to admit more people because their primary focus is to train counselors and only secondarily to do research. Large research institutions, however, generally admit fewer students, because more faculty are involved in major research projects. You can do the numbers and see that the chances of getting admitted to regional institutions are greater than to major research institutions because there are more openings.

The reality of competition for entry into graduate programs is that it may be very great at some institutions but much less at most institutions. People who have strengths in one or more of the key areas of grades, test scores, and experience will be able to be accepted in some programs. The question becomes less one of whether you can get accepted, but of where and when you can get accepted. The task is to match your credentials to the institutions that are seeking people just like yourself.

## Selection Criteria

Most programs consider such criteria as test scores, grade point average, reference letters, autobiographical statements, work experience, and interviews in making admission decisions, although not to the same degree of emphasis. Programs are seeking people with a combination of experience, previous success, and abilities that indicates their potential for success both in the program and as a professional following graduation. One program may decide that test scores get more emphasis while another program's faculty believe that work experience should carry more weight. In the end, each set of program faculty show flexibility in each area to get the mix of traits that seem most important to them.

As an example, Jeffrey and Richard's universities have very different missions, and therefore quite different admission criteria. Because Richard's university places high emphasis on developing major research, prospective students are expected to meet certain academic and experience standards typical of a university that recruits nationally. Jeffrey's university is considered regional in nature. Because most of his students come from marginalized minority groups, and most speak a language other than English at home, tests like the Graduate Record Exam (GRE) are neither required nor appropriate for this population. Instead, primary emphasis is placed on life experience and personal interviews. The main point we wish to make is that universities place different emphases on various factors depending on their mission, their constituency, and their philosophy.

### Test Scores

Usually, the GRE or sometimes the Miller Analogies Test (MAT) is required. These tests give one measure of your abilities that is comparable to the abilities of other people from around the country and the world in ways that grades cannot do because schools differ so much. Sometimes other standardized tests like interest inventories or personality assessments may also be required to gain a better understanding of you as a person. Do not be discouraged if you do not do well on standardized tests. Many programs require a test, but not a minimum score; others allow you to compensate for a low score in one area (quantitative) if you have exceptional strengths in other areas. And as we mentioned earlier, some programs do not require such tests at all.

Preparing for these examinations through self-study programs or formal courses often helps you to raise your performance. Study guides can be found in your campus bookstore. If you are still overly concerned or anxious about your test-taking skills (which are only marginally predictive of your success as a counselor), consider applying to programs that do not emphasize objective tests as a major criterion for admission. Remember, as well, that tests are not a measure of self-worth but rather are considered a limited sample of what you know, and can do.

People who score below minimum test score levels can still be considered for programs. Faculty can, and frequently do, decide to accept students with lower scores when their work experience and other demonstrated abilities seem to fit the program. So a school teacher or case manager who has low test scores, but also has 6 years of directly related experience, excellent references, and good undergraduate grades, might be accepted, whereas a recent college graduate with the same scores and no work experience might not be accepted.

Because test scores can be considered in flexible ways, it is important to check with faculty to see where they place their priorities for admission. This should help you in decisions regarding whether to retake tests or to better spend your time demonstrating other areas of strength.

## Grade Point Average (GPA)

This magic number is another quantitative measure that many programs use as a cutoff point to reduce the number of applicants to manageable proportions. Some schools use total undergraduate GPA; others use undergraduate GPA during the past 2 years or in your major. Doctoral programs expect graduate GPAs to be high, so they generally continue to give weight to undergraduate GPAs as well as any work you may have done in graduate school. Keep in mind that because so many counseling students are adults who may have attended college many years ago, consideration is often given for examining GPA within a historical context. If, for example, 15 years ago you had a GPA of 2.5 in college, but in the last few years you have taken several other courses and received grades of A's and B's, this improvement is often taken into consideration.

If you have taken any graduate-level courses, these grades are also examined. In fact, when applicants are not admitted to a program during their first attempt, they often take courses to demonstrate their ability to complete graduate-level work. Many times faculty will help you identify which courses will carry the most weight in future admissions decisions. Courses in areas in which you have had less success in the past are often the best ones to take because they can show how you have improved, whereas taking courses in areas where you have always done well will not demonstrate your growth. Although this effort will not guarantee you admission the second time around, it certainly strengthens your case.

## Reference Letters

Everybody has good reference letters. After all, you do not ask someone to write you a recommendation unless you are fairly confident that she or he will say something flattering. For a letter to stand out to the admissions committee, it should not simply laud your many wonderful traits, but specifically describe what you have been able to do that provides evidence you will perform well as a student and future counselor. Try to solicit letters from a variety of sources, including a past and present employer, a colleague or supervisor familiar with your work, and a faculty member who is knowledgeable about your verbal, thinking, and writing skills. It may also be useful to have someone testify as to your integrity, honor, morality, and compassion as well as your desire to be a professional counselor.

## Autobiographical Statements

These are critical. In some programs, the autobiographical statement may be the single most important source of data to determine how well you fit into their vision of a qualified applicant. You want to demonstrate your writing skills and your ability to present an organized, fluid, convincing, and effective essay. (In graduate school you will engage in much scholarly writing.) The objective is to present your clear personal goals and identify how you intend to reach them as well as how this particular program will help you meet those goals.

We suggest that you be as honest as possible. No one expects a perfect person; and when a paper suggests this, the readers begin to question the honesty of the writer. Readers want to learn about you, how you see yourself, and how comfortable you are discussing yourself. Remember that you are seeking to be a professional counselor who understands and is not afraid to face strengths, weaknesses, and difficult human issues in yourself or others. Avoidance of difficult issues is usually recognized and never appreciated. Providing a false impression of yourself greatly increases the chances of problems when you enter a program because expectations on your part as well as on the part of faculty will be inaccurate.

## Work Experience

This criterion often presents a paradox: programs want you to have had some experience in the field to demonstrate your commitment, but often you need the particular graduate degree you want to gain such experience. What programs are seeking is people who have done work or had volunteer experience that demonstrates their ability to learn what is required and apply that information in practice.

Master's degree programs present a mixed bag of what people can present as valuable experience. School counseling programs, for example, like it when applicants have been a teacher or even substitute teacher so that they know the school system, its goals, and the people in it, and have shown they can work with children on a daily basis. Employment in children's services, youth organizations, preschools, or children's homes is also greatly appreciated. Other programs look for people who have worked, for example, as case managers or counselor assistants at hospitals, agencies, nursing homes, or prisons, that is, in paraprofessional positions that require only a bachelor's degree. The pay is not great in these positions, but the experience in working with clients is invaluable. Programs know that success in these types of positions greatly increases the chances for success as a student because these students are more likely to understand both the highs and lows of what the counseling profession offers and what it takes to deal with those highs and lows on a consistent basis.

Although working for years at a job in the human services area may create great references, it is not always possible for people to take this kind of time. Fortunately, there are a number of other ways to gain practice in a helping capacity that will be looked at positively by program admissions committees. Schools, agencies, and religious and community organizations are always in need of volunteers. The more volunteer work or summer employment you can acquire working with people, the greater acceptance there will be of your motivation and abilities to deal with the training and work of the professional counselor.

Further, positions like these help you to better understand both the productive and problematic ways that clients, professionals, and agencies interact. Faculty realize the importance of these experiences in preparing counseling students for the realities of the profession and consequently appreciate the students who share such experiences in class and improve the educational experience for everyone. But gaining this experience goes beyond helping you get into a program. Before you invest the time, money, and energy in training to become a counselor you should make sure that you know what you are getting into. Most hospitals, public agencies, community service programs, schools, and charitable organizations offer a number of possibilities you can consider. The more experience you can get, the more likely you will be to be admitted and the better you are likely to do once in a program.

## *Interviews*

Some master's programs require interviews of all applicants; others use them only for finalists or for special cases; and others do not use them at all. In every instance, however, you can request an interview with either the department chair or several faculty members. The interview examines how well you handle yourself in person and how effectively you interact with faculty. Acquiring some form of interview is an excellent idea, not only to become a person rather than just an application but also to gather valuable information about what faculty in the program are seeking. The more they see your strengths in person, the greater the likelihood that they will want to be your instructors.

Most doctoral programs require interviews because of the greater individual work the applicant will be expected to do with faculty. They want to know how the person will work with the relatively small group of faculty and other students in the program as well as whether the person can do the work required. Will the prospective student's ways of learning, expectations, and goals match what the program and faculty offer? Although programs seek a diversity of faculty and students, they are also attempting to put together a group of people who will work effectively together toward accomplishing common goals. Faculty will certainly be looking for what you know and how your experience has molded your views of people and counseling, but often the larger issue is, what will it be like to work together?

Interviewees should keep in mind that the interview process is not just for the faculty to find out about you, but also for you to find out about them. The only way the process works well for everyone is if you present yourself as who you really are and not who you think faculty want you to be. Successfully faking who you really are only sets up the potential for a bad experience when you actually get in the program. But when the real you comes out at the interview and faculty decide you are the kind of person they want, the stage is set for an excellent program experience. You have worked hard to get to be the person you are, so let it show and find out whether this program is a match made in heaven or one to avoid.

## *Your Professionalism*

General criteria around tests, grades, experience, and interviews do not necessarily tell the whole story of your potential as a professional. Demonstrations of your professionalism that make you uniquely interesting to programs often come in the form of professional involvement as a member, leader, or scholar. Anything you can do to develop these demonstrations of professionalism and highlight them will create a major advantage.

The person who is not yet trained as a counselor but who knows the professional organizations, is a member, and attends meetings and conferences is one that most any program wants as a student. This is the individual who does not need to be convinced to get involved, to care about what professionals care about, or to support other counselors. Demonstrating the initiative to become involved with the profession before you are admitted to the program is a major plus on your admissions score card and needs to be highlighted.

Taking on leadership positions in general and particularly in professional or scholarly organizations is another way to show faculty your initiative and desire to go beyond what is required. Programs want leaders and the profession needs them. Taking leadership positions and then highlighting them in the admissions process gives you a significant step up on the majority of others who have good grades and good test scores, and done all the required work.

There are some signs of scholarship potential that carry much more weight than previously acquired good grades. Most applicants will not have them, which makes them very special if they are part of your presentation. Perhaps the two best examples are making professional presentations and developing publishable materials. Individuals who have shown enough knowledge, skill, and confidence to seek and make professional presentations outside of class make clear cases for how their professionalism and desire to achieve go beyond the norm.

An even stronger case is made by the person who has demonstrated enough scholarly expertise and assertiveness to write and publish some work that most others would have put away after receiving a grade of A on their paper. This may seem out of reach for many contemplating graduate school, but it is not. Faculty and practicing counselors are always excited about those individuals who are interested in taking such steps. They may not go searching for you, but if you take the initiative, they are almost always willing to help or even work with you on a project.

## Other Selection Criteria

Additional explicit factors may also come into play in deciding who gains admittance. These include the specialty area that you select because some programs are looking more for students in one area over others. Your race, sexual orientation, or cultural/ethnic background may have an influence because preference is often given to students who can add to the physical, cultural, or emotional diversity of a program so that it better reflects the increasing complexities of society. Life experiences and how well you have handled them, whether you are an in-state or out-of-state student, whether you have an advocate in the department working on your behalf, and the intangible potential that you hold, which may not have been reflected in the other areas, are all possible factors in your gaining acceptance. The homework you do in finding out about the program and its preferences as well as in understanding your own special qualities will help you in planning which of your unique characteristics needs emphasis in the application process.

## When Things Do Not Work Out as You Had Hoped

Applying for admission to a graduate program is stressful. It is almost always uncomfortable to be in a position in which other people are making decisions affecting your life. This is even more the case when you have decided that you want something very badly, and people in positions of power stand at the gate examining you critically, deciding whether you are worthy of admission. It is possible that an admissions committee may decide, based on the limited information at their disposal, that you are not as qualified as other applicants.

It is up to you to decide how to take that information and what to do with it. One possibility is that you do not have the necessary verbal, academic, and quantitative skills or the personal attributes that are needed to be an effective counselor. Another possibility is that the decision was based on information that does not accurately reflect your potential. Yet another possibility is that you are just not a good match (in their judgment) for this particular program but that another one might be more suitable. Remember also that many programs have less room than the number of qualified students who apply. You may be very qualified but perhaps less so than others who were accepted. Such feedback may be used by you to strengthen your application in ways that increase your likelihood of admission next time.

Here is one student describing his trials and tribulations in being denied admission to the same program twice before finally securing a place for himself:

Admittedly, I did not have the strongest academic background. Twenty years ago when I was in college I was working two jobs at the same time. I had to support my family. There was no way that I could devote the time I needed to my studies. Naturally, my grades suffered. I also didn't get the best education that I was capable of.

The first time they rejected my application I was so depressed I didn't know what to do. It took me 20 years to finally figure out what I wanted to do, and now these people were telling me that I couldn't do it. I went to talk to one of the professors, and he encouraged me to try again. I got some help with my essay. I took a writing class. I bought all those test preparation books and started reviewing math and memorizing vocabulary words. Then I applied again. I was still turned down!

Now I was really mad! No way was I going to give up! I met with the chair of the admissions committee. She went over my application and suggested some things that I might do to look better during the next go-around. Meanwhile, I had changed jobs to one that gave me some experience in the field, even though it meant a substantial reduction in money. I registered for a couple of graduate courses too. Got an A– in one and B+ in another. Not bad for someone who hadn't been to school in so long!

When I got the letter I was ecstatic. I had been admitted on probation, but hey, at least they were giving me a chance. School has been a struggle for me. I don't do all that well in heavily academic courses (I have since learned that I have a learning disability), but I am probably one of the best in counseling skills. I have a real feeling for picking things up quickly. I have even been offered a graduate assistantship next year!

The pride this man felt in his accomplishment is well deserved. He worked for over 2 years to gain admittance into the program of his choice. He was willing to make sacrifices, to stretch himself, to make becoming a counselor one of the major priorities of his life. If you are seeking entrance into a program, or have already been admitted into one, it may not be necessary for you to go to the lengths that this person did to make his dream a reality. We promise you, however, that training to be a professional counselor is one of the most difficult, exciting, interesting, and stressful challenges that you will ever undertake.

## Making Your Case for Admission

Now you know something about the criteria for admission, but one other thing you must keep in mind is the presentation of yourself. Faculty are looking for people who know what they are seeking and will put their very best foot forward to get there. There are some key guidelines that will make the difference in whether the information and materials you submit make you appear as a conscientious, budding professional or a careless person looking for something to do. So consider the following when you prepare to make your case for admission:

- Admission letters are neat, thoughtful, and polite, and explain why this program and this institution are the particular ones you believe are best for you.

- Make it clear in writing and conversation what it is that brought you to this decision and what you hope the training will prepare you to do in the future.
- Let your interest and excitement about the program and profession show.
- Use good listening and responding skills with faculty on the phone and in person. You need to be both attentive and verbal without being demanding.
- Highlight your strengths based on your past experiences and how you hope to both use them and improve on them during the program.
- Give recognition to any weaknesses in your admissions materials and explain how you feel you will overcome them.
- Be ready to explain what you can bring to the program that will be of benefit to other students and maybe even faculty.
- Business casual is the best type of dress when making contact with faculty. When in doubt, it is better to overdress at this stage because it shows you care.

## Focus Activities: Making Personal Use of This Chapter

1. **Make a list of programs in your geographical area that you would consider if you are still searching for a compatible department.** You might also wish to look at some national programs, many of which might offer financial aid and scholarships. Based on this investigation of both public and private institutions in your area, make a chart summarizing the features of each program as well as their admission criteria.

2. **Take an inventory of your strengths and weaknesses as a candidate.** If you have a GPA well over 3.0, or a GRE score in the 1,200 range, that might be considered a strength. Likewise, if you have little professional experience, or struggle with your writing skills, that might be considered a weakness. Match your particular strengths with the program(s) that most seem to value what you might bring to the department. Do not let the program faculty be the first to evaluate you objectively. Examine yourself and be ready to present your best case in those areas that will be considered potential weaknesses as well as in those areas that represent your strengths.

3. **Make arrangements as early as possible for taking necessary tests.** Do not wait until the last minute to get ready for taking any of the specific tests required by the programs to which you are applying. The sooner you take them, the easier it will be to determine whether the results meet the necessary criteria and whether you should talk with program faculty about the results, and, if you need to retake them, what it is you should study and how to do it.

4. **Make your case in writing even if you are not asked to do so.** Programs like to see well-stated ideas by prospective students. They will be likely to ask you to write some things like an autobiography, but you do not need to stop there. Put in a copy of the best one or two papers or other materials you have written that can be seen as related to your program. Write a strong one-page letter explaining your interest in this particular program, what you hope to learn, and what your professional plans are after graduation.

5. **Make contact with your references early and follow up later.** References are one thing you have less control over, so make contact early with them. When you are ready to send in your materials, check with the references and let them know that you are sending them. People writing references are busy professionals and a polite reminder at the right time is generally appreciated.

6. **Send a resume with your materials.** It is always a good idea to send a resume along with an application package IF it is well done. Have someone more experienced evaluate it to make sure it looks professional and makes the strong case for your abilities, motivation, and accomplishments.

7. **Make a follow-up phone call.** Initiative is always appreciated until it begins to feel like pestering or badgering. About 2 weeks after sending in your materials is a good time to make a phone call to let the program know that you have sent them, and that if there is anything more they would like from you, you would be pleased to provide it. One phone call is enough. Do not make a pest of yourself.

8. **Prepare yourself for perceived rejections.** We have emphasized the word perceived because nobody can actually reject you; all they can do is to decline to admit you. This is a significant difference that allows you to reframe (this is a counseling skill you will learn in your training) the experience as merely a disappointment or minor setback rather than as what feels to you like a major rejection of you as a person. Sometime in your career, you will be blocked from certain options and opportunities that appeal to you, just as your clients will bring these situations to you in counseling. It is your job—whether talking to yourself or to your clients—to respond with resilience, flexibility, and determination to find other means of getting your needs and desires met. Consider several times in your life in which you have felt rejected. What could you now do to reframe this experience in such a way that it allows you to take it less personally and actually learn from the experience?

9. **If you are already accepted into the program of your choice, congratulations!** Now your task is to reexamine the program and compare it to your abilities and work style. No program perfectly fits anyone, so it is now time to begin preparing for what to expect in the program and how to get the most from it.

# 3

# Program Quality and Your Professional Future

What are the critical characteristics of a quality counselor education program? Understanding and being cognizant of these features will help you to solidify your choice of one program over another and also to get more out of the program you enter. Note, however, that the question of critical characteristics is one that will change for you from time to time. Different things matter depending on the stage of your journey:

Stage 1—Looking for a Program: "Can I get in?"
Stage 2—Once Admitted to a Program: "Will I fit in?"
Stage 3—Immersed in Your Studies: "Why am I studying this?"
Stage 4—Requirements Almost Completed: "Can I get a job?"

At one point, you may be most concerned with flexible admission standards, but later you may be more concerned with whether the workload expected is manageable within your time and energy constraints. Upon graduation, you may be most concerned with how your program and training are viewed by members of the professional community. Thus your view of many program issues you consider most important will change as your status in the profession evolves.

Fortunately for you, most program quality issues are addressed by professional associations that seek to ensure consistency in the characteristics of the training delivered. This chapter provides an overview of the agreed-upon characteristics of quality programs, including accreditation, as well as of general core content areas, experiential components, and academic culminating experiences. The chapter describes how you can identify the characteristics, what they mean to you as a student, and how you can make the best use of them as you progress through your education. This discussion will also help you to understand the big picture of how the counseling profession is viewed nationally and internationally according to consensual standards.

## Program Accreditation

Did you know that you could obtain a master's or doctoral degree by simply writing a letter to certain establishments, explaining your qualifications, and then paying a substantial fee? Before you put this book down, and run to mail off your application, you should know that the piece of paper you get will be worthless as far as providing the training you need and the security your clients require, or as meeting the standards that state licensing boards and national professional organizations accept as evidence of your training competence.

It is easy to see the danger to clients, and the profession, that this type of shoddy operation poses. Even if the motives of such a diploma-mill institution were altruistic (i.e., to supply credentials to those who have already accumulated life experience in helping others), there is no way that an applicant can demonstrate academic and professional competence through the mail.

Even among institutions that are regionally or nationally accredited, there are enormous differences in the quality of programs in terms of their student bodies, curricula, faculty competence, and academic and professional requirements. Accreditation procedures are designed to provide enough consistency among programs to assure students that they receive training that is at least of generally accepted professional quality. Professional organizations often set up accrediting agencies to promote, evaluate, and recognize institutions and programs that meet professionally recognized criteria. Graduation from such recognized programs often carries benefits beyond graduation. More specifically, accreditation standards provide a program with several advantages:

- Employers knowledgeable in the counseling field can have confidence in the quality, content, and type of training a counselor has received.
- Clients can have confidence that the counselor has been adequately trained.
- Programs assure themselves and potential students that they are providing the most modern training available.
- Programs can use program accreditation standards to seek university support for adequate levels of support and lower faculty-student ratios.
- Higher quality students and faculty are attracted to accredited programs.
- Licensing and certification bodies frequently require less academic verification and reduce the length of experiential requirements for graduates of accredited programs. This allows these graduates to receive a license or certification with less hassle and in less time.
- Accreditation standards and exams for licensure and certification are generally based on similar content requirements so that graduates can be confident of their preparation for such exams.

The two accrediting bodies with the strongest impact on the counseling profession are the Council for Accreditation of Counseling and Related Educational Programs and the Council on Rehabilitation Education. CACREP was created by the American Counseling Association and is most directly tied to the current requirements of counselor licensure and certification laws throughout the country. In addition to accreditation for training general counselors, CACREP institutions may also offer specializations in clinical, marriage and family, school, and gerontological counseling, and in student personnel work. CORE accredits programs focused on training rehabilitation counselors.

Graduating from an accredited program is most beneficial to those who want their counselor training to be as widely accepted as possible. This can help with the portability of your license from state to state. You can consult Appendix A for the Web sites that list the most up-to-date accreditation information on programs across the country.

Other accrediting bodies emphasize training in specializations closely associated with counseling. The American Psychological Association accredits programs that train psychologists. Anyone wishing to become a psychologist, as opposed to a counselor, should strongly consider attending an APA-accredited program rather than a CACREP-accredited program. If this seems confusing, it is probably because the situation is complex. Many people do not understand the differences among counselors, psychologists, and social workers; what they are uniquely qualified to do; and how they work similarly and differently. States do not make it any easier with licensing laws that vary widely in the training required and the professional functions allowed (i.e., counseling, testing, diagnosis, psychotherapy) in these different professions.

Psychologists are primarily trained at the doctoral level. They are experts in assessment, diagnosis, and research, and they also receive training in working with more severely disturbed populations. Master's-level social workers are also generally trained to do psychotherapy with more disturbed populations in clinics, hospitals, private practice, and mental health settings. However, these social workers have a unique professional focus on case management: visiting homes, arranging for aftercare services, referring patients (the preferred term by these professions) to places where they can get help.

The profession of counseling is evolving rapidly so that it is becoming more difficult to separate the work of counselors and family therapists from the work of psychologists and even social workers. Some licensing laws and work sites recognize that counselors do much the same work with most of the same clients as psychologists. Traditionally, however, counselors have concentrated on working with relatively normal populations who are experiencing adjustment reactions or developmental problems (rather than personality disorders or grossly distorted reality). Instead of using a medical model that emphasizes psychopathology, counselors have traditionally employed the more developmental models often used in schools, community agencies, and universities.

To complicate matters further, there are a number of clinical settings (mental health and community agencies, private practice) in which what these various professionals do is functionally indistinguishable. Although social workers, marriage and family therapists, psychologists, and counselors may have been trained a bit differently, and belong to different professional associations and identities, there is considerable overlap in the books they read and the kinds of work they do. Naturally, we favor the advantages of counseling because it is a form of helping that is intended for everyone, rather than only those people who have specifically diagnosable mental disorders.

The American Association for Marriage and Family Therapy accredits a smaller number of programs than CACREP, CORE, or APA. For those individuals who desire to specialize exclusively in marriage and family counseling, a program with this accreditation may offer the strongest recommendation upon graduation. CACREP also offers a specialization in marriage and family counseling that, in some ways, places programs with this accreditation in direct competition with AAMFT programs. Perhaps the most important point for the potential marriage and family counseling student to remember is that programs endorsed by either of these accrediting bodies have been cited for their extensive attention to the development of their programs.

One other group of accrediting bodies that you may hear mentioned deals with accrediting institutions rather than programs. For example, regional associations of colleges and schools evaluate participating schools, colleges, and universities as to their credibility as an institution. Graduates of schools that are not accredited by such organizations often have difficulty having transcripts accepted by other schools or agencies. A somewhat different level of accreditation that nearly all counselor education programs encounter is completed by the National Council for Accreditation of Teacher Education (NCATE). This organization accredits colleges of education, in which most counselor education programs reside, but it does not directly evaluate counseling programs as CACREP does.

The true value of getting your training from an appropriately accredited program is often not recognizable until you begin to seek employment. Job announcements often state that graduates of programs with a specific accreditation that matches the training wanted (such as counselor, rehabilitation specialist, psychologist, social worker) will be given preference. New professionals seeking a license or certification to counsel generally find that the process is much easier and direct if they have graduated from a program accredited by the appropriate organization. Although the sheer number of accreditations may seem overwhelming, the important point is that you should thoroughly research the specific implications of your own institution's approvals as they relate to your hopes for professional employment and skill level.

## Core Content Areas

Quality master's degree counseling programs can have great variety in the courses and content they offer. However, most accredited programs are in agreement regarding eight critical core content areas to be covered:

(1) human growth and development, (2) social and cultural foundations, (3) helping relationship skills, (4) group leadership skills, (5) career and lifestyle development, (6) assessment and appraisal, (7) research, and (8) orientation to the profession. These areas are the same ones in which employers and licensing and certification boards have the most interest about your knowledge and skill level. They are often identifiable as individual courses, but at other times, the information is integrated into several courses. For example, the critical area of multicultural sensitivity—social and cultural foundations—is quite often offered as a separate course. Other programs prefer to infuse the subject into every course in the curriculum, but not offer it as a separate course.

Another type of program may choose to both offer a single course and attempt to infuse the content into other courses. There may be different ways to integrate this information into programs, but the main point is that the core areas are deemed essential for producing quality counselors (and passing licensing exams).

## Human Growth and Development

The first of these areas includes a solid understanding of how people develop, and the impact of this on human functioning. The area is generally referred to as human growth and development, and it places a strong emphasis on behaviors and transitions across the full life span. This area provides the foundation for understanding why people are the way they are at different life stages. A thorough understanding of these issues is considered essential for effective selection of counseling techniques that fit the differing needs of people at various transitional times in their lives. Obviously, if you do not know how people develop in terms of their physical, sexual, emotional, spiritual, moral, familial, vocational, psychological, and cultural evolution, it will be very difficult to help facilitate successful progress through the life stages. Counselors are thus prepared to recognize the developmental tasks that people face at various ages and stages and then to help foster increased progress.

## Social and Cultural Foundations

We are living in a rapidly changing and increasingly multicultural world. Believing that all people perceive the world around them in the same way as you do is a bias that leads to inappropriate treatment of others. The African American middle-class female who grows up in the suburbs may not see the world and how to function in it the same way as the Mexican American male who has lived as a migrant farm worker. Neither of those people will believe that the world operates in the same way as the White middle-class businessman or the wealthy heiress believes. Everyone brings a unique view of the world to counseling, and the more we can understand those views and how they develop, the better job we can do as counselors.

This core area of social and cultural foundations is an attempt to broaden your understanding of the multicultural nature of our changing world and the impact it has on clients' lives, as well as of the counseling interventions necessary to deal with this wide variety of people and needs. We use the term *culture* in the broadest sense, as not only including one's race or ethnicity but also religion, geographical region, avocation, profession, sexual orientation, and other such variables. After all, people are made up of many different cultural identities, rather than a single variable.

Our understanding of the area has also grown to the point that a list of expected counselor competencies has been developed (Arredondo et al., 1996). Essentially, this means, first, that you will need to increase your awareness of your own cultural values and biases, especially as they may influence the ways you respond to others who are members of marginalized groups. Second, you will be expected to increase your knowledge of people from various groups, especially those who might come to you for counseling. Third, there are certain culturally relevant skills that you will need to learn that help clients from diverse backgrounds feel heard, understood, respected, and honored. Obviously, you will not want to alienate people because of your own ignorance about customs, rituals, and practices of various groups. This, then, leads to culturally appropriate intervention strategies that are best suited to a particular client's background. The specific competencies in this area expected of counseling professionals can be found by going to the ACA Web site www.counseling.org, clicking on "Resources," and then on "Multicultural and Diversity Issues."

## Helping Relationship Skills and Group Work Skills

All counselors have to develop helping relationship skills, whether in groups, families, or individual settings. It is, therefore, necessary to master all the counseling skills that are involved in building effective relationships, regardless of the helping modality. These generic skills are applicable in most every setting, although there are also specialized skills in leading groups and in counseling families.

- **Examples of Generic Counseling Skills Employed in all Modalities**
  - **Reflecting**: "You are feeling upset about not getting admitted, but you are also saying that you are ready to work on your weak areas like lack of experience so that you can gain acceptance the next time you apply."
  - **Reframing**: "Not getting accepted was a blow to you, but that rejection also opened up this opportunity to try a new job that you are excited about."
  - **Questioning**: "What is it like for you to feel depressed?"
  - **Goal setting**: "So what you want to accomplish is to develop new social skills so that you can make more friends than you now have."
  - **Action planning**: "Applying the skills we've been working on in here by introducing yourself to three new people sounds like a good plan for this week."

- **Summarizing**: "You have been speaking at length about your frustrations at work and how familiar this feeling of being ignored has been throughout your life."
- **Examples of Group Leadership Skills**
  - **Blocking**: "Ty, before you get into this more, I think we need to finish up with Michal first who was not yet finished with what she wanted to say."
  - **Identifying themes**: "Stephan, Cho, and Veronica, each of you has been talking about your fears of taking risks in this group because of concern about being judged critically. Who else would be willing to speak about that?"
- **Examples of Family Counseling Skills**
  - **Redirecting**: "Nyla, rather than talking about your husband, I wonder if you could tell him this directly? Please face him and repeat what you just said."
  - **Structuring**: "I'd like to ask you to switch seats if you wouldn't mind. I like the two parents sitting together on the couch over here, and then I'd like you three children to sit together over there. Grandma, if you wouldn't mind, I'd like you to sit here, next to me."

You can readily see from these examples that counselors use a limited number of core skills in almost every helping situation whether they are working as an individual counselor, group leader, family counselor, life coach, or consultant. Further, these same skills of active listening, reflecting, interpreting, summarizing, and so on, are used universally, with adjustments for multicultural variables and with the addition of those specialized skills that you will learn for specific treatment modalities.

Counseling skills cannot be learned through lectures and discussions and reading alone; they must be practiced. In order to do so, there are often experiential learning structures that require you to apply the skills with your peers. This can include role-playing activities, but also may involve talking about real concerns in your life.

There is considerable debate in the field about how to provide these early experiential learning opportunities while protecting students from the problems of dual relationships. On the one hand, the best way to learn new skills is to experience and practice them yourself; on the other hand, it is difficult to do this without revealing personal things about yourself that may put you in an awkward, vulnerable situation. Counselor educators who teach group and skills courses now generally support experiential learning components when the following conditions are met: (1) you have the right to pass and avoid coercion; (2) you are not graded on your personal disclosures; and (3) you are adequately informed about the consequences of such involvement. The important point about quality programs is that they all provide for ethically responsible experiential learning and self-exploration experiences in some form during training.

## Career and Lifestyle Development

Whether clients come to a counselor for positive growth-related work or reparative clinical work, their problems and their development usually have a potential impact on the choices they make regarding career and lifestyle development. An individual's vocation is one of several crucial agents of human existence that leads to life satisfaction, and all counselors must be ready to understand and deal with these issues.

Most clients, of any age, come to counseling because they are having difficulties with relationships, love, economic constraints, and meaningful work. Career decisions are no longer made once, in high school or college, and then followed through during a lifetime. Nowadays, a person may have as many as a half dozen different careers, each one requiring additional exploration and development. In addition to finding meaningful employment, many clients struggle with problems they have on the job—with colleagues, with conflicts, and with stress.

Traditionally, counselors have been leading experts in the domain of helping people make career choices and sort out the meaning of work-related activities. This still remains a specialty area that distinguishes us from other helping professionals.

## Appraisal

People generally enter the counseling profession because they enjoy and find value in interpersonal relationships. Most do not generally have a similar interest in statistics and testing, so they are often less than excited about finding out that appraisal and research are two areas included in all quality counselor education programs. It may not be immediately evident how studying systematic inquiry in client assessment and research are part of a counselor's roles, but these are indeed as much a part of what we do as offering support and guidance.

Appraisal deals with the process and instruments available to help counselors make critical judgments about clients. No one goes to a brain surgeon and accepts a comment such as "Now that we have talked, I am ready to recommend that we do surgery tomorrow." People expect the doctor to know which tests to perform, interpret the results to the client, and only then come up with a joint decision as to what is best to do. Counseling clients deserve no less thoroughness and quality in the appraisal methods used by their counselor. Unless you have a thorough understanding of the clients' presenting complaints, underlying unresolved issues, personal strengths and weaknesses, and interests and abilities, any helping efforts are likely to miss the mark.

Appraisal is the clinical activity in which you systematically collect and analyze all relevant data and then formulate diagnostic impressions and treatment plans. Is this client a suicidal risk? Should I work with the person in individual, family, or group counseling? What goals are realistic in the time available? How much confrontation can the client handle? Is he or she likely to benefit from meditation? What family-of-origin issues from the past are unresolved? Who else is operating behind the scenes of sabotage/progress? What are this client's interests, abilities, achievements, and deficits? What developmental transition is this client living through now? Which differential diagnoses might apply? These are but a few of the assessment questions you must consider before structuring an effective counseling plan.

Many psychological instruments are available to the modern professional counselor to solidify clinical impressions determined during interviews. How extensive the training you receive in this area depends on the degree to which your program focuses on diagnosis and treatment of clinical problems. Your program could range from a one-course overview of the issues and instruments to several specific courses on administering and interpreting them. The most commonly used diagnostic classification system is the *Diagnostic and Statistical Manual of Mental Disorders* (American Psychiatric Association, 2000), and you will be asked to learn it. You will also be exposed to objective and projective personality tests, intelligence tests, aptitude tests, and achievement tests. Developing an understanding of and an ability to use these assessment tools increases the likelihood that clients get the most appropriate treatment possible.

## *Research*

Learning about research serves a dual purpose in programs for counselors. First, it provides the counselor with the understanding necessary to locate, read, and interpret the most current research on the wide variety of client problems that may be encountered. Without this knowledge, counselors could not offer clients the most current and reliable techniques. Second, research offers counselors a model for how to judge their work and evaluate its effectiveness. Use of this research model in your own practice assures clients that you have evaluated your work and made valid judgments about what works (keep using these methods) and what does not work (stop using these methods or seek improvement).

You will be using research in a variety of ways once you graduate. In order to remain current and up to date on the latest innovations in the field, you will peruse research reports and professional journals. Yet you cannot take what these articles say on faith alone; you must be a critical consumer of research, able to make your own determinations about whether the results are valid for the work that you do.

You will also constantly be called upon to function as a researcher, regardless of your interest in doing systematic research, and publishing the results. Doing research simply means searching and re-searching for meaningful information that informs your practice. You must devise ways to determine the effects of your interventions; otherwise you will have no way of improving your effectiveness. This means, essentially, that you will collect data (qualitatively and quantitatively), analyze the results, and then, based on what you learn, make adjustments in the ways you function in the future. This is research at its best.

## *Professional Orientation*

Most counselor education programs offer an introduction to the counseling profession that includes its history, organizational structures, ethics, and credentialing procedures. This professional orientation area provides understanding of the many dynamics and issues of the complex profession you are entering. This is where you try to gain an understanding of the professionals who have blazed the trail for you and where that path is leading. It is your first opportunity to draw a clear picture of your profession and how you can effectively fit into that picture.

Study of professional orientation issues also helps you to form a clearer identity as a clinician. Clients, colleagues, and family members are going to be asking you, "What IS a counselor anyway? And how is that different from a psychiatrist or a psychologist?" You had better learn to answer that question in such a way that you emphasize our unique history, our specialty in working with adjustment reactions, our developmental rather than exclusively psychopathological diagnostic model, and all the other unique facets that make up your honored profession.

## Experiential Components

Counselor training can be much more complex for the student than other types of academic programs. Whereas gaining knowledge is often the primary goal for many academic programs at all educational levels, knowledge alone does not ensure the development of a quality counselor. You must have opportunities to practice counseling skills and integrate the information you have learned into your personal style.

Quality counselor education programs can generally be expected to include three general types of experiential components. Normally, this process begins early in the program by having new students role-play clients so that beginners can practice the skills and information they are studying. Introductory individual and group counseling skills courses are often the first time you are asked to try your skills and knowledge out with other people. There is certain to be a degree of anxiety going along with the excitement of this first step.

Learn to enjoy seeing yourself improve as a counselor rather than worrying about whether you have done everything exactly right. This is especially true with respect to watching yourself on videotape, during which you should try to attend as much to what you are doing well as to what you might work on to improve.

The first actual clients you will see are in an experience called a practicum, in which you work in a tightly supervised setting. Most programs have some sort of laboratory setting, complete with one-way mirrors and methods to give you feedback during or after the sessions. These laboratories are used for role-playing, observing actual counseling, and, in some cases, seeing actual clients. Clients may come to the center from around the university and/or community.

The practicum, which may involve one semester, or as many as two or three, is followed by an extended internship in the field. The object is for you to accumulate on-the-job experience in one or several different placements. By the time you graduate it is typical that you have logged close to 1,000 hours of clinical experience, nearly 300 of which involve direct contact with actual clients. The remainder of the hours are spent learning about the organization and its ways of handling clients, going to staff meetings, and participating in other activities designed to integrate you into this particular professional setting. Supervision is by on-site and university faculty in both individual and group formats.

Practica occur when you have taken most of your academic and skills courses. They promote your confidence in what you can do, reveal your limitations, and clarify your legal and ethical responsibilities. Faculty and on-site supervisors generally offer opportunities for you to watch counseling first-hand and to do counseling in a closely supervised format. They pay particular attention to how well you work with clients by listening to you on audiotapes and watching you on videotapes, or from behind one-way mirrors, and often by sitting in with you during counseling sessions.

An internship is generally the last experiential component of a counseling program, and it comes at a time when you are ready to take on most professional duties for which you have been trained. It offers a wider range of counseling and work experiences than a practicum. You are generally expected to do whatever a fully qualified counselor in a similar position does.

## Academic Culminating Experiences

The practicum and internship experiences are generally the portions of your program that demonstrate your ability to perform counseling skills. However, the professional counselor also needs to communicate a sound knowledge base to other professionals and the community in general. Most quality programs, therefore, require an academic culminating experience to assure everyone concerned that you know what you should know and that you can communicate that information in professional ways.

Comprehensive examinations are one common form of assessing your degree of mastery. Programs with comprehensives require you to call upon information from your many courses and experiences. The exams may be of the multiple-choice or true/false variety in which objective assessment of information retained is the focus. They may also be essays in which writing skills and abilities to put ideas together are given more emphasis. Of course, they may be some combination of these two alternatives as well. Generally, programs emphasizing the more objective type of items place a higher priority on knowledge, and those emphasizing essay tests place their priorities on your ability to communicate more general concepts in writing.

Comprehensive exams may be a stressful experience. However, there is some therapeutic/educational value in having a structure to review and integrate what you learned in your program. Typically, these exams are designed in such a way that most students pass if they have done adequate preparation. Study groups are often formed during the semester prior to administration, offering students a structured, often playful, and supportive environment for reviewing their studies.

Some programs have a thesis, professional paper, or final project as their choice for a culminating experience, either as an alternative to comprehensive exams or in addition to them. These programs generally place high value on the logical thinking and written communication skills that counselors need to display as professionals. They assume that you have learned information, and that it is most important for you to apply that knowledge to some specific topic of interest. Generally, the most useful theses or professional papers are those in which you have a strong personal, as well as professional, interest in researching a particular area of inquiry.

These culminating papers are expected to be completed in a highly professional manner. Their style and format should match that which makes them appropriate for submission to a professional publication. The content should examine current and previously published research and theory to present new directions for professional counselors that will potentially advance the profession as a whole.

## Focus Activities: Making Personal Use of This Chapter

This chapter addresses the critical characteristics to consider in order to understand the nature and content of a quality counselor education program. Program accreditation, core content areas, experiential components, and academic culminating experiences are the primary issues discussed. Understanding accreditation and being attentive to the core content areas will enable you to finalize your choice of a program and prepare you to get the most from it. Completing the following exercises will help you strengthen your understanding of accreditation and core content areas identified in quality training programs.

### Accreditation

1. **List both what you know about accreditation and the questions you still have about it.** Leave room because you are likely to have more questions as your knowledge and experience increase because accreditation is an important but complex topic. For more information you can talk with faculty or contact the Council for Accreditation of Counseling and Related Educational Programs, 5999 Stevenson Avenue, Alexandria, VA 22304 / 800-347-6647 x301.

2. **Identify what accreditation your narrowed list of programs have and how well they fit your specialization needs.** Use the lists of accredited programs available on the CACREP Web site (http://www.counseling.org/cacrep/directory.htm) to see whether programs you are considering have achieved this status in your area of interest.

## Core Content Areas

1. **Keep the list of the eight core content areas as a quick reference while researching programs**. This will benefit you throughout the program and even after graduation by helping you recognize those things for which you will most be held responsible.
2. **List the courses in the university catalogs that correspond to the eight core content areas.** You can find most university catalogs on their Web sites, but you can also call or write for information. If you are unsure whether the courses fit and fulfill the areas, ask a faculty member at the university and/or contact CACREP to ensure that the courses you take will fulfill the requirements. You may decide not to take courses that fall under the categories, but be aware that if you do fulfill coursework in these categories, it greatly improves your chances for employment and strengthens your career opportunities.
3. **List special course requirements and potential electives.** Some accredited programs require that you take specific courses to fulfill specific accreditation or licensure requirements, which leaves room for you to take only several electives. Explore your personal view of this situation. Will you take required courses with only several electives in order to meet all accreditation and licensure requirements? Or will you take other courses of interest that may fail to meet licensure requirements? Be aware of your views and feelings on this, and make sure to choose a program that meets your needs. This will ensure that you are not disappointed and disgruntled with your choice of a program.
4. **List the eight core areas with situations that might require you to know related information.** Stretch your imagination and also contact counselors in your vicinity, asking them when you might need such information. Reframe any potential negative feelings toward an area with more information so that you will feel more positive and recognize the benefits of each area.

## Academic Culminating Experiences

1. **List your preferences in relation to what each program requires for culminating experiences.** This will enable you to better visualize the match and increase the likelihood that you will choose the program that is right for you.
2. **List any anxieties that you may have from reading this chapter.** Challenge your fears by listing reasons why the experiences are necessary. Finally, list a positive reframing affirmation as necessary. For example,

    - **fear:** "I am afraid of statistics. I have never been good at math."
    - **why necessary:** "Statistics are important to research and growth of our field. Even when I am not actively researching, I will

need to be able to understand statistical concepts and terms when I read and interpret the literature."

- **positive affirmation:** "I am not going to let this one requirement stop me from pursuing what I really want to do. Besides, I am sure not everyone is good at math, and they did it. If all those people did it, I can do it too!"

# 4

# Early Decisions Related to Specialization

The path to becoming a counselor generally begins with a desire to help people and a recognition that you may have the ability to do just that. Once enrolled in a graduate program, however, it quickly becomes clear that there are more decisions to be made regarding what counseling personally means to you and how you can achieve your goals. What kind of counselor will you be? Should you be highly specialized in a particular area or develop a broad range of skills and knowledge? What types of persons do you prefer to work with? What program track should you choose? What course selections should you make? How can you best make this program work for you? Where will these choices lead you?

In counselor education programs—as in most educational endeavors—you usually find that the more you truly learn, the more clearly you recognize what you still do not know and what you cannot yet do. Past experiences may have given you some confidence that you do, in fact, have something to offer others. But then as you learn about theories, techniques, and why people behave the way they do, the whole world of counseling becomes more complex. With your developing skills and knowledge comes increased responsibility and apprehension.

## Personal Reflections on Competence

We want to share with you our own struggles with feeling competent, a challenge that still lives with us today. Even after more than 25 years in the field each, we still go through periods when we do not feel good enough, when we become aware of so many things we cannot do nearly as well as we would like.

> **Richard's story**. My feelings of anxiety as I learned to be a counselor were like those I had when I first began playing soccer in elementary school. I was pretty good, if I do say so myself. The coach was impressed, too, so he took me aside and gave me tips on how to move my arms, make judgments, accelerate, finish a play. He taught me a great deal in a short period of time, and what he taught made lots of sense. Unfortunately, the more I thought about all that he told me, the more tense and awkward I became. The more I knew, the less successful I felt. I was ready to quit the sport altogether.
>
> Fortunately, the coach stayed with me and explained that if I gave it sufficient time, what he was teaching me would become automatic and my natural skills would return. The coach was right. My skills did return, and I became better than I had been before, even though I knew more about what

I was still doing wrong than I ever wanted to know. My soccer career continued to bloom in high school, where the knowledge of the sport taught by my coaches allowed me to make the best use of my natural abilities.

I did not work at soccer with either the degree or consistency that I did at my profession. The result is that my soccer career faded, and my teaching and counseling skills grew. Common to both of these growth experiences, however, was the recognition that a little information takes a lot of practice to become truly valuable.

**Jeffrey's story.** I also experienced tremendous apprehensions and doubts about myself as an emerging counselor. The more I learned about the various therapeutic options that were available in any given moment with a particular client, the more overwhelmed I felt. When I reviewed my videotapes of sessions, all I attended to were my mistakes and errors in judgment. I cringed as I heard myself say the stupidest, most inept things imaginable. I was obsessed with my inadequacies, my imperfections, and my failings as a practitioner. It was not uncommon for me to think, for example, that my supervisors and professor must be lying to me, that they only told me supportive things because they didn't want to hurt my feelings and tell me that I really didn't have what it takes to be a good counselor. After all, how could I possibly do this complex job when I knew so little about what I was doing? Then, in a vicious cycle of self-doubt, I often sought to banish my uncertainties and apprehension by studying even harder: If only I could readjust a few more books, review my tapes one more time, try a bit harder, then maybe I could make it.

How unrealistic I was in expecting that my counseling skills and knowledge would all come together in such a way that I would be able to do all that I learned! It has been 20 years since this struggle began, and I am still waiting for my doubts and apprehension to dissipate. I certainly know more now than I knew then. I can do more, with greater skill and fluency, than I ever could before. Yet I still have not reached my image of the kind of counselor I truly want to be—one who can do all I was taught.

Whether playing a sport or practicing counseling, we all struggle with the challenge of mastering a set of skills and a body of knowledge that can require a dozen lifetimes to understand fully, much less to practice with the success that we might prefer. You, too, will be collecting information about clients and counseling that may seem useless or even harmful to your development at first. Do not disregard this information. It often just needs to be placed in a context you do not presently have available, or it may simply need practice to make it more realistic. This chapter focuses on understanding the context of the counseling professions, making hesitant early decisions, and gaining the experience that will help you make firm decisions later.

## What Kind of Counselor Do You Want to Be?

One way to bring your fantasies and expectations under reasonable and realistic control is to limit your reflections to a concrete arena. Forget your dreams (you can always return to them later at your leisure) of being a supercounselor who never errs and always knows exactly what to do. Help put your skill development in better focus by examining some of the specialties that you might like to develop.

Beginning students often recognize that they want to work with specific populations. They say, for example,

- "I have always liked to be around kids. I feel a special affinity for them and think that I could make the greatest difference with them."
- "The idea appeals to me to reach out to those who are most neglected—the indigent and homeless. They are so often ignored. I would like to do my part to help the people who have not received sufficient care."
- "It seems to me that I could do the most good working with families in trouble, especially those in which one or more members are abusing drugs or alcohol."
- "I want to help older people. I don't think that they have gotten enough attention from our professions."
- "I want to work with people from a culture and background similar to my own. I feel I know these problems and the lifestyle, and I want to make a difference for these people."

Such choices of specific populations are often based on interactions with friends and relatives, or from other personal experiences. The problem, however, is that they often do not reflect what is practical and available, or what the students' abilities or their long-term interests are.

You need to make yourself more knowledgeable about the options available and how they will impact you. This takes reading, asking instructors and other students, and talking with people in the field. However, you need to do much more than read a few books. You are not seeking simple facts. You need information that will match your changing personal and professional self and how you view the world through this profession.

Something that should relieve a little of your anxiety about choosing a specialty is that across most counseling programs there are more common core courses than specialty courses. You are sure to have a general orientation to the field before you are expected to narrow your choices. Taking the introduction, foundations, or orientation course that almost every program has in the beginning of a program will help you get started on exploring these issues. Just make sure that you use this time to learn and ask questions, and to get in the field to see and experience the different kinds of counselors and settings available to you. Perhaps the best way to find out what kind of counselor you wish to be is to talk with as many practitioners in the field as possible. Observe what they do. Ask them about the professional images they once constructed in their minds and how their daily work compares to these expectations.

## What Counseling Specialties Are There?

Counseling specialties can be divided according to client population or work setting. Client populations include children and adolescents, young adults, adults and special populations, and older adults. Thus you can, for example, decide you want to work with a client population that consists of basically healthy functioning children from ages 5 to 12. This decision then has direct impact on the work settings where you may find employment. Your most likely choices will be elementary and middle schools, large mental health centers, or private practice in areas with sufficient client populations to support such a specialization. Grant-funded programs specifically designed for this type of client are other possibilities. If you can broaden your choice to children with mental, physical, or emotional disabilities, then opportunities in large hospitals, rehabilitation centers, and many additional special programs become viable job possibilities.

Your initial task in choosing a specialty is to consider both client and setting factors. Note that in the age group populations (children, adolescents, young adults, older adults), counselors must become experts in the group's unique developmental issues and associated adjustment difficulties. This consistently developmental orientation is part of the identity that helps to make the counseling profession unique. We are specialists in facilitating life transitions for people of various ages and stages in life.

## Working With Children and Adolescents

The concepts related to why and how humans develop at young ages must be of high interest to those who will truly enjoy and be good at counseling children. Memory, language, thinking processes, perceptual abilities, moral development, personality development, and physical nature are all constantly changing in children. The choice to work with this age group must be made based on an interest in facilitating these changes.

Types of problems and techniques to treat children's issues vary greatly for different age and maturity levels. There is no single way to deal with all children, so the counselor must be ready to recognize developmental stages and utilize the techniques to match the child's needs and abilities. Individual and group techniques appropriate for this population are generally more structured, more action oriented, and less verbal than for adults. These factors generally place more responsibility on the counselor to decide what to do and when to do it than is true in working with adults.

People who work with children must also recognize that society has much more direct influence over children than it does over adults. Adults can decide not to practice math or stop going to school. They can decide where and with whom they will live and play, and they can choose to work primarily in those areas in which they have abilities and interests. Children, however, are expected to live where they are told, be good at all school subjects, and get along with everyone. The result is that counselors of children must be ready to recognize the greater impact of society on their clients. They must also be willing and able to work with those organizations and adults that impact the clientele.

Counselors of children often work in agencies, but they also work in private practice. Municipal organizations and mental health and community groups all employ child counselors. However, the greatest single number of people working with children are school counselors. These are the people who work within the schools to help youth and to help provide the most effective atmosphere in which they can learn and grow. Marriage and family counselors also do a great deal of work with young people in a different context: that of the family. Many other programs and individual counseling positions continue to open up due to growing problems for children related to abuse, homelessness, divorce, foster care, and other contemporary social problems.

Adolescents are probably at the most difficult developmental stage. They are considered children and young adults at the same time. Physically, they are ready to be adults, yet society continues to treat them in much the same controlled ways that it did when they were 5-year-olds. Emotionally and socially, adolescents are trying to find a place for themselves at the same time that they are changing rapidly. There is every reason to believe that individuals at this age will have many problems related to issues of self-identity and autonomy.

Counselors of adolescents must recognize the developmental needs of their clients as well as the specific life problems they may face. You may need to work with a client on children's issues this week and then on adult issues the next—using very different techniques. Adolescents are constantly testing their relationships to adults, and counselors can be expected to be tested as much or more than most. Excitement, challenge, change, and variety are key words for the person considering a specialization with adolescents.

### Counseling Young Adults

Many people express initial interest in working with older teenagers and those in their early 20s. The opportunities for these two groups tend to be in college and vocational schools or in programs for individuals having problems involving the legal system.

A specialty in this area requires familiarization with the unique problems of this age group: solidifying career choices, developing greater independence, establishing a romantic life, and building a solid foundation for the future. Such counselors typically work in counseling centers on college campuses, in the mental health system, or in other community agencies.

Testing and assessment skills tend to be especially important when working with young adults because they often require help in making decisions related to vocational development. In addition, you may be expected to become an expert on problems in relationships because so many young adult concerns center around decisions and conflicts with parents, friends, and significant others.

### Counseling Adults and Special Populations

Prospective counselors often want to work with people who are similar to themselves. The most common similarities selected are age, sex, or sociocultural background. Although this makes a lot of common sense, because it may be easier to work with people you perceive to be similar to you, counselors rarely have the opportunity to be that limited. They are instead expected to work with diverse people because our society is becoming more diverse, and people must generally live their lives in this context.

The counseling profession has begun reacting to this diversity by altering an earlier view that all people can be treated the same way. It has long been clear that individuals have many similar attributes. However, in addition to unique differences, individuals also have many differences related to the groups responsible for their development. Reflecting this reaction has been an increase in counseling specializations dealing with select populations. Counselors are more frequently deciding to emphasize specializations in working with males, females, Asian Americans, Native Americans, African Americans, Latinos, people with disabilities, individuals with substance abuse problems, gay men and lesbians, and many other groups, as well as with religious issues and sexuality issues.

You may decide to emphasize work with one or more of these specialized groups or issues that particularly interests you. However, most counselors cannot spend all their time and energy on one or two specialized areas simply because of a lack of sufficient clients. For example, a desire to work with inner-city African American clients requires a counselor to find employment in an inner-city school or agency, and even there, the client population is likely to be made up of other types of individuals and groups. Consequently, counselors must prepare themselves to work with diverse client populations while they also expand their knowledge and skills related to those populations that most interest them.

### Counseling Older Adults

Improvements in lifestyle choices, nutrition, and health care continue to increase life expectancy for many people. The result is that the fastest growing subgroup in America is older adults.

There are quite a number of unique issues that must be considered for this population. Counselors who concentrate on working with older individuals feel a special affinity for this group and particularly enjoy learning as much from them about life as they give in return.

Quite often the primary task of helping efforts with older adults is to aid in their search for meaning as they review their lives. Counselors in this specialty also help with the adjustment to the changing role of parent and the new role of grandparent. They must help clients find and adjust to meaningful leisure and productive activities after retirement. Older clients must also learn to deal with declining health and vigor, adjust to deaths of friends and spouses, and, perhaps most important of all, make necessary emotional and spiritual preparations for their own deaths. These are all normal life processes that counselors can expect to find in some form in all older clients.

### Individual, Group, and Marriage and Family Counseling

Specialties can be developed not only to work with special client populations but also to work in particular therapeutic modalities, such as individual, group, or family. Counseling strategies such as group counseling and marriage and family counseling were at one time considered to be unusual treatments provided by a few maverick practitioners. These modes of practice are now so common that practically all counselors are at least minimally familiar with these interventions.

You are likely to have the opportunity to concentrate your efforts in developing expertise in one of these counseling approaches. Some graduate programs offer specific degrees in marriage and family counseling, preparing graduates for licensure as marriage and family therapists. Other programs offer a sequence of specialty courses in group work for those students who wish to become specialists in this area.

There are specific divisions of the American Counseling Association devoted to specialists in each of these areas (International Association of Marriage and Family Counselors and the Association for Specialists in Group Work), and there are even separate organizations such as the American Group Psychotherapy Association and the American Association for Marriage and Family Therapy. The number, size, and variety of these organizations attest to their popularity and impact on the profession.

## Developing a Flexible Specialty

Whether you wish to work with a particular age group (children, adolescents, adults), in a particular modality (individual, group, family), in a specific setting (agencies, rehabilitation centers, private practice, schools, universities), or in a particular area of expertise (substance abuse, sexual concerns, posttraumatic stress disorders), you should also develop a certain flexibility in your plans. No one can ever be sure what they will do for the rest of their life, and this is particularly true for counselors in a changing profession and society.

Richard recalls his own early struggles to settle on a specialty area:

> Some of my most vivid counseling memories are of being in a university counseling center working with 18- to 21-year-old students on career planning issues. They were often distraught because they felt the success of their whole lives was dependent on making a choice that had to be correct and that they had to live with forever. These memories are particularly vivid for me because I had a wife and two small children, was in my mid 30s, had worked all my life but had never stayed at a job for more than 3 years, and was working on my doctorate in counseling for another work environment change. If they were worrying about having to make quick and permanent career choices, then something was likely to be very wrong with my own career path!

The fact is that most professionals have a varied career path rather than the "one early decision" plan many people expect. This is evidenced in Jeffrey's experience:

> As I look back over my own career, I am astounded at the number of different ways that I have functioned as a counselor—in a preschool, middle school, community college, hospital, corporation, mental health center,

private practice, psychiatric clinic, substance abuse facility, university, and several community agencies. I've worked in a dozen different communities in North America alone, and another dozen in various parts of Asia, Europe, South America, and the South Pacific. When I was a graduate student, preparing for my first position, I had no idea of the different career paths my life would take, each job sparking an interest in another facet of this work.

The concept of a varied career path also holds true as you begin to choose a specialty. Many counseling students assume that they should read the necessary information, weigh the alternatives, and then select the best specialty for the remainder of their career. It is just not that simple. You are likely to experience personal changes that will impact your interests and recognition of your potential. Society will change in ways you had not imagined and so, too, will the demands of the profession.

Because no one can accurately predict the combination of personal and societal changes that will impact your professional future, flexibility in selection of counseling specialization is important to everyone. Your current situation as a graduate student is likely to be influenced by unique circumstances, some deliberately designed and others serendipitous.

The task for you as a counselor in training is to examine personal interests and skills, and the opportunities for specialized work in areas in which you want to work. This may lead you to an interest in a specialization as broad as *adults* or as narrow as *HIV-infected adults in a hospital setting*. Either of these examples serves to give you the necessary direction for making the study of abstract concepts more practical, program planning more rational, and motivation more personalized.

The choices you make should not be viewed as irrevocable. No career choice should end your career exploration activities or reduce your openness to new possibilities. This book could never have been written had the authors not continued to explore career-related aspects of themselves beyond the direct practice of counseling. Perhaps most importantly, career choices should not direct you to put all your energy into learning only about a few specialties. Fortunately, quality counselor training programs demand that you gain a wide variety of skills and areas of knowledge. This ensures that you will be able to function in either the limited area you might choose at this time or the more varied settings that life and societal changes may bring to you.

## Focus Activities: Making Personal Use of This Chapter

This chapter addresses critical decisions about specialization and gaining experience that should be made early in your program. Completing the following exercises—and following the related suggestions in the chapter—should help you clarify your interests and identify those areas in which it will be best for you to specialize. Completing the exercises should also help you find those employment opportunities and work sites that will provide you with the best counseling experiences to match your goals.

## *Choosing a Specialty*

1. **Your first task is to reflect on your interests and needs.** Write about yourself—your personality style, cultural background, experiences, values, attitudes, and beliefs—in your notebook before you begin to answer the following questions. Try to put down as clearly as possible what type of a person you are before deciding the types of clients with whom you want to work.

2. **Identify, from your reflections, those groups with whom you think you want to work, and look for their relationships to the way you see yourself.** Who you are, what you want, and who you should work with should be related in some ways. You need to be looking for these relationships and whether they are healthy or unhealthy.

3. **List your attitudes, thoughts, ideas, and feelings about the following groups:**

   - children,
   - adolescents,
   - young adults,
   - adults,
   - older adults, and
   - special populations (related to gender, race, religion, sexuality).

4. **Consider how you will evaluate and act on your reactions to these special groups of people.** Be honest with yourself and your abilities. You will need to refer clients who you feel you cannot work with due to things like conflicting issues and lack of objectivity. Which groups have the most interest for you? With which could you expect to have the most difficulty? Why? What do you need to do to resolve feelings related to these groups? Will you avoid working with certain groups or tackle your fears or concerns?

5. **Consider the settings in which you might encounter each specialized group.** Contact agencies in your area of interest and inquire as to which groups they serve. This will help you to identify possible practicum, internship, and future employment sites as well as help you to better understand the people you are seeking to serve.

6. **Identify courses to take that best prepare you for the type of counseling you prefer.** List them in your notebook and check out your reasoning with your adviser. Most programs emphasize skills and techniques for individual and group counseling with marriage and family courses as electives. Make sure that the program you choose offers those courses you need to specialize in a certain area.

# 5

## Solidifying Your Specialization

Once you have figured out who the general groups are that you want to work with, and found a program that fits those needs, your next step is to develop your professionalism in that area. Taking the basic courses is certainly a key step, but it is the same one that everyone else in your specialization will also be taking. To make yourself stand out from the crowd of other students and new graduates, you will need to take some personal initiatives to demonstrate your commitment and talents. One way to add to your expertise is to identify extra courses that will add to your knowledge and skills. Seeking professional involvement beyond the classroom is another key step, and making conscious choices about your internship can be critical.

### There Are Always More Classes to Take

The first questions graduate students tend to ask faculty about classes are which ones they should take and when they should take them. These are good student questions, and the answers will keep you on the road to graduation. But there is another set of questions that are generally not asked, either because they involve spending more time, energy, and money, or because the student never thinks to ask. These are the questions about what other courses beyond those that are required might provide additional preparation.

There is much more to learn than any program is ever going to be able to put in a required curriculum. People with the most expertise go well beyond the required courses to take others that could add something more to their knowledge and skills. Here are some examples of how counselors explained the benefits of seeking extra courses.

- **A school counselor:** "One of the best things I did was to take two extra courses outside the department. One was play therapy and the other was community prevention programs. The schools that I got job offers at were really excited that I could work this way with the youngest students, and my knowledge of how to improve relations between the school and community hit right on their needs."
- **A mental health counselor:** "My friends thought I was nuts taking an undergraduate class in physiology and a graduate class in school counseling. I know they sounded strange, but I wanted to know more about how the body worked so I could better understand stress,

relaxation, and even some of why drugs work the way they do. And the school course has been a big help for my clinical work with kids, because so much of their life is focused around the school. The two courses together have helped make me a welcome consultant in the schools as well."

- **A college student personnel graduate:** "My program was less clinical than others and that was basically what I wanted. But I knew from my undergraduate days that students had so many serious problems that I needed to learn more about. So I got permission to take a diagnosis course and a psychopathology course, and I can't tell you how much that information has helped my work with students and also made me the go-to woman when administrators are faced with difficult student issues."

Taking additional courses may not be practical for many students for lots of reasons: not enough time, too expensive, or can't find what you want. But when you do find a course that seems to fit your interests, remember that once you take enough courses to be in the full-time student status (9 credit hours is a common minimum) then it costs no more to take one, two, or even three more courses. If you have the energy, then the financial piece may be available to you. Another possibility is to sign up for a class as an audit rather than for a grade, which takes the pressure off of having to do all the work and get an A grade. So if you chose to explore them, there are financial and effort-saving options that may be available for taking additional courses.

## Professional Involvement in Specialized Organizations

Taking additional classes can certainly give you more information and skills to strengthen your specialization. What they are not likely to do is to provide experience in a specialization and in making contacts with people who can support your professional development. Involving yourself in organizations focused on your specialization or volunteering to work directly with faculty are other ways to expand your professional advancement, potential skills, knowledge, and connections.

Louisa Foss's (2002) development as a group work specialist provides a good example of how organizations can be a major source of support in your advancement. Classes and an experience in a group raised her excitement, but left her with the question, "How do I become a group work specialist?" (p. 30). Her first step was to contact the Association for Specialists in Group Work and ask how she might get more involved. That contact led to some volunteer work at a convention and conversations with experts in the field, and each new contact seemed to provide new and "exciting opportunities for service and learning" (p. 30). Returning home with even more interest and excitement, she contacted her state representative and quickly became involved both as a member and in leadership opportunities.

Professional organizations like the one Louisa selected are always look-ing for interested people to get involved. Students are especially welcome because they bring the new ideas and an enthusiasm these groups need. This is even more of an issue at the state level where there are fewer people with even closer connections to each other. Taking a little initiative to make these first few contacts can add a whole new dimension to your knowl-edge, skills, and sources of support in gaining recognition as an emerging new specialist.

Faculty are always looking for students with the interest and initiative to get involved with their specialized work, and this provides another oppor-tunity for strengthening your professional development in some special-ized area. There is never enough time for faculty to do all the research, publication, teaching, consultation, and organizational work they would like to do. One way they can become more effective is by finding emerging professionals who want to work with them on one project or another. It could be library work, interviewing people in the field, hands-on research, presentation help, or a myriad of other activities in which a student could provide great service for faculty.

But what could you, the student, gain from such involvement? Certainly there is information to gain from working with a faculty member that will not be available in class. Then there is the more specialized mentoring that can come when a faculty member believes someone is interested enough in the work to go beyond the norm to help. And there are also the connections that begin to be made by simply being around faculty when they are work-ing with others. Not only does your knowledge base increase, but you are also building a network of relationships that can be invaluable in finding employment or other professional opportunities.

## Specialization and Choice of a Quality Internship

It is never too early to begin seeking a quality internship—even though it will be at the end of your program. In fact, the process of choosing a qual-ity internship goes hand in hand with the development of your profes-sional style and flexible specialization. Making choices that stand the test of time in any of these areas requires both study and experiential explo-ration. That is, you must read about and discuss counselor roles, responsi-bilities, and functions in different settings and also get out and actually see and practice those factors as they appear in real-life settings.

### Early Interviews

During the introductory courses generally offered early in a program, you are exposed to techniques, counseling settings, and areas of specialization. Some of these you will be familiar with, and others will be new. Reading and passing tests about these concepts and settings are important, but can only go so far in developing true understanding. You must seek out and visit counselors in schools, mental health agencies, inpatient wards, rehabilitation settings, and private practice if you are to have a personalized feel for what is expected in such places. This personal contact is the only way for you to find how well the specialty actually matches your abilities, interests, and needs.

Ask questions early on of faculty and students about potential places to do an internship. Learn the specific requirements for such an experience in your program. Once you have some basic answers, you need to locate potential people and/or places where you might like to work. Interview professionals from these settings to see how they feel about their work and how it matches what you have been learning in class. Many times you find that the view of a specialty or agency from a counselor who works there is very different from the view presented in class or the text. Remember not to generalize from one interview to the whole profession. People in the same specialty can work in very different environments, and they can perceive similar environments in highly personalized ways.

### Sharing With an Adviser

After you have done extensive reading and exploration of the possible settings on your own, start talking to your adviser about selecting an internship site. This can now be an effective two-way conversation in which you describe your ideas and experiences and the adviser can offer his or her own perspective. The adviser has personal experience with specific settings and also knows how valuable specific settings have been to past students. Adding the adviser's knowledge and experience to that which you have been actively acquiring on your own will greatly clarify what might be the best site for you. It will also produce some specific personalized questions for you to get answered about the site or the actual internship.

At least one semester before you are ready to begin, you and your adviser should have reached some consensus on what might be one or more good internship sites for you. This is the time to make more formal contact with an agency about actually doing your internship with them. You must rely on your adviser at this time for the best way to proceed. The adviser's knowledge and experience about the most effective way to approach an individual or agency are very important. The adviser is likely to know, for example, whether the agency wants you to contact it first or whether it prefers that a faculty person do this. The adviser might also know whether there is a more appropriate faculty person who should call the agency, or if there is some specific person in an agency to contact.

### Advanced Interviews

You are likely to have one or more formal interviews at your internship site before you begin, and this situation is good for both of you. You need to get to know the site and those you will work with, and they need to understand you. The site that is good for some or most students is not necessarily going to be a good match for you. These interviews also provide an experience that is similar to interviewing for jobs—a time that is no longer that far away. Therefore, you should treat these interviews as important professional steps. Come prepared, be on time, and dress in a manner that is professionally appropriate for the site. These few basics will ensure that you make a good first impression.

The people at the potential site will want to know some specific things about you. However, you do not need to cram as you might for a big exam. They will want to know mostly general things about you, your program, your needs, and your expectations so that they can make some estimate of how well you will fit their personnel and system. You should prepare by reviewing your professional goals, how those match your program, and why this site might be expected to provide just the right culminating experience for you. Review your professional beliefs and theories as well as how you expect to implement them, but do not be afraid to express some hesitancy and equivocation. Experienced interviewers will recognize that you are new to this level of the profession and that only experience will clarify these issues and make you more confident in your positions.

Professionals from your internship site will have an expectation that you know something about the work they do. Another preparation task is thus to review the roles, function, and work expectations of people in such a setting. The less formal visits you have had to this or similar settings should help you recognize the tasks and issues that are expected of employees. You may not be an employee at this time, but being an intern is the closest thing to being a paid employee.

Make sure you go to the interview ready to ask questions as well as prepared to answer questions about yourself. You will be viewed as more professional if those who meet you see that you can integrate your professional needs with the reasonable, but more student-like, role of simply demonstrating knowledge and skills. Prepare yourself by developing a list of things that are important to your satisfaction in internship, and check that list out with other students currently in internships and with faculty. Once you know what you need and desire from a site, deciding what questions to ask should logically follow:

- What kinds of clients will I see most often?
- What activities other than counseling will I have the opportunity to experience (e.g., training, assessment, management, public relations)?
- To what extent will I be working with individuals, families, or groups?
- What sort of orientation program do you offer?
- Who will do my on-site supervision? How much will I get? What will be the format of the supervision?
- Will I be attending or taking part in staff meetings or other professional meetings?
- Are there particular days or hours that will be best for me to be on site?

Following the method suggested in this section will prepare you to enter your internship with the confidence that your choice was made professionally and that it utilized all possible resources. Of course, you can get an internship without so much work and thought on your part. For example, you could wait until the last minute and leave it all up to your adviser; or pick the most physically convenient site; or pick the site where most people go; or go wherever your best friend goes. However, these alternative methods also greatly increase the chances that the internship will not provide you with all the benefits of quality preparation, supervision, work opportunities, and personal satisfaction that might have been available in another appropriately selected setting. Begin the ground work for selecting your internship site from the first day you enter the program. This will add relevance to all you study and also increase the likelihood that your internship will be the true culminating experiential program component everyone expects it to be.

## Focus Activities: Making Personal Use of This Chapter

This chapter emphasizes the need to go beyond choosing a specialization, to doing those extra things that will actually more fully prepare you in that area. Courses will not be able to provide all you need. Completing the following exercises and following the suggestions in the chapter should provide that extra dimension of expertise that will bring you confidence and greatly increase your professional work opportunities.

### Extra Professional Efforts

1. **Talk to people working in your specialization, including faculty and other professionals, about what kinds of information may not be in your standard program, but that they have found to be particularly helpful in their practice.** Make a list of the kinds of information they suggest.
2. **Look for courses in your campus catalog that could add an extra dimension to your specialization based on the feedback you got from professionals.**
3. **Use the Internet to search for on-line courses, workshops, or other materials on your specialization.** Remember, the issue is not whether you can acquire three more credits, but whether you can get the information that will make you look special.

### Choosing a Practicum, Internship, or Work Site

1. **Begin looking for potential practicum and internship sites from the outset of your program.** Internships are almost always done off campus, and practica generally are. Check with your adviser to see if you have a choice of practicum site or whether your program does all practica at a given place. Remember that being prepared and keeping your eyes open to possibilities improves your chances of finding the

setting that best meets your needs and gives you counseling experiences that will contribute most to your clinical interests and areas of specialization.

2. **Look for sites in multiple ways.** Use the yellow pages, interview counselors in your area, interview other students who have worked in the area, and interview faculty about options. Put the highlights of your findings in your notebook.

3. **Prioritize sites that serve the client populations you prefer.** You want to maximize the usefulness of your practicum and internship experiences.

4. **Once you have narrowed your choices, find out more about each facility.** Knowing who the facility serves and how it works will demonstrate interest and increase your chances of being accepted as an intern.

5. **Practice interviews with family or friends, but do not overprepare.** Be yourself. Refer to the tips in this chapter and jot down the key ones for you. Ask questions, and do not forget to interview your interviewer.

6. **Consider your strengths, weaknesses, interests, and philosophy, and how well they match the needs, philosophy, and practices of the agency.** Choose the facility that appears to be the best match for you to get the most from your practicum and internship experiences.

# 6

# Getting Off on the Right Foot

Once you have chosen and been accepted in a counseling program that appears to meet your needs, you can expect a general feeling of relief. Surely the course work will meet your interests, the faculty will be compatible with your style, and the other students will be a source of inspiration and support. It is also tempting to assume that entering a quality program will ensure that you get exactly what you need in order to be an excellent counselor. Now all will be well if you just take the required classes in the specified order, do what is asked of you by your instructors, and follow along the prescribed road mapped by your adviser. After all, these people are experts in identifying what you will need in the field, and at teaching you these skills and knowledge in such a way that they will be at your permanent disposal. Why shouldn't you trust their judgment and guidance?

Believing that counselor education programs, especially those accredited by the profession, contain what you need is certainly reasonable. Indeed, such curricula are composed of the content that has been found to be most useful over time. The problems, however, are more numerous than you might imagine, and they cannot all be solved by the program or the faculty alone. Your initial feelings of relief at being admitted into a program may very well give way to new concerns about the program and how you fit in. This chapter identifies some common issues that may be troubling. If you are aware of them, and give them proper attention, they may prove to strengthen rather than hinder your education.

## Troubling Issues You May Face

There are several challenging issues you may face in your program. This is not necessarily a problem considering that your very job will be to help people overcome such obstacles. We highlight here some of the more frequently reported complaints to prepare you better for what you might expect to encounter.

1. **Classes are not necessarily taught the same way by all instructors.** A counseling theory course, for example, may emphasize learning a different approach to counseling each week, with the ultimate goal being that you select the theory that you find most attractive. Another way of teaching the same class may involve helping you to view these different theories as historical antecedents of an integrative

approach that you have to create yourself. Both approaches to teaching you about theory are legitimate, but each produces quite different outcomes.

To make things even more interesting (notice we do not use the word *difficult*), each of your instructors may have a stated preference and strong affiliation with one counseling approach that is believed to be superior to others. In one of your courses, you teacher may convince you quite persuasively that psychoanalytic theory is the best place to begin a career, while the next class may stress cognitive behavioral, and the one after that Gestalt. Then to make things still more challenging, your practicum instructor may prefer you to work within an altogether different framework once you are seeing clients.

You may not be able to choose your instructor, but you can make some choices about how you approach your courses. For example, you can willingly follow wherever your instructors lead you, do no more or no less than just exactly what they ask of you, and worry about what you did not learn after you get in the field. Another alternative is to take the instructor's lead and supplement what he or she is offering by doing additional investigations in the library, with faculty, and with peers on your own. This clearly adds to your workload, but it also makes you more the master of your education.

2. **There is not necessarily continuity and consistency from one class to the next.** One course may teach you that the single most important counseling skill for you to master is reflecting client feelings, the means by which you help facilitate self-exploration, clarity, and insight. Your next instructor may tell you that currently the most important skill for you to apply is cognitive interventions, in which you teach clients to think more healthfully. A third instructor may state that although reflecting client feelings and applying cognitive interventions are useful, what you really need to concentrate on are strategic interventions, in which you seek to disrupt dysfunctional behavioral patterns. As a result, you are now standing amid three experts each of whom is telling you to do something quite different.

The example is exaggerated, but you can certainly expect to be presented with widely differing viewpoints in any given program. This is not necessarily a problem with the program but simply a reflection of the current state of our profession. Your task is to look closely at all the viewpoints presented, learn the logic behind them, and incorporate that which makes the most sense and works best for you.

3. **Some of your instructors have not done much counseling in many years.** Faculty are pressured to do many things, and they may not get to do much counseling as a part of their current work. They may wind up teaching concepts and skills based on what they have read most recently, or on what they remember from their past. It is even possible they may be encouraging you to learn strategies that do not work very well in the modern world, even if they sound good in the classroom.

Remember that your training is part theory and part practice. As long as you have varied faculty and varied experiences in the program, you will be exposed to enough opportunities for successful development. A successful program blends many types of people and experiences. You must see and accept each part for what it is, and then make the best possible use of what each part has to offer.

Experts develop credibility for their ideas in a number of ways, some through practice with actual clients and some through systematic research. Ideally, you will have the opportunity to work with faculty who are steeped in both practice and research worlds, but even if you are not, you are still likely to become exposed to a knowledge base that is informed by both important sources of information.

4. **As in any human organization, faculty members in a counseling program sometimes do not get along very well.** There may be rivalries between factions, even hostility between two instructors who do not like one another very well. Inevitably, there will be disagreements even among the most cooperative staff members as to the best way to influence you. You may find yourself left to sort out what you believe in the face of heated disagreement by your mentors.

Imagine, for example, that you are confused about a case. You decide to consult with several different faculty members to get a consensus as to what you should do. The first person tells you that what you are doing is just fine; keep doing it. Unsure of yourself, you decide to get another opinion. The next person you consult tells you to do something quite different. Then you try a third source, and she tells you that both of the other two are wrong, that what you really need to do is something else.

You are thus caught in the middle, among conflicting people and views, and cannot get an answer as to what the right way is. A more positive view is that you are learning about the practical differences in theories and people. These differences, and their impact on you and clients, reflect the true state of affairs in the real world. Agreement among people on what to do and how to do it is not the norm in an evolving profession, except for those who refuse to consider change. What you are actually seeing is real people with evolving ideas about what counseling is and how it works.

5. **The experience and background of each student is different.** Counseling programs try to present what most people require, but they are certainly not customized to address all your unique needs. Given your individual personality, your interpersonal skills, your cultural background, your preferred learning style, your career aspirations, and your previous experiences in the field, what you will benefit from most is probably considerably different from someone else.

Even the best, most comprehensive, thorough, well-integrated, and meticulously planned counselor education program is going to leave out a lot of material and experiences that are crucial to your development. That is why, ultimately, you are the one responsible for filling in those gaps and customizing your educational experiences. You must be in charge of making information and experiences personally useful and professionally relevant. It is imperative that you take responsibility from the very beginning of your counselor education experience to ensure that you get what you will need most. This involves becoming an informed and active consumer of your training, not a passive recipient who does only the minimum of what you are asked to do.

6. **Students don't always get along.** Everyone recognizes that students and faculty have different expectations of each other, so conflicts can arise. The reality is that as many or more conflicts can arise among students than between students and faculty. The obvious hierarchy between students and faculty sets up clear roles for each group from the very beginning, and whether or not everyone likes those roles, they do create confidence in how to react around each other. The same roles and rules do not apply among students, which can make the relationships more complex with more potential for conflict.

You are in a program in which being open with beliefs, feelings, opinions, and reasoning is encouraged in students and in the counseling relationship. As beneficial as openness about these things may be, it also identifies differences that can cause anxiety, tension, and defensiveness. One example comes from a 30-year-old student who always wore a tie to class as a part of his way of demonstrating professional behavior:

> It was in our first semester and the class discussion was on professionalism. I was pretty quiet as I was in most of my classes. During the break a student who always wore cut-offs and dirty sneakers suggested that he thought I was putting him down and showing off for the professor with the way I dressed. I was hurt, but thought this kind of honesty was what we did in counseling, so I told him that this just feels right to me and from my perspective he wasn't dressing professionally.
>
> Well that comment went over like a lead balloon, and we didn't speak for weeks. The worst was that people started taking sides. Hallway conversations stopped when one group went by, and it was almost like we were warring factions. It felt like a competition for other students, faculty, and even grades. It was not a pretty sight for a long time.

Another example comes from a South African student's comments to her adviser:

> People are very unfriendly here. I walk down the hall where a group of students are talking and they ignore me. Why don't they like me?

After a couple of months, this student almost gave up the program and left for home before finally approaching her adviser with her dilemma. Only through exploring differing cultural perceptions did she come to recognize how much more assertive Americans are expected to be in these situations and how much more inviting South Africans were expected to be. These are only two examples of many that emphasize how the differences in students can become serious problems.

# Take Initiative Early

We do not mean to burst your fantasies that faculty know what is best. By and large, faculty are well informed and experienced. In most cases, they have a very good idea of what might be the best experiences for you. But learning, just like counseling, is a partnership. Ultimately, you have to be responsible, be assertive, and initiate enough to make sure that you do your part in directing and monitoring your own learning. Take responsibility for your own growth and development. Ask for what you want most.

There are several things that you might wish do in order to function most effectively in your apprenticeship as a counselor.

## *Teach Your Family and Friends What to Expect*

Attending a graduate program in counseling requires you to invest a tremendous amount of time, money, energy, and commitment. It means making a number of sacrifices. It involves many late nights and early mornings catching up on your reading and class assignments.

Yet your training and degree will eventually provide you with personal and career opportunities that are currently out of reach. Educate the people you are closest to that during the next few years you will be undergoing a major transition in your life. You need these people to be supportive of your efforts. You must keep them informed as to what you are going through in order to have them feel a part of your team. For example, you might say

- "Honey, I have a big exam coming up this week. Could you cover for me with the kids and chores around the house while I spend some time at the library?"
- "Sorry that I haven't been able to spend much time with you. I am a bit overloaded with schoolwork right now, but I want to schedule some quality time when we can be together."
- "Next semester I will be taking a practicum, which will involve a lot of extra time on campus. We need to talk about some changes we can make so I don't put an unfair burden on you."
- "I am feeling a lot of pressure right now, and I don't like the way I have been taking things out on you. I want you to understand what is going on with me."

All these examples indicate a student who is asking for what he or she needs in order to function optimally, and yet who is also being sensitive to the impact of graduate studies on family and friends.

The other part of your responsibility is to recognize that there should be times when you can give more of yourself and that your family and friends need that also. For example:

- "I am done with exams and have nothing to really do for a week. What can I do for you?"
- "I know I've been focused on myself and my school, and I really appreciate your being so supportive. Make sure you let me know when you need more than I have been giving. I want to be there for you, too."

In one sense, you are not the only one who is going to school; your whole family system will be affected by the experience. After a period of time you are going to begin to speak differently, think differently, and behave in different ways. In many cases, you will find this will enhance your relationships with family, friends, and coworkers. But some people in your life may feel threatened by the changes you experience. That is why it is absolutely critical that you involve your loved ones in your learning as much as possible. Tell them about what you are experiencing. Bring them up to date on what you are being exposed to. Keep them a part of your education rather than separate from it.

### Balance Your Lifestyle Between Work and Play

Graduate school is a marathon, not a sprint. You cannot put everything else in your life on hold—your family, your friends, your job, your leisure pursuits, your other interests—and then race to the finish line.

Those students who are working full time, managing households, and taking care of children are particularly at risk for overstressed reactions and burnout. We wish to give you fair warning that many of your friendships and intimate relationships are going to change, irrevocably, as a result of what you learn in your program. As you become aware of dynamics and processes that were previously unknown to you, as you increase your interpersonal sensitivity, as you improve your communication skills, you are going to find out about things in your life that will never remain the same. Divorce or separation from a partner can occur unless you are vigilant and work hard on your relationship. Friendships will change. Perhaps you will find that you no longer have the patience, or the inclination, to hang out with the same people with whom you used to spend time.

Build some time for yourself and the people you care most about into your daily and weekly schedule. Vacations from school are not enough. Diversify your life as much as you can reasonably manage in the time available.

Here are several students describing their efforts to strike a balance:

- "I really don't have time for my participation in a community choir, but I force myself to make the time. With the practices and performances and all, a lot of my time that I could be spending on schoolwork I use to take care of myself. This is the only way I could get through school."

- "Having a youngster playing little league baseball takes a lot of my time. At first, I was trying to avoid going to my son's games. Between work, school, and everything else, I don't have much extra time. But then I realized how important it is for me to spend that time away from professional stuff. For a few hours all I think about is baseball and watching the children play. I need those breaks. I really do."
- "Music used to be such a big part of my life before school. If I gave it up, I just wouldn't feel whole. Playing music helps me to stay centered. I'm not sure if I really have a choice to dump it in order to make room for more school activities."

Other students talk about reading novels, watching old movies, gardening, building something with their hands—anything to give them some time away from school activities to replenish themselves. Indeed, you will want to structure some part of your life so that you can recover from stress, heal your wounds, or just make sure that you are functioning at peak levels.

## Create a Private Place for Study Without Distractions

You will be spending hundreds (if not thousands) of hours reading books and articles, digesting new ideas, studying material for later application on examinations or in counseling sessions. It is not a luxury but rather a necessity that you find a place where you can work best.

The library may offer you some advantages, but you will still need to create some space for yourself within your own domain. Ideally, this should be a place where you can get away from the telephone and interruptions, where you can concentrate fully on the tasks at hand without being distracted. Pick a place that is out of the mainstream traffic of those in your life. It is better to have a small, crowded space than to have plenty of room with multiple distractions.

## Establish Specific Times to Concentrate on Schoolwork

Build into your daily routines a part of every day in which you concentrate on schoolwork. There should be specific time always available for catching up on reading assignments, reviewing class notes, making outlines for projected papers, and preparing for class assignments.

The things you learn in a counseling program do not lend themselves to memorizing for later recitation. You do not just learn a list of terms or concepts that you are expected to spit back out on demand. You should be learning ideas and developing an understanding so that you can actually apply them with real live human beings in need. You may have to answer questions about Piaget's stages of cognitive development, Freud's defense mechanisms, or Adler's stages of treatment, but you will also have to use these concepts in your work, which requires another whole degree of understanding. In order for this process to take place, this material has to become part of you and part of the way that you think and react to others.

This can only happen when you devote considerable time and effort to your studies every day.

You are likely to find that there are specific times of the day when you study and learn best. Some people are fresh and most alert at dawn; others cannot conceive of being out of bed at this time. You need to experiment to find out just which times during the day are the best ones for you to set aside for your studies. Consider the experiences of these two students:

- "I'm a mother of three children in school. At night when I get home from classes, there is dinner to make, clothes to wash, stories of school to hear, homework to help with, and getting kids to bed. After that I'm exhausted and only ready for bed. Once they go off to school in the morning, I'm FREE and awake. A hot cup of coffee and the kitchen table is all mine to spread out on any way I want."
- "Do whatever you want to me, but don't get me up early! I hang out after classes with some friends where we discuss what we are learning and other junk and this seems to relax and encourage me. So around 10 o'clock I'm ready to spend 2 to 4 hours at work in the apartment when everyone else goes to sleep."

We tell our clients that what takes place during sessions is relatively less important than what they do when they are outside the sessions, applying what they learned in the real world. The same holds true in learning to be a counselor. What you do in class is less important than what you do in your own life applying what you truly understand.

### Create an Image of the Kind of Student You Want to Be

How willing are you to take an active role in directing your own education? Do you see yourself as the student who sits in class quietly and dutifully, does what is expected, and tries to draw as little attention to himself or herself as possible? Or can you imagine yourself getting out of your comfort zone and pushing yourself to take some risks?

Constructive risk taking is individualized for each person, depending on your style, personality, and particular needs. Some students already talk way too much, dominating discussions, keeping the focus on themselves, speaking not because they have anything meaningful to say but because they simply feel a need to talk rather than listen. For other students, asking one question, or making one brief comment, may send their hearts into an uncontrolled flutter. Depending on how you need to most challenge yourself, you can push to try those things that are difficult for you.

Richard describes the transformation that took place in creating a new vision of himself as a student:

> I was a C student in grade school, high school, and as an undergraduate. I managed B's and a couple of A's as a master's student, but I became a straight A student in my doctoral program. Only after it was all over did I recognize what made the difference in me. I was never very motivated by doing what I was told to do even when it was good for me. I did it, but with no press to do it particularly well.

It was during my doctoral program, in particular, that I became more interested in directing my own learning than just following what I was told to do. It changed everything. I worked my tail off and loved it. I got involved outside of class, read things that were not required, hunted down people that might have information important to me. I was worrying less about what faculty wanted and finding that what I produced was going well beyond requirements. I was doing this for me, and it made all the difference in the world.

What you get out of your program is directly related to how much you put into it. If you sit back and let others control what you learn, and how you learn it, your education will not specifically address your unique needs and interests. You can certainly complete a program and learn from it through this technique, but do not expect to achieve all you can. You are paying a lot of money and expending enormous energy on this education, so make sure you are making the choices that get you the most out of it.

## Build a Support Network

Make an effort to set up a network of friends and classmates you can rely on. There will be times when you feel discouraged, frustrated, over-whelmed, and ready to give up. It really helps if there are people you can go to for support, to talk things out, to help you sort out what is going on in the program and in your life. Remember that you are in a profession that encourages people to make use of the support of others. Seek support in ways you want for your clients and friends. Give yourself the attention that you give to others.

Support networks can be both informally and formally organized. Informal systems are set up, for example, when students congregate together on a regular basis—as in a car pool, for a meal, or in a study group composed of like-minded folks you enjoy being around. It is important to initiate such groups rather than waiting for someone else to extend to you an invitation to join one.

More formal support systems include student associations and Chi Sigma Iota, the honor society of counseling students, which exists to provide intellectual, social, and emotional support. Many departments also have their own student organizations that arrange field trips, social gatherings, and student-centered workshops. The counseling center, women's center, and various cultural organizations on campus (e.g., African American Student Alliance, Latino Student Association) may also offer support groups for students seeking a trusting environment in which to talk about concerns.

## Find Out How the System Operates

A university is a complex environment composed of a variety of resources and individuals who can help you. Make an effort to learn your way around. This means developing a working relationship with the department chair, with the support staff, and with the secretaries who run things on a daily basis. It also means orienting yourself to the library and learning how to conduct computer-assisted literature searches. In order to get the most from your education, you need to know all of the options and services that are available.

Be aware of your unique needs. Find out what specialized human resources are available to you and make contact. For example, singles groups are generally available on campus or in the local community for those who could benefit. Special organizations and groups for minorities are also available on almost every campus. Such groups often know of financial, housing, transportation, and other forms of support not necessarily included in standard publications.

### Start a Journal

Every time you leave school your mind will be filled to the brim with new things you have learned and complex feelings you are trying to sort out. Your head will hurt trying to make sense of what you were exposed to most recently. Ideas will come to you on the drive home, or when you are trying to fall asleep. There may be hundreds of them on some days. What will you do with all that mental activity? How will you channel it?

We recommend to students that they start keeping a journal and write down everything going on inside them. Create a place for yourself, a private place, where you can talk to yourself about what you find most exciting, most disturbing, most confusing. In such a place, you will be able to write down the things that you wish to remember. You can include memorable quotes, titles of books that you want to read, ideas that you have for pieces that you want to write someday. You can set goals for yourself as to where you want to be a few years in the future. A journal is a great place to talk through conflicts that you are experiencing. (See also chapter 9 for ways to supplement your formal education.)

Here is one example of a student's journal entry:

> Class tonight was a real eye opener. I'm not sure what to make of it. People said some things to me that I don't think I've ever heard before. It started out we were talking about how groups are important in people's lives. The opportunities to get feedback and stuff like that. Then I asked why we weren't looking at our own behavior in the class as a group. That was a pretty big deal for me to speak up like that. I usually don't say much.
>
> I suppose because I was the one to bring it up, the teacher turned things back to me. He was pretty smooth, actually, the way he did it. Now I see what the text means when they talk about how group leaders try to get members to take responsibility for what happens. Anyway . . .

Entries such as this represent just one of the many ways in which students attempt to integrate personally what they are learning academically. A journal can be the tool by which you practice your own self-counseling. It can also serve as a personal summary and review of your most exciting times.

## Meeting Social and Emotional Needs

Academic skills are certainly necessary for success, but other needs periodically take priority, and they cannot be ignored if you are to get the most from your education. Simply put, your school life will suffer if, for example, your love life is unsatisfactory, if you are engaged in conflict with a friend or family member, if you are experiencing some physical ailment, or if you are feeling lonely or empty or sad.

One of the distinct advantages of our field is the emphasis placed on human connections. All the while you are learning about how to be a counselor, you are hopefully applying the emphasis on intimacy, empathy, and sensitivity to other relationships in your life. This should not only be true for the people you live with but also for those in your classes. Here are some examples of how people used the people around them to get them through difficult times.

- **Support during unexpected trauma:**

  "I woke up, took a shower and then I found it—a lump in my right breast." It was naturally a struggle for Cher to find a way through this trauma, but some lessons became very clear and among them was, "Talking to fellow counselors was helpful during this experience . . . reaching out to let others know that I needed support was essential to receiving what I needed." (Igelman, 2000, p. 25)

- **A group approach to the stresses of school:**

  Every few weeks, on a Friday or Saturday night, we pick a few places to go for an outing. Then we discuss amongst ourselves which one would be the most feasible for all of us to make. . . . Once we decide on a location, we proceed to coerce each other into attending that week's activity. It may sound like a cruel way to get us out of the house, but without it, I'm sure that many of us would have stayed home. . . . Each outing the group embarked on has made us all feel much better about life in general. (Davis, 2001, p. 31)

Your dedication to academic studies is certainly crucial to your development as a counselor, but you need to take care of yourself as well. Most often, this means complementing business with pleasure. Make sure you create time for fun as well as work. Seek out those in your program who seem attractive and interesting to you. One of the main messages that we teach our clients is the notion that you have to go after the things you want. You cannot sit around and hope that others read your mind, sense that you are looking for human contact, and initiate relationships. It is probably most helpful to operate under the opposite assumption: pretend that whatever you want in life is only going to take place when you are prepared to make it happen. Look around the room and identify those with whom you seem to share similar interests. Note those who you think might be interesting to spend some time with. Then approach them!

## Getting the Most From Your Faculty

Implicit in much of what we have to say is the idea that you are not a passive recipient of learning but are actively involved in the process. Your task is to find socially appropriate ways to go about getting what you need from faculty. In addition to the usual things that you imagine are available to you in your interactions with faculty, consider the following specific actions.

1. **Ask for feedback whenever you can.** Approach faculty members you particularly respect and trust. Ask them to share with you their assessments of your skills. If you demonstrate a real willingness to gain honest input, rather than fish for compliments, you are likely to hear invaluable suggestions as to ways that you might upgrade your communication skills, your interpersonal style, or your student-related behavior. Keeping quiet will leave you guessing and probably have you missing out on invaluable insights.

2. **Read the research being conducted by the faculty in your department.** Approach those who are writing in areas in which you have particular interest. Engage them in informal discussions about the articles and books. Learn as much as you can about the process by which these works are created. Faculty always have many more ideas and stories beyond the specific details included in what they have written. This is the way to understand what makes a highly successful person in the field tick. The more you understand this, the greater the likelihood is that you can utilize for yourself the best of what you learn about the material, the person, and the process.

3. **Volunteer to collaborate with faculty members on their research.** Even if you are not a graduate assistant assigned to a particular instructor, approach someone who is writing in an area that you find compelling. Ask if there is some aspect of a project in which you might become involved. All faculty can use consistent and knowledgeable support.

4. **Attend social gatherings in which faculty members will be available for informal interactions.** Try to get beyond seeing your professors as godlings and know them as human beings. Remember that counseling, teaching, learning, and growing are combinations of informational, individual, and interpersonal concepts. To make the best use of all that is available to you, combine these concepts.

5. **Don't be afraid to set boundaries.** Historically, students have sometimes been sexually or emotionally exploited by faculty. Professors are in a position of power and authority, so that any personal relationship that develops between faculty and students is not based on equal footing. Be aware that faculty are ethically obligated to avoid dual relationships with students in much the same way as counselors are to avoid them with clients. The boundary line between a personal and professional relationship can be subtle, and both faculty and students should use caution to make certain that students are not exploited.

If you observe or sense that a professor might be acting inappropriately seductive or exploitive with you, the appropriate professional action is to bring this to his or her attention. This action may be risky in that you may fear retribution, but allowing yourself to be taken advantage of has even worse consequences. Should you not feel satisfied with the way the matter has been handled, seek the counsel of another faculty member you trust, or approach the department head for guidance. That is one of the reasons administrators are in those positions.

All universities have two other sources of confidential support when you are feeling mistreated in some way. There will be an office that is often called institutional equity or affirmative action that works to support fairness efforts for anyone who might be suffering from prejudicial treatment based on race, gender, sexual orientation, disability, or other factors. They deal with sensitive issues all the time and will give solid, confidential advice on understanding problem situations and potential actions.

Another source of support is the ombudsperson's office on campus. Students are in clearly one-down power positions with faculty, administrators, and sometimes other students. Universities try to create more of a balance when problems arise by creating an ombudsperson to offer confidential guidance or formal support in working out problems.

You do not need to face a difficult faculty situation alone or without quality guidance. Seek the help that is there for you if and when you might need it.

## Focus Activities: Making Personal Use of This Chapter

This chapter focuses on how to get the most from your program. It begins by addressing five issues that you should consider—because they may cause you problems—as you enter a program. Many students enter programs with unrealistic expectations, failing to consider the realities of organizational policies, procedures, and politics. Review the five issues and consider how you feel about each in relation to your program. Sometimes merely having your eyes opened to things that could occur prepares you for them and helps you put them into a more positive, workable perspective. The key is active involvement on your part. Take responsibility, ask a lot of questions, prepare yourself, and do not hesitate to get involved.

### Getting Started

Preparing yourself and being organized from the outset of your program can go a long way in seeing you through to successful completion of your program. Completion of the following exercises should help you get off on the right foot.

1. **Communicate with family, friends, and coworkers about your needs, expectations, and fears.** Refer to examples in this chapter for ideas.
2. **Balance play and work in your lifestyle.** Many students enter a program feeling they must put everything else in their lives on hold. This is a myth! In fact, the most successful students are those who are able

to maintain a holistic balance in their lives. Although initially you may have to force yourself to put down the books at times, the following suggestions may help:

- *List your hobbies and favorite things to do in your notebook.*
- *Star the top five.* Make sure to engage in your favorite activity several times per week and engage in the other four at least biweekly.
- *Listen to your body and recognize when it needs a break.* Write a paragraph or two in your notebook on how you take a break and also note what happens when you fail to give yourself a break. What are the consequences? Are they really conducive to productive scholastic work? Two hours of work riddled with anxiety, preoccupation, and stress will probably result in your having to redo the work.

3. **Create a private place for yourself where you can study without distractions.** Learn to be assertive in asking for your space and privacy when you are not getting it. Say "no" and give social cues that you need to get back to work (e.g., stand up and walk to the door).

- *List at least five private, quiet places in your notebook.*
- *Explore how you feel and what it means to say "no" to others.* List your fears, write out some ways you can say "no," and practice with family and friends.
- *List social cues you can use to help communicate that you need to get back on task.*

4. **Program into your lifestyle opportunities to concentrate on your schoolwork.**

- *Schedule to do a majority of your work when you are the most focused and do your best work.* Is it morning, afternoon, evening, or some special combination of times?
- *Always keep something with you to do when you are waiting.* Write in your journal, brainstorm for a paper, edit something you have written, or read several pages in a textbook. Working on things for 10 minutes here and there adds up to a lot of saved time.
- *Use the ABC method to prioritize all your tasks.*
  — List all tasks and do not forget things like household duties, errands, and assignments.
  — Write A's next to those things that must be done today.
  — Write B's next to those things that must be done within the week.
  — Write C's next to those things that can be done in the next several weeks.

This method will keep you from clumping all of your responsibilities together and significantly reduce that overwhelming feeling that comes from that clumping.

- *Tape class lectures.* Listen to them while driving, cleaning, working on the car, doing laundry. Design creative study habits and list them.

5. **Create an image of the kind of student you want to be.** Think of others who represent the kind of student you want to be or people who possess certain qualities that could help you as a student. List those qualities in your notebook.

6. **Build a support network system.**

   - *Share your feelings, both positive and negative, with family and friends.* Keep communication open about your and their feelings, needs, and concerns.
   - *Expand your support system by meeting at least two or more people in every class.* Ask to exchange phone numbers and share a bit about yourself. Many students initially feel nervous and anxious and often welcome greetings, exchanges, and invitations from others.
   - *Take others up on their invitations.* Even when they do not sound too exciting, good things often come from slow beginnings.
   - *Ask your adviser about formal and informal options for support.*

7. **Learn how your program and the university operates and what resources they have to offer.**

   - Take a tour of the campus.
   - Go to the orientation programs.
   - Find the organizations that emphasize ethnic, religious, or other special interests that are important to you.
   - Find the library and ask for a tour.
   - Find the copy centers available to you.
   - Find the computer labs and take the introductory sessions on how to use different computer packages if you need them.
   - Find the student center, which is a central location for lots of information.
   - Find the book stores, health facilities, and other campus locations you will use.
   - Be sure to find the best spots for food, fun, and entertainment!
   - Note all of the above, with locations and phone numbers, in your notebook.

8. **Start a journal.** This will help you to get your thoughts in order and be better prepared mentally and physically to take action on those things that require your attention.

## Getting the Most From Your Faculty

1. **Ask for feedback whenever you can.** If you are uncomfortable with this, role-play with a family member or friend. Record the results.

2. **Read about the research being conducted by the faculty in your department.** Knowing their interests can help you to identify those that meet yours. Similar interests may lead to working together in counseling, research, and publications.

3. **Volunteer to collaborate with faculty members on their research.** Take a risk and ask about research opportunities within the program. Once you have made it known that you are interested, motivated, and available to work, more opportunities will come your way!

4. **Attend social gatherings in which faculty members and students are available for informal interactions.** Getting to know faculty as human beings will help reduce some of the intimidation you may feel. It will also allow you to see how they interact with others, thus providing a model for you to follow as you become a professional. Remember that they are people with many similar issues, feelings, and needs, so do not be afraid to show a bit of your human side as well.

5. **Learn to set appropriate boundaries.** Be aware of your rights as a student and a human being. If you feel you are being treated inappropriately, talk with a trusted faculty member about your options.

6. **Find out where the ombudsperson's office is located.** This is the place you can always get confidential advice on problems with faculty, administrators, or other students.

# 7

# Strategies for Academic Success

You have been admitted into a graduate program, in part because you have demonstrated some degree of success in those tasks usually associated with scholarly work. Specifically, this means that you are reasonably proficient at taking exams and writing papers. This is a great start, but there are other kinds of tasks that you will be expected to complete in your graduate education. These include research skills, computer literacy, interpersonal skills, take-home examinations, and, probably at the end of your program, some combination of comprehensive exam, master's project, thesis, or dissertation.

## Research Skills

Richard's story about one of his clients gives clarity to the importance of research for professionals dealing with human needs:

> A client came to me in a panic after a standard physical identified a growth on his head. He was referred to a specialist who informed him that he needed a complicated operation soon. Fear and anxiety were normal reactions, so we worked to reduce them to a level where we could consider what the key things were that he would want to know about his doctor before letting him operate. Two key questions emerged from the discussion. With volumes of new research becoming available and much of it being conflicting, does this doctor effectively evaluate the current research on diagnoses and treatment of problems like mine? Is this doctor involved in the latest research and does he apply it successfully, or does he just read about it in the news?
> The client wanted confidence in a doctor. Clarifying his questions did not make the client ready to jump for joy, but at least he now had key questions to get answered in order to gain confidence in the doctor and the procedure.

You will not be trained to be a brain surgeon who cuts into people, but your work will certainly involve helping people with their thoughts and behaviors surrounding serious issues with major quality-of-life implications. Shouldn't the clients that you work with be able to have the same confidence in us that this client wanted in his surgeon? Of course they should. This is the primary reason why graduate school will place more emphasis on research and your ability to understand, evaluate, and apply it in your practice no matter what kind of people or issues your work entails.

## *Statistics*

Counseling students are often heard to say, "I got into this field because I like to work with people. Why is it that they expect us to be mathematicians as well?"

The apprehension that many students feel in taking research, statistics, and appraisal courses is all too common among prospective counselors. Some people have such a block against quantitative subjects that they save these courses for the very last, hoping that somehow they will be able to avoid them—although such an outcome is highly unlikely. The fact is that you need the information and skills from these courses in order to complete a number of other assignments as well as to do the best possible work with your clients.

The good news is that the emphasis in your quantitative courses is less on mathematical operations and more on understanding the underlying principles involved in making sense of research data or test scores. These skills are crucial in order to understand literature in the field and to be a critical and discerning consumer of what you read. In addition, no small part of a counselor's job involves administering, scoring, and making sense of testing material. Clients have many questions about tests that you or others have given them; and in order to help clients understand what these tests and scores mean, you must have a solid knowledge of statistical methods and appraisal techniques.

Katherine Ziff (2002) was a student interested in people skills and the arts. She could only see stress in the research classes until she found a number of key things that got herself and others through the process successfully:

- Stats are just different—Most of us did not focus on statistics before graduate school, and learning about them is just different than our other studies so we need to just accept this and look for new ways to learn.
- Journal your thoughts and feelings—It will help you clarify your thoughts and fears so that you can express them to peers and faculty who can help.
- Use study groups—You wouldn't ask a client to struggle alone so there is no reason for you to struggle alone.
- Do your homework—Skip this piece and only problems will follow.
- Ask questions in class—Make the class work for you by letting the instructor know what you need when you need it.
- Learn the software—Computers can do much of the work for you, but you need to quickly get familiar with the instruments and the software.
- Seek extra help—There are always research and stat students around who know more than others. Use them. (pp. 24, 29)

Reach out and get help if you are apprehensive about taking quantitative courses and doing well in them. Do not be satisfied with just getting through them. The courses are required because the material and concepts are critical to your work. Make sure you have someone around, such as the instructor, a mentor, a friend, a tutor, or a classmate, who can help you to understand what it is that you are doing and why. The concepts of *standard deviation, Z score, dependent variable,* or *analysis of variance* are ideas not numbers. They are not that complicated if you search out those people who can explain their practical applications to you.

### Computer Literacy

It may still be possible to complete at least a master's degree without mastering word processing software and simple applications for test interpretation and statistical calculations, but it is very difficult. The reality of the counseling profession is that computers have become an indispensable tool for our work. School counselors use computers in their scheduling activities. Career counselors use computer programs that help clients complete assessment instruments and make informed decisions. Rehabilitation and community agency counselors use computer-designed diagnostic programs to help them with treatment planning. Marriage and family counselors construct genograms on computers. All counselors are responsible for reports, case studies, and other paperwork that could bury them without computer assistance.

As a student you will make some use of the computer for statistics, but much more for writing papers. Computer technology is so advanced that faculty are rarely willing to accept anything but professionally prepared materials from students. Even those of us who have been poor spellers and weak at grammar from the first grade on can use the computer to help us correct it. The result is that when faculty see the use of poor spelling and grammar, they know that the student is not only weak in those areas but also has not yet learned to effectively use the computer technology available to him or her.

Computers are so important to school and work that now universities have huge budgets to provide computer labs for students, but it has not been enough, particularly for graduate students. The vast majority of graduate students have found that they need to have their own personal computer so that they can work morning, afternoon, or in the middle of the night while at home or at school, and thus gain the freedom to choose their own best work environments.

It used to be difficult to find the right computer because of the many options and technology changing so quickly. Universities are making it much easier for you now because most have an office or computer store where people will listen to your needs, tell you what others with your needs are doing, and also offer discounts on major brands. This is a good deal, and there is no longer any reason to go about choosing on your own.

### Research Papers

You will be introduced to methodologies and terminology that may be new for you, or at least variations of themes that may seem familiar. The terms *APA style* (which refers to the standardized way in which you use citations and present your paper) and *adequate documentation of your ideas* (which means that you must support the things you say with research and the writings of others) will haunt you again and again.

In many, if not most, of your classes you will be assigned papers encouraging you to develop literacy in the major areas of specialization in the field. Depending on the content of the course, and the approach of the instructor, your papers may involve integrating the literature in a particular area, or they may involve a type of personal research in which you are expected to apply concepts to some aspect of your own life. For example, in a theories class you might be assigned the task of selecting a few of the approaches and discussing how each of them might be used to approach a particular case. Another variation might require you to apply a particular theory to a concern in your life right now. Still another kind of paper might require you to find all the empirical evidence that can be used to support and/or refute the effectiveness of a given approach.

Each of these assignments asks you to demonstrate understanding of course content and become a fluent communicator using the written word. Much of what counselors do involves logical thinking, problem solving, reflective activity, and communication of ideas. Writing papers helps you become more fluent, which will serve you well in your counseling as well as in communicating with those who impact both your clients and yourself. If you have some degree of apprehension or resistance to writing papers, we strongly recommend that you get some help in the form of writing classes or tutoring by someone who can help you develop in this area. The journal writing mentioned earlier will also help.

### Theses and Dissertations

The idea of writing a thesis for a master's degree or a dissertation for a doctoral degree is a common source of high anxiety because it is often the last hurdle. The actual situation is much less of a problem than the anxiety level often suggests. Counselors have already written many papers as undergraduate and graduate students. However, the fear is usually present in the form of, "Sure I can write a 10- or 20-page paper but write a dissertation? That's like writing a book!"

Writing a thesis or dissertation is indeed like writing a book in some ways. However, the task is so tightly structured, and so much support is available during the process, that you will not be asked to do anything that you are not fully prepared to complete. Along the way, you will have lots of practice in constructing assignments that parallel each chapter in the paper. You will have learned how to effectively

1. define a problem under investigation,
2. describe the variables,
3. do a thorough review of relevant literature,
4. construct a study to test your hypotheses, or (in the case of a qualitative study) explore your research questions,
5. select and describe an appropriate research method,
6. analyze and present your data,

7. make sense of what you have discovered,
8. draw reasonable conclusions from your results, and
9. suggest implications for further study.

All of this will be familiar territory to you by the time you complete your course work and begin writing your proposal for what you intend to do. In one sense, this whole process is not unlike the logical process you will follow when doing counseling: identifying problems and issues, designing procedures to resolve the identified issues, and then measuring the results of your interventions.

Perhaps the most important concept to understand about the whole research process is that it is a step-by-step procedure that begins as soon as a program starts. Theory, practical application, research, and writing skills are all part of any quality program, and these are exactly the information and skills needed to complete a professional research study successfully. These requirements come at the end of the program precisely because students must study these areas before they begin their own investigations. This process is virtually the opposite of developing a standard paper, which is made as an assignment the first day of class and rarely mentioned again until it is due. Students will find much more long-term support from the program and faculty in developing theses and dissertations than with any paper they have ever done (or will ever do again).

Faculty and the program committee members seek out the students' interests with the idea that a program can be designed to meet and expand these interests. A well-planned program that incorporates students' interests and needs should also serve to prepare students for a research study that builds on what is studied. Good program planning, therefore, begins preparing students even before they know what the research topic will be.

As an example, one student who had a long-standing interest in working with hyperactive children selected courses that fed this clinical and personal interest. By the time he was ready to complete his study comparing the emotional impact of this disorder on Anglo versus Latino children, he had already completed most of his review of the literature. He already knew more about the subject than most other people alive. That, after all, is one of the intentions of completing such a study as a student: When it is over, you will be one of the experts on a particular topic that is of great personal interest to you.

Your research training will allow you to make sense of what others have done before you (as described in journal articles and dissertations) as well as construct your own hypotheses and research design, and analyze the results. By the way, experimental designed studies are only one of many activities that you may decide to undertake. Qualitative research alternatives could include a historical study, extensive interviews, focus groups, or even a case study.

One of the big professional jumps for most students is the realization that they are being asked to do more than just read and review what others have written and then give their opinions on that information. The research component of a program emphasizes how professionals find, test, verify, and report information that has not already been discovered by someone else. These skills are vital to a research study and to doing highly professional work designed to add new information to the field of counseling.

The tools and information learned in the research component of a program lead to a model for doing original research. Major advisers and doctoral committees for students work with them as closely as possible to use this model in the development of this, their first independent research project. Whether by student choice, or faculty choice, it is critical that a close working relationship be maintained with the thesis or dissertation adviser and committee members from the early planning stages to the end.

The most positive working relationship between students and their committees is one in which the student seeks advice, demonstrates the work he or she has completed, and receives feedback on a regular basis beginning as early as possible. For example, agreement on a topic and method for completing the study should be reached (probably in writing) early in the process. It is a disaster if disagreement on these issues is only discovered after considerable work and effort have already been invested. Most programs recognize these needs and require formal meetings of dissertation committees throughout the process.

Many formal and informal meetings take place with committee members after the initial proposal is approved. This is in addition to weekly, and sometimes even daily, meetings with your adviser planning the next step and going over what you have just completed. Working the bugs out of a plan, making small changes, and planning how most effectively to utilize the data acquired are among the many issues that arise. Then there are the emotional issues that often turn up, such as writer's block, procrastination, lethargy, and even depression, all hopefully worked through with the support of your adviser, committee, and peers. Some students (and occasionally programs even arrange for you to) meet in a support group on a weekly basis during the dissertation phase so that you have the opportunity to test your ideas and obtain help from others who are going through a similar struggle.

The greatest danger during this period occurs when students complete their doctoral course work ABD (all but dissertation), leave the university community to take a job somewhere, and then never get around to finishing their dissertation. Things just came up, and they just could not find the time, structure, and motivation to finish what they had spent so many years working toward. That is why, whenever possible, it is best to get most of the work on your dissertation completed while you are in residence at the university and have the structure to keep you focused on the assignment at hand. Most students who do not finish their degrees do not flunk out; they give up.

Master's students are not expected to do the quantity or quality of work that a doctoral student does, and they are expected to finish the paper within the 2 or 3 years of their course work. The anxiety and process may be very similar, but the expectations and time requirements make the thesis somewhat less of a challenge.

Finally, the doctoral research study is completed and turned in to committee members. But unlike your standard paper, the student's role is not over at this point. Professionals are expected to be able to support their findings and beliefs effectively in person as well as on paper. The last step in the doctoral dissertation process, and often in the master's thesis process as well, is to make an oral defense of the research to the committee. Committee members want to see if you can explain and provide sound justification for the study in general and the data and conclusions in particular. They also want to see how well you explain the potential impact of your work on counseling practice and future research. It should be clear by this time that the more continuous, accurate, and complete the communications with the committee members prior to this time, the greater the likelihood that the oral defense will go well.

## APA Format

Everyone preparing to be a counselor should purchase the latest edition of the *Publication Manual of the American Psychological Association* (American Psychological Association, 2001). You may have used other style manuals in previous schoolwork, but this one will be used throughout your counseling career. All the major counseling, psychology, and educational journals utilize this style, so your papers will follow the same rules as most published articles. It also makes the jump from writing a class paper to getting published a much smoother transition (if you become so motivated).

About the time you first peruse this manual you may feel an increase in anxiety. But this would be like delving into a dictionary and feeling unrealistically that your job is to memorize all the content for instant retrieval. To help you develop a working knowledge of the style without feeling overwhelmed, we offer here a few tips and suggestions.

If you use just a handful of key APA format rules, the paper you turn in will look good, and other style mistakes will generally be considered minor. You may be asked to correct those minor flaws, but you will be viewed as one who knows style issues and turns in professional work, which is what you are seeking as a student and emerging professional. Format conventions that demonstrate professional work start with the following:

- Margins of 1 inch all around the page are normally acceptable.
- Double-space everything.
- The font(s) should be something standard. Times New Roman in 12-point type always works.
- A header and page number go in the top right-hand corner of each page.
- Heading levels follow the format outlined in the APA Manual.
- The title page is a separate page.
- References start on a separate page.

- Citations in text and entries in the reference list follow the formats in the most recent APA Manual.

APA style for in-text reference citations follows essentially two formats. In the first, you are making a statement that needs to be supported by some evidence, some reference from which you borrowed the idea. This looks something like this: "Counseling students attain higher grades on their papers once they have mastered the standard citation style (Hazler & Kottler, 2006)." In this example, the statement is supported by an illustrative citation. Let's forget for a moment all the intricate details related to the use of commas, spaces, and such, and note that in this first format the authors' last names are followed by the year of the publication within parentheses.

In the second format, you use the authors' names in the body of the narrative: "Hazler and Kottler (2006) found that students attained higher grades on their papers when they mastered the standard citation style." In this case, the parentheses contain only the date, and follow the authors' names. In a nutshell, these are the two formats in the standard citation style. Remember that all reference citations within the text must have a corresponding entry in the reference list, and all references in the list must be cited in the text.

Turning in papers with these few issues handled well will make the paper look professional even if there are small errors within it. There is one other suggestion that should make a big difference in how your work looks. Before the first 3 weeks of school are out, find a few advanced students who have gotten A grades on papers and ask them if you can look at their papers for the format issues. Follow exactly the format they use for the title page, header, margins, and references, and you will be off on the right foot. The key is that you do not need to study the whole APA Manual to get off to a good start, and you do not have to learn this all alone. Use the people and examples that are already available to you.

## The Master's Paper

Many programs check to see how well students can integrate their knowledge and skills by requiring some form of master's paper at the end of their program in place of a thesis. This paper does not generally require the student to collect new data or develop statistics. Instead, these papers can take a variety of forms depending on the goal of the particular program. It could be describing the practical application of theory or the implementation of a particular technique or training model, or drawing fresh conclusions from an extensive review of the literature on a particular topic. Whatever model is used, there will be a general goal of seeing how well students can pull together much of what they have learned and apply it in a logical and professional presentation.

One good thing about our profession is that the format of quality papers generally remains the same whether it is research including new data, historical reviews, or logical analyses of concepts and ideas. Almost regardless of the paper you write, you cannot go wrong with a format that includes the following:

- **title page:** vital information about the title, yourself, the nature of the project (e.g., master's project, dissertation, thesis, class assignment), and the date;
- **abstract:** a one-paragraph overview of the whole project;
- **table of contents:** listings of the major headings and on what page each begins;
- **introduction:** logic and basic references to support the rationale for the project and the questions for which answers are being sought;
- **review of the literature:** expanded review of information and studies that support the rationale for the key issues in the project;
- **method:** the who, what, where, and how of the project;
- **results:** what was found after all the work in this project; and
- **discussion/conclusions:** how the results can be applied to the questions raised in the introduction.

Exactly how these sections play out in a particular assignment or for a particular program's requirements can vary although the general model will remain. To find out what adaptations to the model should be made, all you need to do is to find recently produced papers that have been deemed outstanding, and you will have just the combination of models you need.

## Portfolios

Another way of evaluating graduate student overall progress that is gaining popularity is the portfolio model. The essence of the model is that a student collects all relevant proof of accomplishments in an organized way and presents it to the program faculty at various points in the program, to include a final evaluation at the end. This portfolio can include a variety of materials, such as papers from previous classes, written evaluations by clients, observations by peers, or even a sample video of a counseling session. The main idea is that this collection contains a variety of samples of your work, each testifying that you have attained some level of competence in the content and skill areas that matter most.

The portfolio is not intended solely as an evaluation model. It can also serve as an excellent means for you to have ongoing feedback and assessment on your progress. So whether or not your program requires you to develop such a portfolio, it is an idea you should strongly consider adopting for yourself.

## Multiple-Choice Examinations

This old standby may be part of your life in school and probably even after graduation. These examinations may not measure very well what you learned in a class, nor allow you to demonstrate all you really know about a subject, but they are convenient and efficient, and can measure a variety of things reasonably well.

Performing on multiple-choice examinations takes a set of skills beyond your knowledge of the material. How you study for such an exam is often just as important as what you study. Because these tasks require recognition of a correct answer, or discrimination skills in which you are able to eliminate choices that are obviously wrong, preparation efforts should be targeted toward those goals.

The key in taking multiple-choice tests is to remember that good items have several *wrong* answers as well as one *right* or *best* one. All answers may have some truth to them, but something will be missing or incorrect in the ones that are wrong. Each time you can identify an answer that can be eliminated because it is incorrect, you increase your chances of then picking the right answer. Test takers who do a combination of eliminating wrong answers and selecting the best from what remains do much better than those who only look for the right answer.

Get some help if this type of exam has been a problem for you in the past (as it has been for Jeffrey!). Many universities offer courses on test-taking skills, and university learning centers have a variety of pamphlets and books on the subject. The most important point for you to recognize is that just because you have not done well on these types of tests in the past, you are not doomed to continued weakness in the area. Study and test-taking skills can be learned if you take the initiative and time to find and use the necessary resources.

## Take-Home Exams

Some students (and faculty) believe these are the only fair means by which to evaluate learning in counseling courses because they more closely approximate what happens in the real world. When a client comes in with a set of presenting complaints about which you know little, you are not required to select a correct treatment plan from four that are provided. After the client leaves, you consult with everyone you can, and read everything that is available, so that when the client comes back you are knowledgeable on the subject.

That is the reasoning behind take-home exams. The good news is that there is nothing to memorize. There is no need to try to guess what the questions will be. The challenge, however, is that you are required to think, to form your own opinions supported by evidence. You are expected to apply what you learned in the class to situations in which you demonstrate your understanding and then effectively explain that learning in writing.

This orientation is sometimes difficult to grasp because you are not necessarily trying to give instructors what they want to hear. Typically, there are not even any perfectly right answers! Instead, the key is to demonstrate in writing that you have mastered the material to the extent that you have integrated the ideas into your own way of functioning. Like everything else we have discussed in this chapter, these skills take practice. The more specific the feedback you ask for, the better you become at developing these skills.

## Interpersonal Skills

Counselor training involves much more than academic performance. You will be expected to demonstrate competence in interpersonal skills in some way, shape, or form in virtually every class you take. Furthermore, you will be graded on your degree of proficiency.

What this means is that you have to overcome the natural propensity to freeze when others are watching you apply what you have learned. Imagine, for example, that your instructor has just demonstrated to the class how to help clients translate elusive problems into specific goals. Now it is your turn to practice with a partner. You are concentrating intently, trying to remember everything that you are supposed to do at the same time that you are listening to what your partner is saying, and then the instructor comes over to watch. A number of things go through your mind, all unpleasant. Will you be able to continue, to show yourself at your best, when you are being watched, even videotaped?

The answer to this question is that it takes practice but you can. The more experience you gain functioning under the spotlight, the smoother your behavior becomes. If this is a particular area of concern for you, approach an instructor you trust especially. Ask him or her to observe you and offer feedback. As your confidence grows, you will reach the point where you can even volunteer in front of the whole class to demonstrate some counseling skill. The expectation is not that you will perform perfectly, but that you have conquered your own fear of failure. There is nothing faculty respect more in students than their willingness to try doing some things that are difficult and to learn from mistakes.

## Focus Activities: Making Personal Use of This Chapter

This chapter focused on the academic challenges that you are likely to face in graduate school. Completing the following exercises—and following the related suggestions in the chapter—should help you deal with those times when the academic challenges boost your anxiety to unproductive levels.

### Skills and Strategies for Academic Success

1. **List the skills and strategies from this chapter in your notebook or computer file.**
2. **Rate yourself from 1 to 5 (1 being poor, 5 being excellent) on the strategies and skills.** If your score is 2 or below, consider getting some additional instruction in those areas. Ask your adviser about tutoring services and other options for improving your skills in certain areas.

3. **Seek out peers in the program who might be interested in forming study groups and set up initial study times when you can meet.** This will not happen by itself. You have to take the initiative.
4. **Create a corner of your office space for** *My Academic Support Information*. This is where you should put the APA Publication Manual, dictionary, thesaurus, and a grammar guide to get started. Also include any student guides on writing projects that your program, department, or college makes available.
5. **Develop a resource file of people who can be called on for help with writing, statistics, and other areas in which assistance could be valuable to you.** This file could include faculty, students, books, or Internet sites.
6. **Create a container in which you can begin collecting items that demonstrate your accomplishments.** This is the beginning of your portfolio. You should be collecting papers, tests, tapes made, information on interviews done, and any other information that will help you remember and perhaps show others your skills and how they have progressively improved.

# 8

## Overcoming Some Difficult
## Personal Challenges

Visions of academic life pop into your mind when you first think about going to graduate school. You see yourself sitting attentively in class and perhaps pointing out some brilliant insight that others have missed. You imagine yourself isolated in a private place, books and papers spread out before you as you prepare for class. You can see yourself in the library, where you are more of a master of computer-generated literature searches than you ever could have believed. Perhaps you can also picture yourself sitting with a few classmates over coffee, passionately discussing the nuances of a professional issue or the latest counseling technique.

These are indeed the images of academic life at its best. You are a sponge soaking up learning and reworking it in new ways. You are focused on tasks at hand, memorizing the new terms that will become part of your professional vocabulary, studying the differences among theories that appear suspiciously alike, learning new methodologies of research design and of appraisal and assessment techniques, mastering the core therapeutic skills and interventions. This is the content of your program, the academic core of graduate education in counseling.

Implicit in this description of your role as student are the expectations that most of your challenges will be related to the acquisition of knowledge. How will you prepare for examinations? What system will you develop to read texts and prepare for class? How will you write the innumerable class assignments and term papers that will be due?

These questions are obviously worthy of your attention because they form the core of what graduate education is all about. You will, however, confront other personal challenges for which you may be less well prepared. You probably understand by now that learning to be a counselor is quite different from preparing to be an attorney, physician, or public administrator. You are expected to learn a body of knowledge, master a set of competencies, and assume a professional identity as in other professions. But you also face a number of personal challenges that are the inevitable consequences of becoming an expert in dealing with human struggles. In no other field is the content of what you study so personally relevant or the professional skills so personally applicable.

There is no way to study human development without reviewing your own progress through the process. Each time you explore a different facet of human existence, you cannot help but reflect on where you stand. You are thus likely to enjoy more than the usual amount of personal relevance in your professional training. This comes with a price, however, because you will also suffer stress as you look at your own issues and attempt to stay focused on the academic content. Among the difficult challenges you will need to overcome are dealing with personal issues, need for approval, demands for perfection versus nonperfection, working through conflicts, and identifying your strengths and weaknesses.

## Dealing With Personal Issues

Cigarette packages come with a warning notifying potential consumers that there are risks associated with that particular indulgence. Applications to graduate counseling programs might similarly carry the following advertisement:

> **Warning:** This experience may be upsetting to your physical and emotional health. You may be subjected to new information about yourself as well as to stress and pressures potentially destabilizing to your significant relationships.

Any structured experience that encourages you to question the meaning of your life, reflect on the choices you have made and will make in the future, experiment with new behaviors, alter your beliefs and attitudes, and equip yourself with skills and the commitment to use them is going to change you in a profound way. This is true for the process of counseling as well as for the graduate school experience.

There is no way that you could be the same person after counselor training that you were before you started. Your interests will change. Your interactive style, value system, and understanding of yourself and others will be different. The implications of these alterations are worth considering.

1. **Your perceptions of yourself and the world will change**. You have a particular image of the way you see yourself and the ways you are viewed by others. This is not a static condition, but rather one that evolves as you collect new information and integrate these perceptions into your views of self and others.

2. **Your relationships will change**. You will relate to people differently whether they are your associates, spouse, lover, friends, parents, or children. You will have higher expectations for intimacy and feel a greater need for emotional support. You will be much more highly skilled at communication and, therefore, will expect better skills from others. The consequences of these changes are that it is unlikely your relationships can stay the same. Some are likely to deteriorate because others do not accept the new you while others will improve considerably as a result of your new efforts. Because you are likely to prefer the improved relationships rather than the deteriorating ones

(unless you decide that some of your relationships are dysfunctional), we suggest you take some important steps:

- Involve your family and friends in school. Tell them about what you are learning. Keep them abreast of the changes you are making.
- Understand that some people may feel threatened. Some family members and friends will not like the new you who is more knowledgeable, assertive, proactive, and confident. They may feel that you are leaving them behind. Address these concerns rather than ignoring them.
- Monitor the ways you may be taking out the pressures you feel on those closest to you.

3. **Your values will change.** Consistent with your identity as a counselor, you will find that the changes you undergo involve your belief system as well as your interpersonal skills and intellectual development. Specifically, this may involve movement from

| | | |
|---|---|---|
| self-involvement | to | other involvement, |
| emphasis on content | to | emphasis on process, and |
| focus on events | to | focus on meaning. |

In general, you are likely to become more flexible, empathic, and interpersonally sensitive. You will value relationships more in your life and feel a greater demand for intimacy. You will be different not only in the new skills and knowledge at your disposal but also in your views of the world, its people, and your expectations of them.

4. **Your core issues will crop up repeatedly and compel you to manage/resolve them to the extent you are presently able.** The concerns that clients present to you, the discussions you have in class, and the soulful conversations you have with faculty, supervisors, and peers will provoke you to examine those subjects you fear the most. You may ask yourself, for example,

- What do I want to do before I die?
- Where am I most wounded?
- What have I been hiding from in my whole life?
- What could make life unlivable?
- How have I been lying to myself and what will I do about it?
- What if my past life is deemed worthless or unacceptable by the new me?

These are questions that an engineer or computer programmer may be able to avoid but that a counselor must face on a daily basis. Every session you ever conduct will touch you in a personal way, stir up your core issues, leave you feeling both exhilarated and frightened by the depth and intensity of what lies beneath your surface. You have less choice than you think to face your own unresolved concerns. Not only will they affect your work with clients but also your ability to sleep at night.

## Need for Approval

A recurrent issue, and one that students struggle with most, is seeking external validation by faculty members at a time when students feel most vulnerable and insecure. Professors are perceived as the folks with power who decide whether students are deserving enough to enter their domain, and worthy enough to stay there.

The less confident student can perceive a grade lower than expected (anywhere from a C- to an A-), or even an ambiguous facial expression, as evidence that total and complete rejection is not far behind. Professors control the content, pace, style, and the very atmosphere of classrooms, so you, as the student, may feel at their mercy. Will they agree with what you have to say? Will they like you? Will they think you are smart and talented?

All of us at one time or another have valued the input and feedback of mentors, although we need it in very different amounts. However, when your very self-worth, your standing as a human being, hangs on what a professor believes about your behavior in a given moment, trouble is bound to result. It is bad enough to be in a position in which others with power evaluate your performance or decide your fate. The only thing worse is when you give to these people not only the opportunity to assess your skills or products but also to judge you as a person. Consider what happened to Nando:

> Nando was twice denied admission to a graduate counseling program. He was told his GRE scores were too low, and his grades in college were found wanting. It was his opinion that if these people wanted to use a culturally biased test and a limited sample of his academic behavior from many years ago as the best predictors of his potential as a counselor, there was clearly something wrong with their methods. He had devoted the last 10 years of his life to helping his people, migrant workers and their families, cope with life as "invisible ones." He was not going to let them stop him from his goal of being a professional counselor!
>
> When he attended his first class as a probationary student, he was concerned about the amount of deference he was expected to show the professor. Respect was one thing, but no way was he going to play docile just to appease the instructor's ego. When he received a B- on his first paper, he was tempted to give up. Maybe he was kidding himself. Perhaps he did not have what it takes to succeed among the Anglos?
>
> Nando redoubled his efforts to win the approval of certain faculty who seemed to treat him with disdain. Maybe it was his imagination. Perhaps they were not judging him as harshly as he believed, but in any case, he felt that he was losing his own dignity in the process. He hated himself for "kissing butt." He seethed at the ways he trolled for strokes, did most anything to receive a pat on the head or a few reassuring words that he was okay.
>
> Somewhere during this time of humiliation, he could no longer decide what he truly believed. He was so preoccupied with pleasing his professors, with gaining their approval, he could no longer figure out what he consid-

ered important. It was downright undignified for a grown adult to grovel so much!

It was after this revelation that Nando decided he would no longer give away his power to these professors. It was true that they had experience and expertise in areas in which he aspired to similar competence. He would continue to value their suggestions, but no longer would he live for their approval. Better that he go back to the orchards and pick apples than to give away his power to others.

We are not encouraging you to ignore what your professors offer to you, nor are we suggesting that you not care about how they assess your academic and counseling skills. These are important aspects of your training. What is of concern is the extent to which you look to authorities—faculty, supervisors, and mentors—to validate your worth as a person. Ask for as much feedback as possible on how you can improve your functioning, but do not mistake this input for an appraisal of your standing as a human being. You must seek and use the evaluations of others but not become addicted to approval in others. Otherwise you will be so busy trying to figure out what your instructors want, and how to deliver it exactly as you believe they expect, that you will lose yourself in the process. You will become a slave to meeting the perceived wants of others in power, and this is among the worst mentalities for learning.

## Demands for Perfection Versus Nonperfection

Overcoming an excessive need for approval by others is one challenge for graduate students; another is attempting to meet their own unrealistic demands for perfection. Grades are used as a continual measure of how well students are doing, but when it becomes not enough to do well, when you have to be the absolutely best student and counselor and everyone must grade you as such, your learning and growth may be impeded.

### The Problem of Perfection

An ambition to be perfect can be admirable: we need more people in the world, and in the profession, who strive for excellence in their service to others. The problem, however, is that your goal to be the best counselor you can may be overwhelmed by the burning need to meet standards of perfection that are out of reach.

Most students admit that there is often little correlation between how much they learn in a class and the grade they receive. However, they often still have the belief that excellence should always be rewarded according to their own expectations—even though A's do not reflect learning acquisition as much as they measure the ability to read what a given instructor wants and then delivering that.

A related issue is the misguided belief that grades are fair and representative assessments of your performance and behavior. Certainly they reflect an evaluation of a few samples of your behavior, for example, your performance on an examination, in an interview, or on a particular set of assignments. However, such an evaluation does not necessarily imply that you learned very much that is important.

We have heard more than a few employers express deep suspicion toward counselors who are driven to achieve academic trophies or who are otherwise perfectionistic. If you are unforgiving of yourself and need great grades to show others your skills, how will you accept the imperfections of others?

Much of counseling involves operating in isolation when you do not know how you are doing. Is the client getting better or just pretending? When your client does not return, is that because you failed or succeeded? When your client performs well in sessions but does not make needed changes in his or her life, is it because of something you are doing—or not doing?

You will find dozens of things in each session that you could have done differently. You will recall innumerable ways you could have expressed yourself more eloquently or clearly. You will notice, in retrospect, several cues you might have recognized. You need to reach a balance between reflecting on ways you could improve your functioning and running yourself through a gauntlet of self-recriminations such as the following:

- "I should have known better."
- "How could I have missed that?"
- "Because I got a B, I'll never be a good counselor."
- "It's not fair that my effort hasn't been recognized the way I want."
- "This proves I'm not worthy to be in this program."
- "Anything less than an A is unacceptable!"

## The Nonperfectionist Model

In writing about her own struggle around "good enough," Naomi Krause (2000) came to realize that "no matter how hard anyone tries or how long they strive, in the end everyone must still be content with being good enough" (p. 25). Thus you might as well recognize it in yourself sooner or later. But how do you know if you are nearing the balanced life of a nonperfectionist? Naomi, from her experiences, advised asking yourself these questions:

- Do you spend more time actually doing the assignment than organizing it or worrying about it?
- Are you okay with not getting all As?
- Do you balance your schoolwork with other interests?
- When you have finished an assignment, can you let go of it even if you could spend more time on it?
- Are you able to leave your e-mail unopened for more than 2 days? (p. 25)

Nonperfectionsts are not slouches, either! Nonperfectionists, Krause noted (p. 25),

- agonize over assignments. . . . Assignments require time and effort, thought and research. They don't require our souls.

- do our best on assignments. . . . When the assignment is finished, it is finished, done.
- care about how we do. . . . Just because we could do better does not mean we will choose to do so on each and everything in our life.
- give time and attention to our work.
- acknowledge that the amount of time and attention given depends on the time available to complete the work.
- are motivated by our work and our study. . . . Taking breaks gives real-life perspective to the work.
- have clear convictions. . . . Just because we don't do everything exactly the way the manual states does not mean we aren't just as concerned about our education and profession.
- are busy. . . . Being busy isn't the goal, getting things done is.
- are intelligent . . . defined by our creativity and ability to find solutions.

## Working Through Conflicts

A preoccupation with grades is one part of the perfectionistic strivings that may get in the way of your growth as a counselor. Another important source of potential stress has to do with interpersonal conflicts that may arise with your peers or instructors.

Just as most of the clients you will see are struggling with relationships in their lives, you, too, may have a degree of difficulty getting along with people as well as you prefer. This holds true not only for those loved ones who are part of your life but also for the peers, supervisors, and instructors who now populate your graduate school world.

Whenever students gather informally—in the hallways before class begins, driving home in car pools, or over a meal—conversation often revolves around how you feel others treat you. Particular attention is given to those individuals you believe are creating problems for you. This could mean a professor you sense does not like you, a classmate who has been giving you a hard time, or a supervisor who seems to be treating you unfairly. Any of these conflicts can be a source of unending anguish that exacerbates the stress you are already feeling from schoolwork.

You will hear all too often from your own clients that interpersonal conflicts drain their energy, affect their morale and motivation, and lead to feelings of discouragement and despondency. Students who are struggling more often than not are experiencing relationship problems as well as academic problems. Here is one student describing her own experience in this regard:

> I was doing fine in my classes. Maybe even better than fine; I was doing great, and quite proud of myself. I don't know if I did anything to deserve how I have been treated by some of my classmates, but nobody should be treated like this. Apparently, I offended this woman in one of my work groups by being too assertive for her tastes. She then decided that I was some kind of threat to her so she started badmouthing me to others. I began to notice, in quite small ways, how I was being isolated more and more. The harder I tried to make friends, the worse it seemed to become.

This woman had been highly motivated and successful in her studies. The conflict that developed with a few others ended up demoralizing her to the point that she dropped out of her program for a while. She certainly played a role in creating her own difficulties, as is the case with all interpersonal problems. Unfortunately, whether in her own mind or in reality, the problems escalated to the point where she could concentrate on little else.

You may vow that such a predicament will not happen to you, but we have seen all too often instances when conflicts develop with particular instructors or classmates and become blown out of all proportion. A professor does not seem to value your input in the way that you prefer. You do not feel part of the group that you believe to be highest in status. A classmate is rude to you. You have a disagreement with the department chair or secretary over a scheduling conflict. Your adviser does not seem to have time for you. Such situations are potentially discouraging and energy sapping depending on how you handle them, both internally and externally.

Those of us in this profession tend to be a bit more sensitive than others. Perhaps we gravitated to this field precisely because of our high needs for interpersonal satisfaction. One consequence of the training to be a counselor is that you learn to relate better not only to people in client roles but also to those who are colleagues. Hopefully, the skills you learn become an actual part of you and not just a role that you play when the clock is running. Being able to apply what you have learned to the conflicts that inevitably develop in your personal life at home or at school will improve the lives of all concerned. Certain steps can be taken in your relationships with others that are direct applications of what you have learned in your work with clients:

- Face the conflict rather than ignoring it and hoping it will go away.
- Talk to yourself in such a way that keeps things in perspective rather than exaggerates the significance of what is taking place.
- When you address the person with whom you are in conflict, use "I" messages to take responsibility for your role in what is going on.
- Set appropriate limits and boundaries as to what you are willing to tolerate and what you will not.
- Look at the present conflict in the context of ongoing issues in your life. How is this related to things in the past?
- Try to move beyond blame in assigning guilt as to who is most at fault.
- Figure out what you have been doing that produces a result you do not much like; do something else other than that.
- When all else fails, get some help from a friend or neutral party who can mediate on your behalf.

Trina, for example, applied what she had learned and took many of these steps when she became fairly certain that her faculty adviser had some problem with her. Every time she met with her, she sensed a coldness and withdrawal that felt punitive. A few times she attempted to engage the professor in discussion about the matter. On one occasion, she even asked directly whether there was some conflict between them, but her query was put off as ridiculous. It had reached a point at which Trina was so reluctant to meet with the adviser that she decided to take a semester off rather than have to subject herself to further rejection.

In discussing the matter with a classmate, Trina came to realize that maybe both she and her adviser needed some help to work the matter through. Until this point, Trina naturally assumed that the problem must be all her fault. Professors, after all, are never wrong. She must have done something to deserve this neglectful treatment. But now she began considering that perhaps there was some interactive effect operating (a natural assumption if she remembered her family dynamics course). She consulted with another faculty member she felt more comfortable with. She did not complain about the adviser as much as own she was having some trouble that she very much wanted to work out but could not seem to do so alone. Might this other instructor be willing to act as a mediator to help them work things out?

Such an action took quite a bit of courage on the part of this student, as you can imagine. Confronting a conflict like this takes a lot more work, effort, and risk in the short run than just letting it go. But there are some conflicts that loom so large in your mind that ignoring them is out of the question. And unless you are willing to work things through, to face the challenge of interpersonal conflicts, what kind of model will you be for your clients who are struggling with similar issues?

Practicing what you preach to others requires you to act as a living example of what you advocate. Conflicts with peers or instructors offer you the opportunity to face some of the most difficult personal challenges. Taking up these challenges is both good for you as a person and student and will help you to better understand the process in your clients.

## Exploring Strengths and Weaknesses

Each of the challenges described so far can help you to explore areas of personal strength and weakness. Many of these characteristics, qualities, behavioral patterns, and interpersonal styles have served you well throughout your life. Others have repeatedly gotten you in trouble.

Much of counseling work involves not only the professional skills and interventions you apply but also the personal style in which you interact with others. Your individual characteristics are at least as important to your counseling relationships as the skills and information that you learn in graduate school. You have considerable work to do: you need to identify your personal strengths, become aware of your personal weaknesses, assess personal areas you want to upgrade, and continuously monitor the interactive effects of your personal and professional functioning.

### *Identify Personal Strengths That Lend Power to Your Counseling Interventions*

Counseling skills, interventions, and techniques are tools that you can use to help promote client change. How effective you are in your efforts depends not only on your proficiency in applying these methods but also on how well you incorporate them into your personal style.

What is it about you that others may gravitate toward and lead them to trust you? What personal qualities make you most proud? What do you have to offer others? Strengths that may be considered especially useful include

- a sense of honor and integrity;
- a playful sense of humor;
- a reservoir of love, caring, compassion, and empathy for others;
- an altruistic desire to be helpful to others;
- a flexibility and openness to new experiences and ideas;
- a degree of confidence in yourself and what you can do;
- a realistic perception of what is not within your power to do;
- a high degree of functional intelligence (street smarts);
- an intuitive ability to sense and read what others think and feel;
- a willingness to do whatever you need to in order to accomplish goals;
- an interest in understanding the lives and actions of others; and
- a willingness to verify your thoughts and beliefs with accurate information.

These traits are by no means required of every counselor in equal measure. We are suggesting instead that counseling is a uniquely human endeavor, and the more you can make yourself as attractive as possible to clients the more likely they are to hear what it is that you have to offer.

### *Become Aware of the Personal Weaknesses That May Interfere With Your Ability to Remain Clearheaded and Appropriately Empathetic*

What are some areas of your life that you will need to bring under greater control if you hope to be successful as a counselor? Most students enter a graduate program with a host of unresolved personal issues, some more incapacitating than others. Because of recent concerns for your right to privacy, and problems of dual relationships, you may very well be able to get through your program without revealing very much about your current personal struggles. Do you honestly believe, however, that these problems will not interfere with your interactions with clients?

Some of the more common unresolved issues that students bring to graduate school, and that interfere with their counseling efforts, include

- being adult children of alcoholics/addicts;
- being victims of childhood sexual/physical/verbal abuse;

- undergoing a separation, divorce, or other family problem;
- living through an age-related developmental transition;
- being substance abusers or having other addictions;
- living through culture-, race-, or gender-related developmental transitions;
- lacking self-confidence and/or self-esteem; and
- dealing with dependence/independence issues with a significant other.

In addition to these issues are personal qualities that could be problematic. Students can be, for example,

- dogmatic, rigid, authoritarian;
- manipulative and controlling;
- easily threatened;
- extremely vulnerable and fragile; and
- unusually self-centered and narcissistic.

Individuals with these qualities often struggle in their interactions with peers, with faculty, and especially with their clients. The major problem, however, is that the people who most need to assess honestly the extent to which these qualities are weaknesses for them are precisely those who will skip over these words or tell themselves that they do not apply to them.

### Assess Areas in Your Personal Functioning That You May Wish to Upgrade

Consider what you need to improve in much the same way that you would help a client to take inventory of those aspects of behavior that he or she might choose to strengthen. What are some aspects of the ways that you relate to others personally, or relate to yourself internally, that you could work to improve?

If you were engaging in such an assessment activity with a client, you might check out the following areas:

- To what extent do you worry about things over which you have little control?
- In what ways do you spend time inside your head rehashing or feeling guilty over things in your life that have already taken place?
- How often do you end up in a conflict with others in which you are puzzled as to your contributions to the disagreement?
- When you feel depressed, frustrated, or anxious, what do you know how to do in order to work things through?
- How well do you handle spending time in your own company without feeling bored, restless, or lonely?
- How often do you take constructive risks and venture into the unknown?
- To what extent are you free of prejudices and biases toward people of diverse ethnic, cultural, and gender backgrounds?

- In what ways are you limited by your own definition of sex roles?
- How well do you take care of yourself physically, emotionally, spiritually, and intellectually?
- What is your degree of comfort discussing intimate issues related to sex, relationships, and love?
- What are your unresolved personal issues from the past that may interfere with your professional functioning?
- How easily do you change your views when you are faced with evidence that contradicts your previous perspective?
- How upset do you become with yourself when you do not meet your own expectations?
- To what extent do you model for others those qualities that you consider to be most important for others?

These are exactly the areas that you will work on with clients in their sessions. How do you expect to help people deal with problems and issues that you have not yet worked on with some success yourself?

### *Monitor Continuously the Interactive Effects of Your Personal and Professional Functioning*

We have made the point several times before that the greatest strain of this kind of work, as well as its greatest privilege, is the reality that whatever you learn personally will help you in your work, and whatever you learn at school will help you in your personal life. Given this kind of continual interaction, it will be crucial for you to be able to insulate yourself and your family (as much as is possible) from the negative side effects that result from being so close to others' pain. Similarly, whatever is going on in your own life, such as the struggles you are facing, the crises you are living through, the challenges you are attempting to overcome, cannot be allowed to pollute your interactions with clients.

## Preventing Burnout

More than a few idealistic, enthusiastic graduate students, just like you, promise themselves that they will never become like some of the counselors, supervisors, and professors they have known. They will not turn into the tired, cynical, frustrated individuals who no longer seem to care very much about what they do or about what others think about that. They will not be one of the burnt-out professionals who have lost their compassion and are now simply living out their workdays waiting for retirement. But once upon a time, those burnt-out professionals were just like you.

Nobody starts out in the profession planning for the days when work no longer seems vibrant and exciting. New professionals are filled with fantasies of doing good and being the kind of counselor who really makes a difference. Consider, however, that it was not all that long ago that you entertained similar notions about your previous career. The fact of the matter is that it is difficult for most of us to stick with any form of work for very long without feeling the need for a change.

This is why we bring the depressing subject of burnout to your attention from the very beginning. Anticipating the certain predictable stresses and strains in this type of work, and the toll on your physical and emotional health that they will take, allows you to take steps to minimize the negative effects.

What are the stresses and strains that many counselors experience after years in the field? What are the symptoms of burnout that professionals in any field might anticipate? In describing strains, stresses, and symptoms, we do not wish to alarm you but merely to warn you of the realistic stresses and strains that you are sure to face. Among them are boredom, isolation, abuse, and the limits of your own abilities.

Burnout can also impact you as a student as well as when you enter the professional counseling field. There is an unlimited amount of information to learn, and programs try and get in as much as possible. Then there are the skills, which will always need improving and work. If that were not enough, there is you and the specialization things you want to learn. Perhaps you even want to volunteer or work with faculty, as has been suggested, to get the most from your program. You cannot get it all at once in a program, but you can burn yourself out trying.

At the end of semesters and the further you get into your program, the more likely you are to see burnout emerging in yourself or your peers. It is a drooping head, minimal conversation, no time for anything, discouraging talk, and tons of statements that emphasize "I can't relax," "I just have too much work to do." This is the time when students lose the creativity and excitement that makes learning fun, when work becomes agony, and when quality of learning goes down.

There are an endless number of books that tell you how to avoid burnout, and the problem with most of them is that they take so much time to go through that people avoid them, fearing more stress. We may not be able to talk you into planning the healthiest lifestyle while in graduate school, but perhaps you will try some of the following that should keep you physically and emotionally healthier with minimal effort:

- **Walk**: Use the stairs. Park your car one lot farther away. Don't stand in the hall, but walk to the next building to get some refreshment.
- **Eat healthy**: Donuts taste great, and you should have one for a treat on a regular basis. But for the rest of the day at school or work bring, for example, some carrots, cut-up apples, or celery to eat while you are studying. Drinking plenty of water is wonderful because it keeps your system going while filling you up.
- **Deal directly and quickly with conflicts**: Nothing will keep your mind off of learning like worrying about a conflict. Find some way to get through it directly and quickly.
- **Study what YOU want to learn**: Make a list of things you want to learn and take a couple of minutes each day to review the list and

decide on one way to get a little more of what you want. Make learning for you and not the instructor.

- **Support your healthiest relationships**: It is easy for people in our profession to begin helping others rather than using others to help ourselves. Whether it is family, friends, colleagues, or a faculty member, do things that promote those relationships on a regular basis.
- **Do joy**: Don't just look for the joy in life; do it. Laughing, dancing, singing, and even crying are things you do yourself. Don't wait for the feeling to hit you. Do it and the feeling will come along with those endorphins that will make you feel better and be more productive.

## Boredom

Hour after hour, day after day, year after year, clients enter your office, tell you their stories, ask you very similar questions, and expect you to do essentially the same things. After a while, the discussions you have and the directions you take may become predictable and seemingly repetitious.

One client will tell you, in more detail than you ever wish to know, about the accounting procedure in which she has particular pride. Another client will ramble endlessly about the same incidents that you have already heard about twice before. Still another client speaks in such a soft, monotone that you can feel yourself being lulled to sleep. A young child who does not talk much at all forces you to strain to follow the tenuous threads of meaning. Each of these common instances tends to make a counselor tired, frustrated, and often simply bored. The problem of burnout arises when this state of listlessness becomes not episodic, or situation specific, but chronic.

As experienced counselors, we can recall times in our careers when we became bored with a particular aspect of work. The quality of our counseling suffered, as did the satisfaction we felt. During such times, we both seriously considered entering another field. However, by making some changes in the ways that we operated, altering our style of counseling, making moves in our setting or specialty, getting different supervision, taking on new challenges, and using other such tactics we were able to once again restore a state of vitality until the next bout of ennui.

You are encouraged to take steps, before it is too late (as when you are a graduate student), and to plan for predictable bouts of boredom and burnout. This involves developing a flexible enough specialty, and state of mind, that you can make continual alterations in the ways you practice.

Here is a school counselor, who has been practicing for over two decades, describing how important it is to take proactive steps to address issues of boredom before they get out of hand:

> Every year, probably every month, I change something about the way I do business. I get a kick out of seeing the kids' reactions. They come back to see me, expecting things to be the same, and I tell them that I am now working a bit differently. I would just get so bored if I did the same things, the same way.

Here is another counselor, who works in a public agency, describing a similar commitment:

> Over the years I have been an Adlerian, a reality therapist, and a gestalt counselor. I was into REBT [rational emotive behavior therapy] for a while. Now I am heavily invested in learning all I can about Bowenian family counseling. I am seeing this adolescent now, who I also saw a few months ago, and then 2 years before that. He kids me that I am really not the same person he saw before because I don't do counseling the same way. Actually, he is right. I am not the same person I was a year ago. I hope that will always be the case.

The testimonies of these two counselors emphasize how important it is for you to manage boredom in your professional life by making a commitment to keep changing the way you work. The time to make such a promise to yourself is now. You will probably also get a chance to test your techniques while still in graduate school as there will come a time when you are bored with school, too.

### Isolation, Abuse, and the Limits of Your Abilities

Boredom is but one of many of the stress factors that may lead to burnout. Another is the isolation that you may experience. Practicing counseling is one of the few jobs in which you feel utterly alone even though you are always with people. You may not be physically isolated, like a truck driver on the road, but your psychological isolation can be even greater. You are not permitted to even talk about your work, except to a select few, and you must hold the secrets within yourself. Even during a counseling session, you tolerate no interruptions. Privacy and secrecy are the hallmarks of the counselor's work, and they can leave you feeling very much alone if you do not work actively to find appropriate support.

Yet another stress factor is the abuse you may suffer at the hands (or the mouths) of people who nobody else will tolerate. Belligerent adolescents will call you names, swear at you, threaten you, or refuse to cooperate. Young children will look at you as if you are an agent of the devil. Parents will ridicule you and demean the value of the work you do. Adult clients will attempt to manipulate and control you and try to get underneath your skin in order to keep you away from their secrets. You will see couples who hate each other but who turn on you when you attempt to break up their fights. Utter chaos will reign during grossly dysfunctional family sessions.

Not all stresses and strains come from difficult clients. More often than you prefer, you will feel utterly helpless. You will see a client in pain, want so badly to help, and yet feel that what you have to offer is not nearly enough. The abused child you are offering comfort to is about to go back to the abusing home by court order. The grieving widow you are talking to sees no other way out except suicide. The AIDS patient you are working with screams out the indignity and injustice of it all, and then looks to you for solace. How will you handle all of this? How will you metabolize the pain of others without driving yourself crazy? How will you stay focused on that which is within your power to do something about?

Confronting the limits of your own abilities may be the greatest challenge you will face. The place to start with that task is right now in your graduate training. Learn to accept what is within your control and let go of what is not.

## Focus Activities: Making Personal Use of This Chapter

This chapter addresses personal challenges that you may face as a graduate student. Completing the following exercises should help you to better deal with some of the personal conflicts you may encounter as you journey through graduate school. Keep in mind that these conflicts always involve yourself and may also involve others. You can always impact the conflict some way because you are always a part of it.

### Dealing With Personal Issues

Self-exploration at this stage of your development will enable you to better view the inevitable changes as exciting and necessary parts of your personal and professional growth. Do not be surprised if some of your beliefs have changed: that is to be expected. Do not look for a right answer in the following tasks, but instead use your gut reactions, that is, what comes immediately to mind. There are no right answers for everyone in all situations.

1. **Explore your perceptions of yourself by describing *you* and *who you are* in your notebook or computer file.** How does the work of counseling and how you see it relate to this self-defined you?
2. **Discuss the type and number of relationships you have.** What purposes do your relationships serve? What do you expect to give in your relationships? What do you expect to get from them?
3. **Explore your value system.** What are some of the values and beliefs you have about people, yourself, society, current issues?
4. **Identify some core issues you struggle with or have struggled with in the past.** How might they impact you in the future?

After you complete these exercises, refer back to the Dealing With Personal Issues section in the chapter and reread it. Comparing information should make you feel more attuned to your perceptions and views of yourself, others, and the world around you.

### Need for Approval

Most of us rely a great deal upon the approval of others. Graduate students, in particular, often experience insecurity as they seek approval from faculty members, peers, and family. The desire is for counselor trainees to feel increasing confidence in themselves, who they are, and what they know as the program progresses. Exploring the following issues may help you become one of those confident students who does not rely solely on the approval of others for self-verification.

1. **What does it mean if someone does not approve of you?** If someone disapproves of you or what you are doing, does it mean that you are wrong? Or could it be that you merely have a different opinion or view of a situation? What if something you have done could have been handled more appropriately? How can you assess the accuracy of your ideas?
2. **What are the consequences of always agreeing with everyone, besides that of life becoming extremely boring?**
3. **List all of your accomplishments.** Do not minimize them. Reread them when you are feeling less than confident.
4. **Keep a folder of things that make you feel good.** These could be things like letters of recommendation, good evaluations, well-written papers and exams, cards from friends and family, acceptance letters to the program. When you feel down, turn to the folder for some reassurance about how you are really thought of by others.
5. **Learn to reframe criticism.** Consider your strengths and sandwich the criticized behavior between them. For example, "I am generally very understanding and considerate of others, but occasionally I do become too critical of others when I feel stressed and may hurt their feelings. I do really care about people, though; I have good intentions so I will try to be more attentive to the feelings of others, especially when I begin to experience stressful feelings." Learn to reframe the more bluntly negative comments of others into more accurate total statements.

## Demands for Perfection Versus Nonperfection

**Show a bit of yourself and an occasional tendency to err.** People who cannot or will not show some of their flaws and humanness are often annoying and hard to approach. Regularly allowing your less than perfect side to show reduces stress for you and those around you. We know that no one is perfect, but sometimes we need reminding in difficult situations. It not only strengthens your ability to accept yourself unconditionally, but it also models for others that it is acceptable to be less than perfect.

## Working Through Conflicts

Learning to see conflicts as challenges when facing them, and working through them, can lead to growth and achievement. Consider the following suggestions for dealing with conflicts that may arise:

1. **Keep a daily journal to vent your feelings, identify what they are, and explore ways of dealing with them.**
2. **Take responsibility for your feelings by owning a part of the conflict rather than blaming how you are feeling on others.** Take risks and approach those with whom you have conflict using "I" statements and explain how you feel, what you are willing to take responsibility for, and why you think it will be beneficial for both of you to

resolve the conflict. Refer back to the steps given in the Working Through Conflicts section of this chapter.

3. **Seek consultation prior to confrontation to check on your objectivity.** Role-play the situation and how you might best approach it with a friend or colleague.

4. **Consider the negative consequences of avoiding confrontation.** What happens if you do not resolve your feelings? How could this be detrimental to you personally and professionally?

5. **Take a course or workshop on conflict management.**

6. **Remember these key tips in all of your interactions:**

   - Before you say anything to anyone, ask yourself three things: Is it true? Is it kind? Is it necessary?
   - Make promises sparingly and keep them faithfully.
   - Never miss the opportunity to compliment or to say something encouraging to or about someone.
   - Refuse to talk negatively about others. Do not gossip and do not listen to gossip.
   - Have a forgiving view of people because most people are doing the best they can.
   - Keep an open mind. Discuss, but do not argue. Disagree without being disagreeable.
   - Forget about counting to 10. Count to 1,000 before doing or saying anything that could make matters worse.
   - Let your virtues speak for themselves.
   - When someone criticizes you, see if there is any truth to what he or she is saying. If so, make changes. If there is no truth to the criticism, ignore it and live so that no one will believe the negative remarks.
   - Cultivate your sense of humor. Laughter is often the shortest distance between two people.
   - Do not seek so much to be consoled as to console. Do not seek so much to be understood as to understand. Do not seek so much to be loved as to love.

# 9

## Supplementing Your Formal Education

The average full-time graduate student takes three to four classes per quarter or semester. Part-time students construct a somewhat lighter load, taking one or two classes at a time. This works out to spending from 9 to 15 hours per week in class. A legitimate question that you might ask yourself about this is, "What do you do with all the rest of your time?"

Reading, studying, researching, writing papers, and practicing new skills that you learn take up much of your out-of-class time. Reflective time is also needed to simply think about the material you are studying and to integrate the concepts into your thinking and life. The content of counselor education does not lend itself to memorization; rather, you have to spend endless hours throughout the rest of your life trying to make sense of the material presented.

Public learning time includes interacting with peers in informal settings, talking about ideas, testing their applicability to various situations, gossiping about others, complaining about the burdens of being overworked, and reveling in especially exciting class sessions or grueling counseling experiences. You may need to use outside employment just to keep the bills paid, food on the table, and gas in the car. Then there are your various household chores, time with your family and friends, and maintaining some semblance of a social and leisure life.

Obviously, there is plenty to do in your life, so why might you ever be interested in supplementing your formal education with more work? The simple answer is that the more you do beyond the formal classes, tests, papers, and demonstrations, the more realistic, practical, and valuable will be your learning experiences. Oh yes, and the more employable you become for the best jobs!

Much of your education involves academic tasks like reading texts, studying for examinations, and writing papers; but learning to be a counselor involves acquiring a far broader set of attitudes, thinking patterns, and skills in addition to accumulating specific knowledge. This broader, more practical educational mission involves much more than you could ever learn in the classroom or library. Your professors get you started with a structure and process that provides you with much of what you need to know, but it is up to you to supplement your learning with the additional experiences likely to prepare you for what lies ahead.

Counseling programs, in general, do a fine job of adding practicality to training in comparison to graduate programs in other areas. However, there is no way that programs can force all the realities and practical dimensions of professional development on students. Faculty, peers, and other professionals, therefore, make many suggestions of where additional learning opportunities are available, but leave the decisions to get involved up to individual students. So much depends on your own time availability, commitment, ambition, and passion.

The students who take the greatest advantage of the extra learning opportunities available to them are also the ones who enjoy their programs most, perform optimally, make the most practical use of textbook information, and develop useful professional connections. They are also the students who get the best jobs. Prospective employers look for candidates who show initiative, who have gone beyond the call of duty to distinguish themselves as resourceful and truly dedicated.

The supplementary activities described in this chapter include interviewing and interacting with professionals in the field, volunteering to support professionals and agencies, finding and using a guide or mentor, involvement in professional organizations, experiencing counseling as a client, acquiring diversity experiences, keeping a journal, turning experiences into first publications, reading novels, and traveling and exploring different cultures. Many of these supplementary activities do not even require students to add additional work time to their schedules. Some could be classified as recreational activities that offer a break from studies as well as provide professional development. Others can be exciting adventures for vacations and extended break periods.

These opportunities can integrate your academic and professional development into your personal life. They are the same things that professional counselors find themselves doing to improve their effectiveness once they leave school. Initiating these efforts while you are in school will result in more effective learning of knowledge and skills as well as help you personalize what you have learned. They will help you develop a professional counselor lifestyle that can be built upon throughout your career.

## Interviewing and Interacting With Professionals in Your Field

Study, practice, reflection, more study, and more practice are actions that prepare people to deal with real-life experiences. However, study and practice are never quite the same as the real thing. Talking about a client to a supervisor, studying clients, and preparing to help them can only do so much to equip you with what you need during actual sessions. The same is true for a couple preparing for the birth of their child. They study materials, make all conceivable preparations, and practice their birthing skills. These efforts certainly pay off for the new parents, but no new parents ever fully realize all the joys and pains of birth until they have experienced it. The same is true of understanding the work of the counselor. Only people who have been counselors have a clear perception of what the work is like.

Interviewing counselors in the professional areas that interest you, and in those that you know the least about, will help you get a clearer picture of the real work of counselors. What they know and believe never matches exactly what you have read about because no one quite leads a textbook life. You will find as many similarities and differences among professionals as you do among your professors and textbooks. Learning about the personalized perspective of these people and their work will help you develop a more realistic picture of how the factors in your life will interact with the everyday demands on a counselor in different settings. This, in turn, should help you clarify both your future directions and how to make practical use of the information and skills you are learning in the program.

Here is one student reporting on what she learned from a series of interviews she conducted with several school counselors in her specialty:

> My head is still reeling from what they told me. I feel discouraged in some ways, yet inspired in others. I had no idea how difficult it was for school counselors to find time to actually do counseling with kids. That's why I want to get out of the classroom; I just never have enough time to talk with the children. I learned that counselors are also so overburdened with their various administrative and scheduling chores, processing paperwork like glorified clerks, that they rarely have time to help kids with their personal concerns. Applying for college, making schedule changes, finding jobs—these are certainly important areas, but so are their relationships with their parents, with their friends, with their struggles with acceptance, with drugs and stuff. Yet it seemed rare that counselors had the time to deal with these issues.
>
> What I learned that was most important is that it is up to me to create the job that I really want. They advised me to negotiate with a prospective principal before I accept a position, to make sure that I really can function as a counselor rather than an administrator. They also gave me some great ideas about how I could start making some contacts right now for a job I will want later. Basically, they said that school could only do so much to prepare me; most of the details of work I will learn once I get out.

The conversations you could be having with counselors in the field should combine practical, theoretical, professional, and personal dynamics, just as every person's life combines each of these. A conversation about how to do counseling is a good example. Few practitioners ever truly practice only one specific theory of counseling. Like you, most counselors studied many theories, found those aspects that best fit their preferences and priorities as well as their clients' needs, and then expanded their skills and knowledge around that foundation. The particular approach selected/invented is clearly affected by a number of factors, including personality, values, beliefs, philosophy, specialty area, setting, and life experiences. But you must also be aware of the cultural, environmental, and personal dimensions that affected the individual counselor's selection of his or her personalized theory. Interviewing counselors in the field helps you find out how their individual styles of practice evolved. What was most and least helpful to them? What advice can they offer you about how you might best get started?

Once you have settled on the professionals you want to interview, we recommend that you explore several areas with them. Sample questions that you might ask in each area follow. Think of these not as a formal interview protocol but rather as a broad outline of issues to discuss.

- **Counseling Theory**
  - Which counseling theories have the most impact on what you do?
  - How do some theories hold more weight for you than others?
  - How have you integrated specific counseling theory into your work and counseling behaviors?
  - How do counseling theories relate to your personal beliefs about people?
  - How has your view of theory changed since you completed your training?
  - What advice do you have as to the best ways that I could learn about the practical applications of theory while I am in my program?
- **Practical Issues**
  - How much of your time do you actually spend with clients?
  - What kind of client problems and issues do you handle most?
  - What client issues are different than you expected while in school?
  - What administrative and record-keeping duties do you have?
  - Describe a typical day for you.
  - What were you best and least prepared for in graduate school?
  - What are some of the greatest challenges you face on a daily basis?
  - What do you wish someone had told you when you were at the point that I am?
- **Personal Issues**
  - What do you struggle with the most?
  - What are the most stressful parts of the job for you?
  - What are some of your greatest joys and satisfactions in this work?
  - What side effects do you notice as a result of being in this profession?
  - How do you control your worrying about clients?
  - How have you noticed that you have changed since you have been in this field?
  - How do you keep yourself energized and excited about what you do?
- **Professional Development**
  - What do you do to stay current on issues that are important?
  - Who are the people that help you stay fresh and develop as a professional?
  - How do you maintain contact and share ideas with other professionals?
  - What kinds of additional professional goals do you have?
  - Where do you see yourself headed in the next 5 years?

- **Work Environment**
  - What are the best parts of where you work and which ones do you dislike most?
  - How does your current work environment compare to others you have experienced?
  - What do you do to make your work environment more satisfying?
  - What does it take to be successful in this environment?
- **Finding Jobs**
  - What would be the most important things you would look for in a job?
  - What kinds of positions does your organization frequently look to fill?
  - If you were going to look for another position, how would you go about the search?
  - What suggestions do you have as to how I might find a quality job after graduation?
  - Can I stay in contact with you after this interview?

You should feel inspired with some of the answers to these questions. But we must warn you that, as in most things in life worth doing, you may also encounter some difficulty finding people who will talk to you in a frank and honest manner. Some students report difficulty even being able to find counselors who will agree to see them. Others have been successful in setting up interviews but found that what they learned was not as personalized as they had hoped.

Much depends on your own persistence and interviewing style. Many counselors in the field will want to talk with you at length, to tell you their stories, to help you learn from their mistakes—if you can fit into their life pattern. It is your job to find them and, once you do, to create the kind of relationship in which they trust you, want to open up, and share with you a lifetime of accumulated experience.

## Volunteering to Support Professionals and Agencies

Counselors and counselor educators are busy people. They almost invariably have more clients and tasks that need their attention than they have time to give. If you become perceived as another burden, they may be willing to speak to you only for a short period of time. But if you can identify their needs and interests, and be perceived as helpful, they may be willing to devote more time to you.

Counselor needs for assistance provide excellent opportunities for students to learn, get firsthand experience, develop professional relationships, and strengthen that professional resume, which is often rather thin for new counselors. It can also prove valuable to class work by opening up a variety of in-the-field sources for research papers and class presentations.

Consider selecting from among the counselors you meet the one with whom you have the best rapport. Try ending your conversation with an offer to volunteer your assistance with activities that could provide a valuable service and also give you needed experience in the field.

Sometimes interviews will not open doors in this regard. In that case a next step might be to approach a number of organizations to offer your services (and also look at your interviewing style for flaws). A form of practical volunteer experience can often be found at local mental health agencies and on the college campus itself. Most community mental health agencies offer some form of crisis line that requires trained volunteers to answer phones and assist callers. They may also offer other types of work for volunteers, ranging from assisting people with severe mental disabilities to participating in recreational opportunities for children. Any type of volunteer work with people in need or with human research provides not only training and excellent experience but also numerous contacts in the mental health field.

Most universities now offer peer support programs and tutorial services for students. These can be in the form of one-to-one or small group interactions on general concerns or related to specific topics. Student housing, fraternities, and sororities are continually looking for individuals to provide interesting and meaningful presentations on the social and personal issues that residents encounter. Just like the counselor in the field, students who seek out and volunteer for such activities are often given opportunities to help. When that volunteer help also proves to be well and useful, the volunteer will often find that many additional opportunities develop from his or her initial work. Experience, professional references, and job opportunities frequently follow those students who take the initiative in these areas.

Another kind of volunteer work that can bring knowledge, experience, and professional opportunities to students is assisting faculty with their many projects. Faculty are called upon to do much more than teach. They are often part-time counselors, presenters, writers, administrators, leaders of the profession, and researchers. The expectations of faculty members are both to educate counselor education students and to be the leaders in the growth of the counseling profession and their university. These expectations are many for the limited time and resources available. Even those lucky faculty who have been assigned graduate assistants to help them with these tasks are usually happy to involve resourceful students who initiate contact in their work.

One of the most frequent ways students provide valuable assistance to faculty is by doing library research. It does not take a lot of training to do literature reviews and hunt down difficult-to-find materials. It does take energy, dedication, a degree of independence, and determination. Such efforts can save faculty hours of work, or even allow them to pursue a topic that they might otherwise have avoided because of an inability to find the necessary time. Student researchers get firsthand involvement in the development of research studies, presentations, courses, or grant preparation—involvement that will be greatly appreciated by potential employers.

Most students believe that volunteering to work for a counselor or faculty member is very worthwhile, but few ever fully follow through on their intentions. (You will hear this same pattern quite a lot in your clients as well.) But volunteering must not be taken lightly. Remember that volunteer help is only truly valuable if it can be counted on to be there when needed. A good discussion of potential areas for volunteer work should be followed by student actions that demonstrate the commitment to learn and work with the professional. When professionals can see that you are interested, able, and committed to working with them, they will reward you with trust and involvement that you will get from few other opportunities as a student.

Some students become so involved in a project with a faculty member that they wind up having their work formally cited in a paper, being identified as a coauthor, or taking the role of copresenter at a professional meeting. As an example, several students are cited for their assistance with the original edition of this book. They helped with library research, collected materials, and evaluated our ideas; and one person helped in the development of exercises at the close of each chapter. This experience provided them with an apprenticeship that may be useful to them at a later time when they are interested in writing books or articles of their own.

## Finding and Using a Guide or a Mentor

Most master's degree programs have enough required course work that students could chart out a program pretty much on their own. But this type of planning, although it usually includes the basics, never leads to getting the most from a program. Individuals who know the program and the field of counseling are almost always able to provide more effective guidance and support to a new student than the new student, planning on his or her own, could ever secure. It is the providing of this extra understanding and direction that can change a program from acceptable to great.

Here is one student describing how this process worked for him:

> As a potential school counselor, it never occurred to me that I could profit from some of the course work in the marriage and family area. I knew that I wouldn't be doing any marital and family therapy, but I had not considered how useful understanding family dynamics could be in working with children. These courses opened a whole new avenue to me that I would never have thought about. Even though I will be graduating shortly, I now intend to finish the sequence of marriage and family courses to give myself some other options. I feel so grateful to this one person who graduated ahead of me. She sort of took me under her wing and filled me in on stuff I was unaware of.

Once you have made a point to interact with professionals in the field, you are likely to have made some contacts that could develop into mentor relationships. Such guidance-providing relationships usually are the result of interactions with counselors in the field, faculty members (including your assigned adviser or others with whom you have developed an alliance), and/or advanced counseling students who are further along than you are. These three mentor sources have different advantages (and disadvantages because other students can give you inaccurate information) that can improve your training and advance your professional future.

An effective guide or mentor from any of these sources can provide you with direction and support for professional development that is not available through more casual relationships. Using one or two individuals as primary sources of guidance on what courses to take, how to interact with faculty and other professionals, how to deal with students, and how generally to get the most from a program is extremely valuable. Note, however, that most everyone you consult will have different ideas about what you should do, how you should do it, and why you should do it in a certain way. Thus using too many sources for this type of information virtually ensures that your program and the ways you approach it will be inconsistent, and the results you get will be confusing and unsatisfactory.

A guide or mentor is invaluable for dealing with the many personal and professional development issues that arise during and right after your training. This person can help you check on how realistic your anxiety over a test is. A mentor can help prepare you for your first counseling session or review the results of that session in a way that will feel more supportive than threatening. When you are ready to look for an internship or a job, it is the mentor or guide who inspires confidence and provides the regular support that gives you the stability you need. This is the individual to whom you can turn when times are tough and you need explicit directions from someone who fully understands you.

One of the most satisfying, exciting, and worthwhile professional relationships that you can ever have is with a faculty member acting as a mentor. Although this is a relatively common experience between doctoral students and their advisers, who develop a kind of collegial friendship and supervisory partnership that is based on mutual respect, it is also possible for master's students to develop such relationships. Such mentor relationships may not endure when both participants relate to one another on an equal footing, but they can serve an important transitional role for young professionals in any field.

A student who has an effective mentor (ethical, competent, caring, and a good role model) may also be able to rely on that person when the program is over. The nature of this relationship must change after graduation when roles, responsibilities, social structures, and geographic location are altered. Relationships that continue to be effective evolve to new forms at this stage rather than remain the same. Some relationships continue to find great professional or personal commonality and become stronger as more equality enters the relationship. Others continue to be positive but with little direct professional involvement. Whatever the continuing development of the relationship is, most new counselors find that it is often their guide or mentor during their program who can provide the key recommendations and references to support their continued professional growth for many years.

Faculty can be excellent mentors in some cases. They have more experience with the ins and outs of specific programs, the students in them, and the career paths of people who complete the programs than anyone else. This almost unquestionably makes them the best advisers although not always the best mentors. Faculty are busy people and have many students to advise, so they cannot get fully involved in a mentoring relationship with every student. However, all faculty have some students with whom they seem to work most effectively. Common interests, personalities, and work habits are good clues to the potential for an effective mentoring relationship with a faculty member. Faculty as mentors are particularly valuable to students who have professional goals that match those of the faculty. Students who are interested in the research of the faculty members, the types of clients they counsel, or their professional leadership work and want to become personally involved outside of course requirements make attractive protégés.

Most counselor education master's degrees now require approximately 2 to 4 years to complete, depending on the student's pace. One result of this is that there is always a mixture of fourth-, third-, second- and first-year students in the program at the same time. Many institutions also have doctoral students who have completed their master's and are back on campus to do additional work. These advanced students can often make excellent mentors. Experienced students have seen the program, understand the intricacies of individual faculty, have experienced the associated emotional ups and downs, and know how to make the best use of university resources. They are particularly useful to students at the beginning of the program when everything seems new and uncertain.

Professional counselors also make wonderful mentors when the student's personality, work style, past experience, program, and goals are compatible. It is not simply a matter of finding a counselor with a job you like or from a social environment similar to yours. Counselors who feel secure and satisfied with their professional lives have matched the many aspects of their cultural experiences, work, training, personality, and social life to form a combination unique to them. A student must match several of these criteria in order to be a good mentoring match. Finding such a match and making use of it is the most practical mentoring match possible.

Everyone needs someone consistent to lean on when change and growth are occurring. It is a good idea to identify that person or persons for yourself, whether it is a counselor, faculty member, or advanced student. The important point is that you will benefit from finding the consistent sources of professional support that can help you through your program and your transition into the professional counseling world.

## Involvement in Professional Organizations

Expectations of student involvement beyond the classroom are generally limited, although almost all professionals encourage it. Everyone understands that the demands on students are enough to keep most adults busy, and paying professional organization dues can feel like just one more burden when a student's personal expenses are high and income low or nonexistent. What many students do not realize is that professional involvement can make their student life easier, more productive, and more likely to lead to future professional advancement.

Professional organizations like the American Counseling Association, American Association for Marriage and Family Therapy, American Mental Health Counselors Association, American School Counselor Association, and American Psychological Association were developed to provide support systems for professionals with similar needs. Increasing acceptance of the counseling profession has led to the establishment of more jobs, better wages, and greater recognition of our value to society. Resources on knowledge and skill development have also increased tremendously so that clients can benefit from counselors having the most up-to-date information available. But these things do not happen by accident. Professional counselors have backed their respective organizations with ideas, time, and money in order to support these efforts.

Students are seen as the future members and leaders of the profession and are therefore given special attention. Most professional organizations have significantly reduced rates for student membership, purchase of materials, attendance at workshops, insurance, and other services. The goal is to encourage students to begin viewing themselves and acting as professionals from the beginning of their training.

Comments typifying the benefits that students report as a result of their activities in professional organizations include the following:

- "I like the mail I get. Seriously. Every week I get something in the mail—a journal or newsletter, a workshop announcement, advertisements for new books. It helps me feel connected every time I receive any correspondence."
- "I look forward to the state and annual convention every year. I've only gone twice so far, but what a rush! Meeting students from all over the place. Going to programs. Seeing all the leaders in the field. Just all that energy at one place and time is amazing!"
- "I'm not really that active in the organization, but I do read the journals every month. I belong to several different divisions, so I subscribe to a number of publications that bring me up to date on what is going on in the field."
- "At a local meeting of school counselors I met several great counselors, and one of them offered me an internship at their school. It turned out to be great, and eventually I even got a job in the school

district. I've made good professional contacts and friends at these meetings."

- "I'm basically a shy person and don't reach out to others easily. Going to my local chapter of Chi Sigma Iota (the counseling honor society) got me to meet second-year master's students, doctoral students, and faculty in some neat, casual ways. I would never have found these relationships on my own, and they have really helped me personally and professionally."

These disclosures illustrate what students report they enjoy best about being involved in professional organizations. It is not even necessary to be all that active; some belong mostly for their professional identity. Even this limited involvement brings many benefits. One or more professional journals that speak to the most timely issues being studied in classes begin to arrive on a regular basis. Within the various organizations are numerous specialty divisions that address every conceivable interest—including prisons, group work, family counseling, school or mental health counseling, sex counseling, substance abuse, cultural issues, rehabilitation counseling, gay and lesbian issues, spiritual issues, supervision, and behavioral, humanistic, or systemic approaches. There are also smaller network groups that get together at conventions, or by correspondence, to share information and strategies about working with specific populations such as dual-diagnosed substance abusers, multiple personality disorders, sexual abuse survivors, closed head injuries, learning disabled students, and African Americans.

Newsletters are also sent to members with additional practical information on what is happening in the profession, job listings, and descriptions of innovative practices. Increasingly, these organization periodicals are including information specifically directed to students and new counselors in the field. This book, in fact, resulted from our collaboration as editors of two such columns in the American Counseling Association's *Counseling Today* entitled "Student Focus" and "Finding Your Way."

Professional organizations realize that students do not have the financial resources of other members. Therefore, they use a portion of their resources to subsidize student involvement in a number of ways. For example, most students must acquire some form of liability insurance when they enter practica or internships. This can be very expensive when purchased individually ($400 to $1,000 per year) but is quite reasonable when purchased through a large professional organization (as little as $20 to $40 in some cases, such as through ACA). Obviously, this is a major bargain for student members.

Members of professional organizations continue the development of their skills and knowledge base by taking professional development workshops and attending conferences. These events almost always have significantly reduced student rates and offer excellent opportunities to take part in specialized training and information sessions beyond what any single university program can offer. For example, if you have a particular interest in learning about a subject that is not ordinarily part of your program's curriculum, you could supplement your education with this training. A quick perusal of the current offerings in any given week (depending on your proximity to a large city) might find workshops on such topics as play therapy, feminist approaches to family intervention, the *DSM-IV-TR*, strategic family therapy, AIDS prevention and intervention, attention deficit disorders, personal growth for helpers, or using various assessment instruments for clinical applications. Membership in these organizations keeps you informed regarding the content, times, locations, and costs of these events, and offers you rates that are less than half of what nonmember professionals must pay.

Attending professional conferences also offers students the opportunity to make valuable professional connections. Meeting practicing counselors and leaders in the field broadens the network of any professional. This is especially true for students who come from smaller departments or who live in rural areas.

In addition, many students attend specific universities because they believe faculty have insights and professional connections that should help them find initial positions and promote their career advancement. These connections and professional relationships are very often started and continued at state and national professional gatherings. Students who attend such meetings can get the full benefits of the connections their faculty have and begin to develop their own personal professional support network.

Other individual services that professional organizations offer to support member needs include credit cards, life insurance, 800 numbers, and travel discounts. An additional service offered by ACA provides a uniquely valuable service to members and particularly to students. ACA maintains a library containing all the historical documents of the organization and its divisions, copies of out-of-date pamphlets produced by the organization, and copies of all journals produced by the organization since its inception.

Major national organizations also have state, and sometimes local, affiliates that provide similar services but on a more regional scale. State journals, newsletters, and conferences often provide very specific information and contacts regarding the critical issues and employment opportunities in a given area.

## Experiencing Counseling as a Client

What is it like to be a client in counseling? What does the client think of me and our counseling experience? Why is the client only able to see or express one side of the issues? How does the client perceive these issues in comparison to my view? Why don't clients do what they need to do in order to reach their goals?

These are just a few of the questions that run through counselors' minds. There are no easy answers because clients and counselors are individually complex and the relationship between them is even more so. Although there is now considerable debate in the field about ethical problems inherent in dual relationships in which students are asked to serve in client roles, revealing personal issues to those who may be in positions to evaluate them, we encountered few such prohibitions when we were going through school. It was simply understood that before you could ever hope to function as a counselor, you had to first know what it was like to be a client, to experience firsthand all of the apprehensions, doubts, and exhilaration that are part of this process. It was routine to require students to participate as a client in various classes, to volunteer to serve as a client for practicum students, and to participate in experiential exercises in many classes. Some programs even had as a requirement for admission that the student participate in a counseling group or report on another counseling experience. The reasoning is that being a counselor involves much more than the mastery of skills and knowledge. It also involves a degree of personal effectiveness and self-understanding. No matter how well trained counselors might be, if they are personally dysfunctional, they could do as much damage as if they made a clinical error.

Looking back on our own experiences as clients in various forms of individual and group counseling, we are convinced that these situations taught us more about being a counselor than any single course we ever took. We know what it feels like to be understood by a professional. We remember all too well what it feels like to experience lousy counseling. We draw on these experiences constantly in our roles as practitioners and educators, so that every few years we reenter some form of counseling as a tune-up. What kind of hypocrites would we be if we believed that counseling is for others but not for ourselves?

Students can usually no longer be required to participate as clients in counseling, although other structures may be set up to simulate these experiences. For example, all quality counseling programs require students to at least role-play the client in practice situations. Most go further in suggesting that students seek counseling for themselves. The benefits relate both to developing a better understanding of clients and for personal self-growth.

It is ironic, and a bit disconcerting, when professionals encourage self-growth counseling for virtually everyone but do not follow this suggestion themselves. Counseling students, as well, may find it difficult to enter counseling even though they may see the potential value. They offer the same excuses as do other prospective clients:

- "I don't have time right now. Maybe later."
- "I can't afford it."
- "I should be able to work things out myself."
- "Seeing a counselor is a sign of weakness."

- "I will get around to it eventually."
- "I don't know how to find someone really good."
- "There is no sense in stirring things up right now. I already have enough pressure."
- "There is a stigma attached to being a client. I wouldn't want others to know."
- "My husband/wife/mother/father/children/roommate/friend wouldn't approve."
- "I'm just not good at this sort of thing."

Perhaps some of these excuses sound familiar to you. We promise that you will hear them a lot during your career from others. People often do not contact us until they are desperate or have given up hope of working things out themselves. Even if you cannot justify counseling as necessary for your emotional health right now, we still urge you to undergo it as an educational experience. Whether you go to the counseling center on campus, attend an experiential workshop, join a support group, or find a private practitioner, going to counseling as a client will provide you valuable experience for when you are sitting in the other chair.

Increased personal understanding and competency are other obvious benefits you will accrue. The more you learn and grow as a human being, the better equipped you are to help others to do the same. The theories you have read about in your books, and heard about in your classes, become real for you because you know they have worked for you.

Cody Dickman (2003) described his personal client experience that began as an elective class assignment and turned into meaningful professional growth.

> The motivation was to arrange for counseling, but I was dragging my feet on this assignment because of my uncertainty. The bottom line was that seeking counseling was something I was more afraid to do than I had expected. When I finally called to set up an appointment, the urge hit me to hang up the phone and play it safe once again. What I had to do was minimal at best compared with what it must be like having to seek counseling for a more serious problem. I realize more fully now how true the cliché is about knowing you have a problem is only half the battle. The other half is actually doing something about it. Empathy for clients became much more obvious to me.
>
> During counseling it seemed like I was talking in circles and at times didn't even know what I was saying. My train of thought kept escaping me and still she never really answered by questions, but let me work through them myself, giving me assurance when I was on the right track.
>
> The hour flew by. Standing up and thanking her, shaking her hand, and leaving the office, I realized that she didn't have to tell me anything; I figured it out myself!
>
> The adage of counselors needing their own counseling rings true to me, because now I understand a little about how a client must feel. I learned more from this assignment than any other individual assignment I have done thus far in my master's program. I'm proud of myself for pushing past the fears and uncertainty, learning about what it takes to have empathy, and keeping my eyes focused on the process and not the outcome. (p. 27)

## Acquiring Diversity Experiences

You understand your family and friends better than others largely because you experience their world with them. You probably never read about or studied them in a class, yet who they are and why they are that way is clear to you. What you have with these people is not academic knowledge but common life experiences. You have been an active participant in their eating habits, dress preferences, religious beliefs, political positions, cultural traditions, and the ways they are treated by others. The multicultural counseling studies you will have in class are good steps forward in helping you understand the way others see the world, but they will not get you the kind of direct experience you have with family and friends. Those experiential contacts will make you a much better counselor, but you will need to seek outside the program requirements to find them.

Direct experiences with other cultures provide two major benefits. The first and most obvious benefit is that you will better understand the feelings, thoughts, behaviors, and expectations of those from cultures different than your own. Of course, none of us will ever be able to experience every different culture because their number is virtually unlimited. We can, however, find ways to experience those that we are most likely to find in counseling situations. The growing numbers of African Americans, Hispanic/ Latino Americans, Asian Americans, and Arab Americans make them key groups to get to know in addition to the current majority European Americans. Then you can look at rural, inner-city, and suburban cultures to recognize the unique experiences of people living in these areas. You also need to work to understand the ways that males and females experience the world differently as well as the different views of those who, for example, have alternative gender preferences, physical differences, disabilities, or religious beliefs unlike your own.

The second major benefit from seeking ways to place yourself in another person's shoes is your self-understanding of how you deal with the differences between yourself and those you serve. This is the more general value in gaining cross-cultural experiences that will help you better deal with people from cultures you have not yet experienced. You will learn your reactions to cultural differences, to times when your values conflict with your clients, and why at times you cannot understand why someone would think the way they do. Lack of understanding is always due in part to not fully empathizing with other people's experience of the world around them. It causes expectations that others should surely see things the same way as you. The only way to help yourself is to gain some firsthand experience with that conflict between your worldview and how others experience it. Consider how the following three students sought such experiences and what they gained from them.

- Kelly Kozlowski (2004) borrowed the traditional clothes from a friend who was a practicing Muslim and wore them to the local mall. What sounded like a simple experience turned out much more of an emotional challenge:

> I almost chickened out! . . . Lacking confidence and personal pride, I wanted to be what society seemed to deem the norm. . . . I wanted my jeans back. . . . I assumed that being open to the cultures, lifestyles, and appearances of others was enough, but it wasn't. (pp. 9, 21)

Kelly realized that saying she was culturally aware and accepting of others is not enough to really be understanding of others. "This innocent brief experience showed me how much easier it is to say that when you are part of the norm as compared to being outside the norm" (p. 21).

- When Katey Baruth (2002) asked her adviser how she could continue to expand her cultural awareness, the advice she got led to a small college with numerous Korean and Chinese exchange students.

> All the anxiety about taking risks and meeting new people came back in a flood of self-doubt. Then I remembered Keisha's [a previous roommate from a different culture] lessons about dealing with the discomfort attached to taking risks, and that putting myself out there was essential if I was going to grow. (p. 29)

Katey faced the obvious problems of language and the less expected ones of clients showing up early and standing at her door out of respect, and being bombarded with gifts that ethically she was not supposed to take. Her other experience was in an addictions unit where her first client confronted her with, "What does a young white girl know?" These were no easy choices, but the experiences "opened my eyes in ways I could never have imagined. Taking the risk to step into different cultures has made me a better counselor and person" (p. 24).

- Stephen Snow (2002) spent some time working in a homeless shelter that gave him

> amazing new insights to myself as a person and a counselor. . . . I began to feel a sense of honor being with the clients. . . . These were people discarded by society with little education, few social or work skills, and often with mental or physical illnesses. They have been ignored, rejected, forgotten with no reason to trust just one more middle-aged white guy. . . . I learned that being truly present to another person is far more important than any technique or theory. Hearing the unheard was liberating for them and for me. It was a humbling, spiritual experience. (p. 24)

## Keeping a Journal

Chapter 8 emphasized that you will experience many cognitive, emotional, and physical reactions during your tenure as a student and that these need to be recognized and handled effectively to get the most from your program. Seeing a counselor for each problem you encounter is neither necessary nor feasible. Talking with friends and faculty helps to a certain extent, but there remains a need to deal with some aspects of these issues on your own. Keeping a personal journal is a way to help you recognize and work through some of your struggles while also developing a record of your own development.

A journal can serve your needs in a number of distinct ways. By keeping a journal you can

- **keep track of all the unique ideas that you want to hold on to**: "There are so many new names to keep track of, leaders in the field whose ideas I can't keep straight. I forgot who said this, but we talked in class yesterday about what makes any relationship, professional or otherwise, trustworthy. I must remember this . . . "
- **jot down representative direct quotes of authors you have read**: "I intend to create a kind of catalog of the best, representative quotes from people I have read. I want to try and find a particularly insightful message from each of the theorists we are studying."
- **practice your counseling skills on yourself**: "If this idea of disputing irrational beliefs is supposed to be so powerful, let's see if I can put a dent in all this guilt I feel about going to school and leaving my family at home to fend for themselves. OK. I am supposed to start with the Activating Event. What is it that I believe is causing my suffering?"
- **work through personal struggles you are living through**: "This one professor is giving me a hard time. I don't know what I did to offend him, but nothing I say seems to please him. Perhaps I am overreacting. I do tend to spend too much time watching his reactions to everything I do and say. Now that I recall, there are times when he does support me, just not as much as I would like. I wonder why his opinion, in particular, is so important to me?"
- **personally apply the new concepts you are learning to your own life**: "We learned today about the differences between circular and linear causality in explaining human actions. It occurs to me that although I have been blaming my brother for treating me so poorly, he has just been reacting to stuff that I have done, which in turn are knee-jerk reactions to what Dad says to me."
- **work on your writing skills in learning to be a better communicator**: "I am feeling so clear this moment. I know exactly what I want and how to get there. So often I can't quite put what is going on inside me into words. I know that being a counselor means becoming good at expressing exactly what I am thinking. This has been a problem for me but one I intend to work on right here in this journal. Every day I plan to practice, for at least a few minutes, putting my thoughts down on paper."
- **set goals for yourself**: "It seems like every week I change my mind about what I want to do. My confusion only muddles things for me so that I can't concentrate on my work with the attention I would prefer. I think it would be best to stay away, for now, from trying to make a decision about my future with such limited information and experi-

ence. In fact, I want to make a promise to myself that for the next month I will practice staying focused on the present rather than the future. Every time I catch myself fantasizing about what I may want to do, I am going to compensate by writing down some awareness I have about what is going on in the present."

- **keep track of your progress and growth in important dimensions:** "Just a few short months ago I could not figure out how to do reframing to save my life. It reminded me of trying to do algebra in high school, another one of those mysterious things that I just couldn't master. Yet now this reframing business is second nature to me. I routinely think of various perspectives that are presented in a number of different ways, and then pick the one that has the highest probability of proving to be most useful."

- **try to make sense of your own past:** "What is it about this graduate degree that I am hoping will somehow validate me? It is as if I can add a few letters after my name that will prove to my parents that I really am competent. This is another in a series of endless attempts on my part to prove myself. Each time I don't really enjoy or profit that much from the experience because I put so much pressure on myself. If I could just let some of that stuff go, I could really concentrate on learning for myself, rather than to win my parents' approval."

- **keep a record of significant events that occur in your life:** "Today, I role-played my first session as a counselor. I can't believe how overwhelmed I felt. There is just so much to try and remember to do at the same time. Yet I am amazed at how good it felt. I think I am going to be quite good at this!"

- **continue a dialogue with yourself about issues that you find perplexing or that matter the most:** "I feel unfinished about what we did in class tonight. I don't agree with how the instructor handled things. I think she was uncomfortable with the way things were going, so she cut things off before we could finish what we started. I can think of several ways I might have dealt with matters differently. I wonder if I should say something to her before class next week? She might be offended. On the other hand, somebody should tell her what many of us were feeling after class last time."

- **continue a dialogue with significant people in your life with whom you have unfinished business:** "My husband seems to feel threatened by the new friends I am making at school. When I try to reassure him, he just clams up and acts like he doesn't care. I think what I really want to tell him is 'Honey, just because I am excited about new relationships does not mean that I want to dump the old ones. Yes, I wish you wanted to be more involved in my professional life as I have been in yours. And yes, I do resent it when you make fun of the new stuff I am learning. But I know we can work things out if you would just talk with me about it.'"

# Turning Experiences Into First Publications

You are working day and night to do assignments, and hang on to some semblance of a social life, and if you are acting on the guidance we are offering, you are volunteering, finding a mentor, interviewing, and journaling. Why in the world would you want to also think about publishing something?

## Taking Advantage of Extensive Opportunities

Most professional counseling organizations are always seeking short pieces of work for publication in their newsletters. These are publications that generally focus on practical application and direct experiences, unlike the scholarly journals that require strong theoretical arguments supported by new data and/or references to numerous articles. Scholarly articles are often lengthy, whereas newsletter article manuscripts generally range from two to eight double-spaced pages. This means that they are shorter in length than most of the papers that graduate students have to write for classes.

## Seeing Yourself in Print

The first time you see your own work published, the feeling is a very special one. You are moving from having close friends, colleagues, and instructors knowing what you think to having thousands or tens of thousands of people being interested in what you say. People like what you say and the way you say it enough to put it in print. The feeling is different from any other. It is about pride, confidence, belief in yourself, and seeing yourself as important to the larger world. You do not get many opportunities in life to make such a jump, and the feeling is unique.

## Growing as a Professional

We all exist with rather limited views of the world and who we are in it. The people we see every day and the tasks we do give us feedback about who we are. When you work in a clinic, you come to understand that clinic, your roles in it, and how your work is accepted. You do not know much about how you would do in other clinics, or in a school, or in a prison, or in private practice. What if you would be great as a consultant, but were never around consultants? How would you ever know who you could be? Understanding who you could be as a writer of things people want to read carries similar problems when no one outside your day-to-day circle sees what you can do.

The extensive need for articles in newsletters means that editors are consistently ready to evaluate and help you improve your writing. Many times they will take your work and do a lot of editing themselves to help get a good idea into publishable form. So you do not have to get it perfect the first time, but instead can learn about yourself and the process at the same time. It is a kind of growth you can never get by writing only for yourself.

## Gaining Recognition

It is a very nice thing when coworkers, friends, and family know who you are and the qualities you possess. But it is a major personal and professional plus when people outside that circle begin to recognize who you are and what value you bring to them. Listen to what one student said about the reactions of others to being published:

> I couldn't believe it that a professional from Canada wrote me, this mere student, to tell me how much my words meant to her. She said my words confirmed things that she had believed, but had not heard in the way I said them. She even said she was going to deal with her own children differently because of what I wrote. I'm so excited that we are going to meet at the next ACA convention and talk.

Earning recognition is not just about feeding your pride; it is about creating opportunities for yourself. It is by publishing your ideas that you not only help to advance the state of knowledge in the field but also help to create a reputation for yourself that may allow you to expand your work in areas that you could not have foreseen.

## Reading Novels

One of the things most conducive to burnout in graduate students is immersing themselves so thoroughly in their school-related reading that they lose a larger perspective of the human experience. Fiction is about life as it is lived by the characters who inhabit novels and stories. We are privy not only to their actions but also to their histories, their motives, and their inner experiences.

Freud found the novels of Dostoyevsky and the plays of Shakespeare to be just as helpful to him in the development of his theories and understanding of his clients as anything he studied in the sciences. Indeed, reading fiction is, according to some of the field's leaders such as the existentialist Rollo May, the best way to learn to be a counselor. It is from reading novels that we expand our knowledge and understanding of human experiences. We are able to travel to a hundred different cultures and learn the languages and customs of each one.

Whether you prefer psychologically complex novels such as those by Fyodor Dostoyevsky, Albert Camus, Jean Paul Sartre, and Henry James, or contemporary stories of how counselors and therapists function in their daily life, fiction teaches us about why people act the way they do. We are offered the opportunity to follow characters throughout their lifetimes, or through a particularly stressful transition. We observe how people make decisions and what contributes to their most constructive and destructive choices. During those days or weeks that we are living the novel, we are transported to another world. We enter the lives and bodies of others, almost seeming to feel their emotions and think their thoughts.

Watching television or movies also provides ways to view other people's lives. Yet there is something about the activity of reading that requires a degree of imagination and more active involvement that is not present during watching lives on the screen. Books allow us to proceed at our own pace, to stop and reflect on what we have taken in, to think about what is happening, to go back and review sections, to reread poetic passages, to draw personal meaning from the scenes, and to use our own imaginations to create the sounds of voices, the images of characters, the texture of scenes. Reading can be a form of supplemental education for you in learning to be a counselor that both promotes relaxation and helps broaden your interests and appreciation for human experience.

## Traveling and Exploring Different Cultures

What reading fiction and watching movies can do for you vicariously, traveling gives you more directly. Traveling and being away from your things, your possessions, and your support system can free you to be more adventurous. Your job as a traveler, besides negotiating yourself from place to place, is to observe what is going on around you, meet people, see new sights, and find new experiences. Such adventures broaden your awareness of different peoples and help you to be more knowledgeable and tolerant of those who are different from you. All of these things will benefit you as a student, as a professional counselor, and as a person.

You can learn about multicultural perspectives in the classroom or read about different cultures in books, but nothing can replace the experience of actually visiting or even living in these cultures. It is not necessary to buy a ticket to Asia or Africa to enjoy the benefits of adventurous travel. Places quite close to home can provide opportunities for seeing people, customs, behaviors, and values that are very different from your own. These experiences help you remain more flexible, look at things from a more relative perspective, and meet each client with openness to his or her unique view of life.

John Barletta's (1995) experience as an Australian studying in the United States enabled him to effectively summarize some of the key advantages that he derived and that others experience by studying in another country. These advantages include

- **living in and learning about another culture:** This can be daunting, but a lot of fun, as a whole different way of life opens up for you. Studying overseas provides firsthand experience and knowledge of the multicultural issues you learn about in class. Different people, foods, music, values, gender roles, philosophies, clothes, and weather are experienced every day.
- **broadening your cultural perspective of counseling:** Looking at the profession from another culture's perspective presents new approaches and ideas on how society and values impact people. Another culture will view and practice counseling in ways different to your previous experience.
- **expanding your professional network around the world:** It is a wonderful opportunity to make friends and develop collegial relationships with people from around the world.

- **impressing prospective employers:** Gaining an education abroad clearly demonstrates courage and foresight. You will be seen as fearless and flexible—good qualities for most employers. (p. 42)

## Focus Activities: Making Personal Use of This Chapter

This chapter addresses why and how busy graduate students should supplement their education with activities such as those suggested. These experiences will set you apart from others when you graduate. You will know more and have more useful skills, and employers will recognize you as someone who has accomplished much more than the average good student. Remember that you need to take time to invest yourself in a holistic education rather than putting things off until you get out of school. Completing the following exercises should enable you to implement this chapter's information and get far more from your program than course work alone allows.

1. **Identify your strengths already written in your notebook for chapter 8 focus activities.** Use your strengths to supplement your education and make opportunities for yourself. For example, if you are organized and a good leader, become involved in or start a student group. If you have specific knowledge in an area, offer to give a workshop within your program. This is good practice for presentations at the state and national levels.

2. **Strengthen your writing skills as they can affect your career positively in many ways.**

   - Start by identifying three topics that really interest you, and use these topics in class papers to begin developing expertise.
   - Be sure to write in the publishable form you see in journals for all your papers.
   - Take a class or workshop on publishing and begin to take risks by submitting your work. Start by submitting brief works to newsletters. Do not set unrealistic expectations for these first submissions. Expect numerous rejections, not just because you are new but also because even the best of writers get them. Be ready to modify and rewrite as necessary.
   - Read *Writing for Professional Publication: Keys to Academic and Business Success* (1999) by K. T. Henson. This is an excellent resource for getting you started with your publishing endeavors.

3. **Give development of your public speaking skills a high priority because they will strengthen your education and marketability.** Offer brief presentations or workshops within your program, at your place of employment, or at state and national conferences. If you have trouble speaking in front of others, practice first within a group of your peers within your program, or copresent a topic with a faculty member or colleague. Doing these presentations will make you more

comfortable with public speaking and open doors for you by high-lighting your professionalism.

4. **Look for a mentor with expertise in your field that you believe can be trustworthy and objective with you.** Valuable relationships take time to develop and are based on shared interests, experiences, and feelings, so begin developing these relationships early when you can do it in a relaxed and genuine manner. List in your notebook several individuals who might be mentor possibilities.

5. **Join and get involved in professional organizations that best meet your interests.** The American Counseling Association and Chi Sigma Iota offer opportunities for involvement from the international to local levels. Volunteering to work in organizations is a great way to develop a professional network, and the various publications that come with membership keep you abreast of the latest issues and employment opportunities.

6. **Volunteer time to work with faculty on research projects or with local agencies as a way to get experience and to get your foot in the door.** Once word is out that you are motivated and seek opportunities for yourself, you will find that more and more opportunities come your way.

7. **Experience counseling as a client.** Seeking counseling for yourself will enable you to grow and develop as a person as well as help you see what it is like to be a client. Contact the health services at your university. Most offer free counseling to students.

# 10

# Strategies for Finding and Securing a Job

The primary purposes of attending graduate school are to acquire knowledge and to prepare yourself for a position as an employed professional counselor. You can learn more than you ever dreamed possible, change in positive ways that you never expected, receive marvelous accolades from your instructors, and attain a sterling record of achievement; but if you cannot find a desirable job following graduation, you may justifiably wonder if it was worth all the effort. The emphasis in this chapter is on recognizing what can help you find a job in the field and also lead to additional opportunities throughout your career.

There are several effective strategies to increase your likelihood of finding a job. These include

- avoiding misconceptions about the job search and opportunities available;
- clarifying your preferences and choices;
- interviewing practicing counselors as early in your program as possible;
- attending as many state, regional, and national conferences as you can;
- networking with colleagues in your targeted areas;
- subscribing to professional newsletters;
- developing flexibility in terms of your mobility and options;
- volunteering to work without pay during a trial period;
- being initiating and assertive in going after what you want;
- learning to reframe rejection so you do not become discouraged and dispirited;
- presenting yourself in the best possible way in person and on paper;
- building good references; and
- being as honest as possible about your strengths and limitations.

## Clarifying Your Choices and Avoiding Misconceptions

Before you can hope to prepare yourself for finding the job of your dreams, you first have to clarify exactly what it is you are seeking. You need to know what your training and employment options are. A sound footing can be gained by reviewing chapter 4, which emphasizes the development of a flexible specialty area. This begins early in your program as you create the expertise you need and as you gain information on where and under what conditions people in your specialty area(s) work.

The possibilities include the broad categories in Table 3, which are typical of the kinds of work choices that counseling students make. Keep in mind that these are only a few of the current possibilities. The evolving needs of our profession, society, and local communities will cause this list to change continually.

The many options should stimulate your excitement over what is possible with your graduate degree, but be careful not to become overwhelmed or anxious. Remember that the more clearly you focus your attention on the job(s) in which you want most to function, the easier your transition will be from the role of student to that of satisfied professional.

Students often have misconceptions about what life is like after graduate school. Among these myths are that finding a job will be easy, as will be the adjustment from student to professional; that your years of apprenticeship and deference are over; and that you will absolutely love all aspects of your new job. Another myth is the unrealistic expectation that whatever problems you had in graduate school—problems with authority, fear of failure, resentment at being evaluated, the need to prove yourself, interpersonal conflicts with peers—will be left behind when you enter the work world. Life just does not work that way. It is important for you to avoid such misconceptions and work to achieve a clear, realistic vision of what your transition to professional life will be like.

•   Table 3   •
## Jobs for Counselors

| | |
|---|---|
| Elementary school counselor | Adult education specialist |
| Secondary school counselor | Gerontological counselor |
| Parent education instructor | Ministerial/spiritual counselor |
| Prevention specialist | Lifestyle coach |
| College counselor | Personnel manager |
| University student affairs officer | Personal growth group leader |
| Community agency counselor | Management supervisor |
| Mental health counselor | Human relations specialist |
| Private practitioner | Affirmative action officer |
| Adventure-based counselor | Organizational consultant |
| Rehabilitation counselor | Marriage and family counselor |
| Substance abuse specialist | Family mediation specialist |
| Correctional facilities counselor | Divorce mediation specialist |
| Probation officer | Child welfare agent |
| Career counselor | Crisis intervention team member |
| Employee assistance specialist | Assessment specialist |
| Employment counselor | Hospice counselor |
| Military counselor | Psychological educator |

# Interview Practicing Counselors Early in Your Program

Students are often assigned, as part of their introductory courses, the task of researching systematically what counselors actually do in the field. For example, students may be required to interview a minimum of six counselors, with half working in the specialty they are most interested in and half in areas that might be of interest. The primary goal of the assignment is to find out how these professionals were best and least prepared, as well as to solicit advice on how students might make the best use of their educational experiences. Side benefits that these students often report are the establishment of valuable contacts that were later instrumental in securing internship placements and jobs upon graduation.

Here is one student describing how this experience developed:

> I was initially kind of hesitant about approaching these people. You know, they are so busy and all. Why would they take time out to talk with me? At first, my worst fears were confirmed. I got put off a lot. When I could get through to a few counselors, they only wanted to talk with me on the phone. My first interview was even a disaster, so I felt pretty discouraged. I was so nervous that I just asked a bunch of questions, got brief answers that said very little, and was out of there in about 15 minutes.
>
> After I regained my composure, I tried a few more times and eventually made some wonderful contacts. It was through these interviews that I met my current internship supervisor, who invited me to come back there when I was ready. I made an effort to stay in contact with her, sort of keeping her up to date on what I was up to. Amazingly, when I was ready for my first field placement, she accepted me immediately.
>
> Since that time, she has moved on to another agency. We have a great relationship, and after I finished my internship, it seemed natural for me to approach her for a job. I will forever be grateful for that first assignment in my introduction to counseling course when I did those interviews.

You do not have to be assigned this task by an instructor in order to give yourself an excuse to start making contacts with professionals in the field. You may be surprised at how receptive many counselors are to your serious inquiries about what they do. They may be very busy, but they also feel honored when a counseling student calls on the phone asking for help.

Another benefit is that interviewing practicing counselors will help you determine which aspects of counseling employment are most important to you. Some of the more common values that beginning counselors consider include a good salary, excellent supervision, a pleasant working environment, supportive colleagues, opportunities for advancement, a variety of tasks, freedom to pursue their own interests, a benevolent administration, good benefits (including reimbursement for attending workshops), flexible hours, and opportunities to work in their preferred specialty. These items probably all sound pretty good to you. Unfortunately, you are usually forced to choose among these characteristics. For example, you may have to decide on the relative importance of job security versus good supervision, on a relatively high salary versus working in your preferred specialty, or on a brief commute to work versus a better group of coworkers. The task of making such choices is more easily accomplished when you have had the opportunity to observe professionals operating in diverse settings and situations.

## Attend as Many Conferences as You Can

Going into counselors' offices is not the only way to make valuable contacts. Many jobs are filled at professional meetings in which people get together from around the state, region, country, or world and share ideas about what works and what does not. For the industrious professional, the benefits of these meetings can go far beyond the formal presentations, structured discussions on a variety of subjects, scheduled interest groups, and committee meetings. These are the places where important professional contacts are made that may later lead to otherwise unknown employment opportunities.

A number of national conferences, such as those sponsored by the American Counseling Association, American Association for Marriage and Family Therapy, and American Psychological Association, go a step further and formally organize job placement services in which employers from all over meet with prospective applicants. In a few brief days you can meet with dozens of agency and school representatives in person. Even if an offer of employment does not immediately result, you have established contacts with people in supervisory roles who may be of assistance to you at a later time if you maintain contact. You also gain valuable feedback from them on the way you present yourself. This is particularly important because most employers are not looking to hire a degree but instead a quality person who has the right training.

The informal contacts you make at national conferences, and especially at local and state conventions or workshops, are likely to be just as important as formal interviews. It is during such encounters that you can meet many of the counselors in your city, state, or region and find out about what they are doing and how they are doing it. Counselors often make it a priority during such annual pilgrimages not only to attend seminars and programs but also to meet other professionals they did not know previously.

It is relatively common for students and others to create employment opportunities for themselves at such conventions, as well as to network with students from other institutions and swap information. More than a few counselors chuckle as they tell how they got their jobs not during formal interviews in which they responded to announcements, nor even during attendance at scheduled gatherings, but rather during serendipitous meetings in which they found themselves talking with someone in a lounge, restaurant, or social event who just happened to be looking for someone to hire.

If this strikes you as improbable, or even unfair, consider the way the world works: who you know is often as important as what you know.

Employers are looking for people who are trustworthy and can fit into an organization as well as people who are competent, knowledgeable, and experienced. What better forum to impress people with what you have to offer as a person, and as a professional, than at the professional and leisure activities at a conference?

Here are what some people who have done lots of hiring for years have to say about contacts made at conferences:

- "Lots of candidates for beginning positions look similarly good on paper. The interview helps see their differences, but it doesn't show what you are like outside that formal setting. You see more of the real person at a conference. How they interact with you and others is more like what can be expected at work."
- "Any student I meet at a conference who does not have to be there gets a plus in my book. They are putting out money and time they probably don't have to do something I feel is important. I immediately see them as more of a professional, and it makes me interested in their potential as an employee."
- "When I've read dozens of applications and a couple are names of people I recognize from meeting at a conference, I'm immediately drawn to them. That personal connection may not get them the job, but it does automatically get them more attention at the application stage."

It is expensive to go to conferences, but it is also an investment in your future that is just as important as the tuition you pay. Professionals establish friendships and collegial relationships at these meetings that last a lifetime, and this is the time in your career when these friendships may benefit you most. There is also good economic news for students who attend professional conferences. Just as you receive reduced rates (usually 50% or more) when you join professional organizations, you also are entitled to substantial discounts in registering for conferences. Also check with faculty members or student organizations to see if there are organized trips planned in which groups of students share expenses to reduce costs further.

## Networking

You should recognize that three of the first four strategies described in this chapter refer to making human contacts. These are critical because people in general, and counselor types in particular, respond most favorably to personal contact as a means of impressing others.

The ways you find to meet professionals on a daily, or weekly, basis may be just as important as the interviews you do or the conferences you attend. Start by interacting with every faculty member within your own department so they get to know you better. Try to develop especially good rapport with a few you particularly admire. Such contacts will not only be important when it comes time to write letters of reference, but often faculty members are the first to know about jobs when they come up. It is common for professors to be called by contacts at various agencies and schools (sometimes by former graduates of the program) in order to see if they can recommend someone graduating who might be a good match for a particular position. The same process takes place for those who are interested in applying for doctoral programs (described in greater detail in chapter 11) in that associates from one institution might call another on behalf of a student to recommend him or her for admission.

Reach out to fellow students as well. Rather than sitting with the same people in every class, or hanging out with the same comfortable group, try to develop relationships with as many peers as you can. These contacts can lead to support as a student, and throughout your professional life, by providing a wide network of friends and associates with whom you may consult. A directly work-related benefit from such proactive efforts is that (because many jobs are filled from within) it may just be one of your contacts who is asked to recommend someone for a position. In fact, one of the first ways that many jobs are filled is by asking current employees for recommendations.

## Subscribe to Professional Publications

You must know what opportunities are available in order to apply for them. One of the principal ways that such openings are advertised is in the professional publications such as *Counseling Today* (American Counseling Association), the *APA Monitor* (American Psychological Association), and various state and regional newsletters for family therapists or counselors. In addition, the *Chronicle of Higher Education* lists jobs for counselors, counselor educators, and university administrators. *Black Issues in Higher Education* provides job listings as well. Once you decide on the kind of job you want and its particular setting, location, and responsibilities, you can then review those journals, newsletters, and other publications that are concentrated in that area.

## Scour the Internet

The professional associations you belong to will provide directions to Web sites where you can locate jobs. Virtually all major professional publications as well as local newspapers also have Internet editions that give much more current information on employment opportunities. State education, mental health, social services, and criminal justice agencies are other great sources of Web sites that either advertise directly or point you to other sources of jobs. The use of Web sites by agencies to find employees has become the norm because the process has minimal cost, has nationwide and even international distribution, and attracts those people who have the technology skills needed in today's modern work force.

The most common question from people starting out with Internet searches for employment is how to begin. That has become an easy one to answer. Anyone can develop a solid Internet search plan using just a few initial steps.

- **Go to newspapers and professional publications.** Use the paper editions of professional publications and local newspapers to find their Web sites. An even more direct step is to go to a search engine like Google.com and simply type in the name of the newspaper or publication. It will lead you right to its Web site. Once there, look for employment opportunities, and you are in.

- **Locate state and local agencies.** Go to an Internet search engine and type in the name of the state agency you are seeking. If you do not find what you are looking for, find a phone number from the Web site and call to see where such information might be.

- **Locate local employment offices.** Find your local employment office on the Web, and it will list a wide variety of opportunities available in your area.

- **Look up professional associations.** These organizations need you to be involved, and they know you want employment, so they will either have job announcements on their Web sites or links to other sites that will give you leads.

- **Go to university career centers.** Find the career center at your institution and ask for its Web site, which most will have. But even if it does not, it will be able to point you to Web sites that will give you the information you need and the sites most commonly used by people from your school.

- **Ask your colleagues near graduation.** February and March of the second-year master's student program is when the best job hunters really shine. They know where to look and have options available while others are just beginning to worry about where to look. Find these people, and they will be happy to put you onto some key sources. They are proud of what they can do and love the feeling that comes with sharing with appreciative peers.

- **Consider your professors.** Faculty are sometimes great sources and sometimes of no value to your Internet employment search. They have a million things to do, and maintaining expertise in the job hunting area is not generally a top priority. The faculty most likely to help you with Internet searches are either the ones who traditionally teach students in their graduating semester or who are really into technology and the Internet themselves.

Still need more direction? Appendix B lists Internet Web sites that will direct you to employment opportunities identified nationally and for individual states. One set of sites is specific for those seeking jobs as school counselors; the others provide information on more general employment opportunities that include the wide variety of positions for which professional counselors will qualify.

## Be Geographically Mobile

Graduates who cannot find satisfactory employment are most often those who have rigid parameters for what they are willing to do and where they are willing to work. If family commitments or other responsibilities make you unwilling to move, you will obviously have a more difficult time than if you are willing to relocate most anywhere to find the right job.

Some geographical regions and counseling specialties present relatively few employment opportunities (e.g., private practice in an affluent area or school counselor in a highly desirable district), but others cannot find enough counselors to fill their positions (e.g., inner-city agencies, rural mental health centers, or private rehabilitation centers in some states). You may have to make some hard choices, in consultation with your family, about what you are willing to do, and where you are willing to live.

## Volunteer to Work Without Pay During a Trial Period

The less experience you have, the less likely you are to get the job you want. Yet how can you gain experience if you cannot find anyone who will give you the opportunity? One answer is to work for free as you prove yourself. Here is one student describing how he applied this very strategy to secure a job he really wanted:

> I had heard about this unit at a local hospital that had a great program working with hospitalized dual-diagnosed patients who had a likelihood of getting back out into the community. They specialized in using group work as the preferred treatment, which is of special interest to me. I love working in groups.
>
> When I first approached them about a job, they were fairly lukewarm about the idea. The only people they had ever hired were social workers and psychologists. They were very skeptical that someone with training in a counseling program could do the job, even after I explained my unique qualifications as a skilled group leader and mental health specialist.
>
> As a last ditch effort, I presented them with the idea that I would work for free during a trial period. If they didn't like my work, fine, they had nothing to lose. But if I could perform according to the standards that they expect, then they would hire me.
>
> Well, they bought it. At first, I was kind of nervous having to prove myself, but in a matter of days it was clear to me, and to them, that I was more than capable and well prepared for the job. They offered me a permanent position before the trial period was even up!

Here is another student describing how she utilized part-time volunteer work to increase her employability:

> While in the counseling program I took the training offered by a mental health center and worked the crisis phone a few hours per week for 2 full years. I got to know the people who worked there, and they got to trust my

competence. Even before I graduated they were asking if I would help in other areas, and eventually they suggested a paid internship at the end of my program. I accepted the offer even though it was not a great financial deal. By the time I completed my degree, the agency was working hard to make a spot for me even though funding was tight. They saw me as a competent and reliable person who had proven to them that my interests and motivation were ones they could count on.

Even if these students had not ended up with job offers, they still had gained valuable experience that could have been used in marketing themselves later. Part-time or full-time volunteer work is a way to beef up your resume and create a portfolio that represents you as qualified and experienced. What these positions lack in monetary compensation they can make up for in providing you with valuable opportunities to make contacts in the field and apply what you learned to real-life situations.

## Start With the Less Desirable Job in the Right Place

You are looking for a career as a professional counselor, and there is virtually no chance that your final career position will be the first one you take. Everyone learns more about themselves and employment in their field after they begin working, and when you learn, your ideas, hopes, and dreams change. The overwhelming majority of people change positions multiple times as they decide one type of work, or one geographic area, or one agency to work for fits them better than another. It therefore becomes most important to acquire a first position that will get you started and help you to see the field firsthand. At times that first position might not even match the credentials you have acquired, but it can get your foot in the door.

Many mental health counselors have started out as a case manager in an agency, proven their abilities, and moved quickly into counseling and supervisory positions. Teachers with new school counseling degrees frequently take the available teaching position in a district where they want to work, prove their abilities, help out the local counselors, and when the right school counseling position comes open, they are in the lead position. If your ego is too big to take the less attractive or lower level job in the place you really want, you may be passing up significant future professional advancement opportunities.

## Prepare a Compelling Resume

The new counseling graduate often has only limited counseling experience so the resume will be a relatively short one. Putting in the extra time to gain more from your program than others will allow you to put in volunteer, leadership, and writing experiences that others may not have. Whether you have the extras or not, there are visual differences in resumes that set some apart from others. Skip the multiple colors and fancy print style on specially designed paper. They might get you an artist position, but they do not do much for people seeking counseling positions. What does catch the eye of employers is a resume that is specific, easy to read, developed in a logical format, and highlights what the employer is seeking.

The basics of a visually appealing resume can easily be applied.

- **Put contact information first.** Name, address, phone, and e-mail information go right at the top with the name highlighted in bold.
- **Make headings bold.** Use bold type for the major headings, such as education and additional training. These will make reading easier and quicker for the reviewer, and that will be a plus in your favor.
- **Use logical order.** Put things in the order that matters to reviewers.

  - *Name and Address* tells who you are and how to contact you.
  - *Education* assures them of your training and may include both degrees and other training such as workshops, seminars, or certification courses.
  - *Licenses and Certifications* emphasizes your professional status that employers will need to know about.
  - *Professional Experience* confirms that you have the appropriate experience.
  - *Other Experience* shows how other work and volunteer experiences may have shaped who you are and how you work.
  - *Leadership Positions* tells something about how others respect you and your willingness to work with others.
  - *Honors and Unique Accomplishments* allows you to show off those special honors or accomplishments that highlight the differences between yourself and others.
  - *Professional Affiliations* makes the case for your commitment to professionalism through your investment in general and specialization organizations.
  - *References* is the final section that lets people know how to follow up on your qualifications and potential.

- **Tell what you did.** You were more than an intern at some site so let people know what you did. Because the work you did there defines your intern experience, be sure to list your individual and group counseling, teaching, program development, and other activities while at the site. And if there was something special you did in your practicum, such as develop a new group or create a brochure, this is the place to state it.
- **Be neat and accurate.** This is no time to have spelling mistakes, use cheap paper, or make little errors in names or addresses. Get someone you trust to look it over to see how it reads and to check for mistakes. It needs to be and look professional.

Ironically, the area in which students invest most of their energy— grades—is probably the least helpful. Rarely will an employer even look at your transcript, and there is no formal place on a resume for your grades.

Academic achievement as demonstrated by grades is important, but even more important is to concentrate on learning and learning experiences rather than on achieving grades. Diversify your educational experiences so you may present yourself as much more than a scholar.

## Write a Personalized Cover Letter

The cover letter you send will be the first impression the reviewer gets of you. The sense of you the reviewer takes away from reading the letter sends him or her to the resume with a specific mind-set that you want to be positive. Does the reviewer sense you to be logical and thoughtful or scattered and shallow? Do you appear personal and knowledgeable about the position, or cold and just hoping for any job? You can emphasize the positive characteristics by following a few simple guidelines.

- **Be direct and personal first.** The first sentence in the first paragraph should say what position you are applying for, and the following sentences in the first paragraph should say why you think the job would be good for you. Usually this means why it would be good for you professionally and what it is about the agency or location that makes it your choice. Employers want people who know how the job will be good for them as well as for the employer.
- **Summarize your qualifications.** It is useful to have a two- or three-sentence paragraph that gives a summary of your qualifications and where they can be seen in the resume. This will help direct the reviewers' thinking as they read the rest of the letter and go on to the resume.
- **Explain why you fit the criteria.** Following the first paragraph or two, your job is to show how well you meet the needs of the position. If criteria have been listed in a job announcement, speak to each one of them individually. Let the reviewer know that you know the requirements of the position as well as what it is about you and your experience that makes you well qualified.
- **Be personal and grateful last.** Let the reviewer know in two sentences that you appreciate him or her taking the time to evaluate your credentials and that you look forward to hearing the reviewer's reactions. If you plan to follow up with a phone call, this is the place to say it.
- **Say it all in one page.** Your job is to guide the reviewer and not to tell your whole story. Reviewers are reading lots of material, and they need concise wording in front of them or they will either not read the whole letter or, worse yet, read it and be frustrated as they go on to your resume.

## Be Your Professional Best at the Interview

When you get offered an interview, the key issue changes from how qualified you are to how well you demonstrate your qualifications. The unqualified are generally weeded out during the paper reviews. What interviewers seek are the professional and personal qualities that will make one person stand out among others as an effective participant in an organization. The questions they are asking will not be the ones they are truly trying to answer for themselves. Their key concerns will be more general, as the following questions suggest:

- How much supervision, direction, and energy will it take to help this person be effective?
- How long will it take this applicant to become a fully functioning member of our staff?
- How much can we trust the honesty of this applicant? Do we feel sure that if this person runs into problem situations he or she will tell us?
- Will this person be a leader in our organization or a follower?
- Does this person understand the pressures of the work and how to handle both the tasks and the pressures?
- Will this person bring new strengths to the organization that will move us forward?
- When this applicant becomes effective in the position, will he or she stay in it or look for another job—in which case we'll have to hire someone new again?
- Will this person's personality fit in with the others working here or will it cause frictions that will reduce the agency's effectiveness?
- Is this person flexible enough to adapt to the changes that naturally take place in this workplace?

Whatever the questions you are being asked, the interviewers are trying to learn how professionally you behave and what kind of person you are. You will need to show both aspects to be most effective. The more you can show them how your personal and professional sides are complementary to each other and to the agency, the better you will be perceived.

Your professional side will be off to a good start if you have spent some time learning about the organization, what it does, who the clients are, and how the agency seeks to deal with client needs. Employers are most comfortable with applicants who understand the kinds of problems the agency encounters; whether the agency emphasizes crisis counseling, prevention, or consultation efforts; and how the clientele, societal changes, or funding issues are pressing the agency to change. This is why people who have had relationships with an agency as paraprofessional workers are often chosen for professional positions when they become qualified. They know the system and how to be effective in it.

One key underlying issue in an interview is how this person will get along with the rest of the staff if hired. It is never directly stated in the job announcement, and rarely mentioned in an interview, but the biggest headaches that employers have are around workers that do not get along with others. The whole organization is disrupted and becomes unpleasant for everyone when this happens, so clients do not get the best care, and the staff either starts giving less of themselves at the office or looking for other places to work.

You should present yourself professionally but also authentically. You do not want to work in a place where you got the job by pretending to be someone you are not. So although you will be on your best behavior at an interview, it is essential to also let them know who the real you is that they would be hiring.

## Go After What You Want

Once you have found a few places where you want to work, be polite but do not take "no" for an answer. Keep trying again and again to get the interview you want. Even after you are turned down for one position, do not walk away in dejection but immediately begin a campaign for the next opening. This is how one person handled a disappointing phone call:

> I really appreciate the time you took to see me. Although I am sorry I did not get the job, I was so impressed with your organization and the way you work, that I would like to stay in touch with you in case another position opens up shortly. Would you mind if I called or stopped by occasionally to see how things are going? Even if you can't hire me, I have found that what I have already learned during this process was quite interesting.

The average school principal or agency director receives hundreds of inquiries about jobs every month. Resumes are often routinely filed without even being looked at. Phone calls are screened in such a way that it is often difficult to get through to those in positions of power who make hiring decisions. When you do get through to the gatekeepers, you may feel that your conversation was less than satisfactory. Rather than giving up, keep in contact and show your continuing interest. You do not really have to make yourself a pest in order to communicate that you are someone who goes after what you really want, and that a position in this organization is one that would benefit both you and the organization.

## Reframe Rejection

You may have to distribute 200 resumes to get 15 interviews to get 3 offers to get 1 opportunity that meets your needs. This means that a high percentage of your attempts to find a job may result in a less-than-desirable response. How you process those experiences can lead to feelings of frustration, demoralization, and helplessness—or can spark you to work even more persistently in the future.

Reframing is the attempt to interpret a problem in such a way that it may more easily be solved. Choosing to think about your unsuccessful attempts to secure employment as failures or rejections makes you much more likely to experience them as discouraging than if you decide to think of them as learning experiences. Failure may be a source of great anguish and aggravation, or it may be reframed as an opportunity for growth.

One of the most challenging tasks you face in your search for a job is to bounce back from results that are not what you prefer. Try viewing such outcomes not as uniformly negative or extremely discouraging but as mildly annoying or slightly disappointing. By thinking differently about your predicament, by framing these problems as challenges, or by reframing your experiences as opportunities for learning rather than as failures, you are more likely to retain the energy and commitment you require to find eventually what you are seeking.

This is much easier than it sounds to put into practice. The time to practice this skill is now, when you receive a disappointing grade for instance, rather than waiting until your job search. Get in the habit of talking to yourself on a regular basis. Any of the skills you learn in your program—cognitive interventions, reframing, self-talk—will be a lot more accessible and effective if you have some experience applying them in your own life. For example, it is quite easy for us to sell these ideas to you because we know they have worked in our own lives. Time and time again, when we have encountered difficulties and discouragements, an internal signal reminds us to ask ourselves the questions, "How might I frame this problem differently?" "What might I say to myself that is more constructive?" "How can I choose to think differently about what I am experiencing?"

## Get Feedback and Move Forward

Get feedback on your interviewing skills and resume. It is forgivable to make a mistake in the way you present yourself once, but it is stupid to continue such ineffective methods, oblivious to how you may be turning people off.

As counselors, we must be sensitive to how we come across to others. Such awareness is what allows us to know when clients are responding well to what we are doing and when they are not. When we notice that a client tends to withdraw after direct confrontation, hopefully we stop doing that and do something else instead. When we observe that a client stiffens when we address her by her first name, we alter our behavior accordingly, or at least deal with its implications. Similarly, if there is something in the way you present yourself to prospective employers that is perceived as threatening, it is important to know that. If there is something in the way your resume is put together that does not highlight your strengths as well as possible, it is good to know that as well. The problem is finding honest feedback on how you come across.

Your experientially oriented classes (such as group counseling) provide the first opportunities to give and receive professional feedback with peers. Take the risks that are necessary in order to find out what it is about you that others find most and least attractive.

Ask your instructors and supervisors for as much honest feedback as possible. The key is to communicate as authentically as possible that you really do wish to hear the truth about how you are perceived, rather than a watered-down but more polite version; that you are strong enough to handle constructive criticism without feeling offended; and that you will be grateful for their efforts. Of course, these conditions are predicated on the reality that you really do wish to hear the truth about how you are perceived by others.

We can think of no excuse for a counselor not to want constructive feedback, considering how important such data are to improving effectiveness. Nevertheless, we have encountered numerous students who engage in obviously self-defeating behaviors while also communicating clearly that they are not open to hearing what is offered. Keep in mind that grades are not the only indications as to how you are doing. Most faculty members have also constructed professional judgments (hopefully separate from personal feelings) regarding what you could do differently to improve your functioning. Ask yourself which instructors you trust the most to tell you some ways you might improve your behavior and then approach them.

Another important source of feedback can come from those who interviewed you. Make an appointment with the interviewer after a job search is ended to go over how you might improve your interviewing skills. Such things as your body language, your dress, and the style in which you present yourself can all be altered if needed. You may have been perceived as too passive or too aggressive, too timid or too controlling. You may not have asked enough questions or asked too many. Your own responses may have been too evasive or too verbose. You may have appeared too rigid or too indecisive. Whether they tell you or not, these interviewers had reasons why they did not select you, and you are more likely to be selected next time if you understand and can take actions on those reasons.

## Asking for References

Everyone has letters sent that speak glowingly about what wonderful people they are. What sets a particular letter apart is when it comes from someone who is fairly well known in your area or who has a contact with the particular organization in which you are interested. It also helps if the letter is written in such a way that it specifically discusses what you can do (and what you cannot do) and the ways in which you are qualified as a counselor.

Sometimes the people who write reference letters are grateful for your efforts to help organize your background information for them. For example, when a student asks one of us to write a letter, the following information may be critical: How long have I known you? In what capacity? What courses did you take from me? What feedback have you received from me? What specific jobs are you seeking? What do you see as your greatest strengths and weaknesses? What are some things that could be important for me to say in the letter?

Although it could be perceived as presumptuous for you to supply the answers to these questions before they are solicited, we have usually appreciated the effort in that it saves us a lot of time and energy trying to recall specifics. Of course, we will not write these things unless we believe they are true. In some instances, we are not willing to write a letter at all. Nevertheless, this subject may be approached by asking the person writing the reference if he or she would like to have you summarize some background information that may be used in the letter. Providing a resume and transcript is always useful.

## Plan to Meet the Necessary Legal Requirements

You need different licenses and certifications to qualify for the jobs you really want, depending on the state in which you reside or wish to practice. It will certainly be unfortunate to graduate from your program, plan on moving to a particular area, and then discover that you are not eligible for licensure in that state.

You need to research this subject carefully, keeping in mind that the situation changes from year to year. A sampling of the possibilities include licensed professional counselor, marriage and family therapist, limited licensed psychologist, licensed mental health counselor, certified rehabilitation counselor, certified school counselor (secondary or primary), and national certified counselor. There are also specific certifications for a number of specialties, including hypnosis, sex counseling, behavior therapy, and play therapy. If you want to supervise other counselors eventually, that often requires a separate level of certification.

The acquisition of most licenses or certifications takes some planning with your adviser during your program. For example,

> Morgan is now an elementary school teacher. He is currently enrolled in the school counseling track, K–12 (both elementary and secondary schools). He knows that he wants to keep a number of options open, including possible retirement in a few years from the school system and working with children in a community agency. He also wants to maintain a small private practice to keep his hand in direct service activities outside of school.
>
> Morgan planned with his adviser to take the necessary courses to receive endorsement as a school counselor. He also took two electives so that he could be eligible to join the Association for Play Therapy and to be a licensed professional counselor (LPC). Finally, because he may wish to retire in another state that has a Marriage and Family Therapist (MFT) as the credential to operate in private practice, he decided that after graduation he will continue taking another four courses plus another internship in order to be eligible for that license.

Morgan's intentional and specific career plan may strike you as remarkably well constructed, and we agree that it is unusual for a student to know so clearly what he or she wants upon graduation. Nevertheless, be vigilant and make sure you take the necessary courses to qualify you for the license or certification you need for your preferred job choice.

## Postpone Private Practice

Some in our field believe that because a master's program in counseling is not considered a terminal degree (a doctorate is the terminal degree), graduates are not prepared to function as independent practitioners. There is some merit to this idea, considering the limitations of what can be offered in a 2-year (full-time equivalent) training program. Given the variety of problems that a human being can present, it is unrealistic to expect a master's-level practitioner, with minimal experience, to recognize all of the possibilities and take all necessary clinical steps. Even doctoral-level practitioners have limitations based on what they learned, when they learned it, and how much they have used it in practice.

Imagine, for example, that a client comes to you complaining that she feels depressed. Before you attempt to implement your favorite counseling interventions, whether they are cognitively, affectively, or behaviorally based, consider all of the other factors that could be operating. Among the questions that might need to be considered are the following: Is this depression situationally ignited? Or is it more of a chronic, biologically based disorder? Could this person be suffering from an undiagnosed neurological disease, such as multiple sclerosis, in which depression is a side effect? What about hormonal studies and other biochemical tests run to determine if there is an underlying physiological problem causing the emotional symptoms? Could dietary imbalances be a factor? Is this client a candidate for psychotropic medication? Or is she best treated by counseling? What are the consequences of referring the client for a medical consultation, given the history of substance abuse in the family?

The private practice of counseling, with its complex commercial, entrepreneurial, and independent characteristics, requires a high degree of clinical judgment, ethical responsibility, and professional competence, far more that anyone could expect to learn in a master's-level training program alone. Even with doctoral training, it is expected in most states that candidates will complete a 1-year (full-time) internship and then log an additional 2 to 4 years of supervised experience before even being eligible for licensure as an independent practitioner.

It is for these reasons that we highly recommend that you not consider independent private practice as an occupation for at least a few years after graduation. It is most difficult to try and scratch out a living by simply opening your doors for business without the necessary years of contacts to develop adequate referral sources. Perhaps more importantly, you could do your prospective clients a disservice trying to help them without sufficient experience in all of the varieties of problems that you might encounter.

Concentrate on gaining the most varied experiences you possibly can, with the best supervision available. Even after practicing for a few decades, we are still apprehensive about the awesome responsibility that accompanies seeing private paying clients. There are simply not the opportunities for consultation and professional interaction that are available for those who work within a school or agency. Regular staff meetings and case conferences are often rare for the independent practitioner, as are opportunities to talk about clients informally with colleagues. Being paid by the hour makes you tend to think differently about how you spend your time. Even going out for lunch with friends may cost you not only the price of the meal but also an hour of lost income when you could have been seeing a client. These added challenges are part of the reason why we urge you to develop your professional identity and solid work habits before you enter the private sector as a therapeutic entrepreneur.

## Be Honest With Yourself

Our final piece of advice is to integrate what we have offered you in all of these other points in such a way that you have a clear idea of what you want, what is available, and what is realistically within your domain. If doors are not opening for you the way you wish, look at yourself rather than at the obstacles others might present. What are some of the reasons you may not be presenting yourself in the best possible light? How have your expectations been unrealistic? What is within your power to change? What can you do differently?

In closing, we want to remind you about a phenomenon that you learned (or will learn) about in your studies of career development. In our world today, it is most likely that you (and your clients) will have three, four, or even five or more distinct careers throughout your life span. You are in the midst of a career transition right now, preparing for practice as a counselor, but this will probably not be your last such vocational change. It is important to remain open to new possibilities and opportunities as they make themselves known, or as you create them.

## Focus Activities: Making Personal Use of This Chapter

This chapter addresses strategies for finding a job and improving your marketability. The information is closely associated with that in chapters 6 and 7, which emphasizes the different areas of counseling, and chapter 9, which outlines what you may do to supplement your education. You will also want to refer back to the sections in your notebook where you listed those areas that particularly interest you and how to develop your marketability while in school. The suggestions included here aim to help you find the job that is right for you. Remember always to be realistic, active, and motivated, and consider that those who go the extra mile usually come out ahead!

1. **Do those informal interviews.** You should have already interviewed counselors as you explored various specialties to find out what a typical day is like for them, what they do, expectations of such a posi-

tion, positives and negatives of the job. Interviewing not only helps you to make a more informed choice regarding employment, but it also allows you to meet others in your field and further strengthen your system of contacts.

2. **Attend as many conferences and workshops as you can for the information, professional contacts, and job-placement opportunities.** Ask faculty members, peers, and coworkers about upcoming conferences or workshops, and find out what each costs, paying special attention to finding out about reduced student rates.

3. **Keep a professional resume that is up to date, and hand it out.** Swap resumes with peers and colleagues, and seek feedback from faculty members as to what makes your resume stronger. Make personal contact with agencies in the areas in which you will be seeking employment, and drop off a resume with them for future reference. Be sure to get the name of the person with whom you spoke, ask him or her to whom you should direct further inquiries regarding employment, leave your name, and thank the person for the attention. You can follow up the visit with a thank-you note, a summary of your conversation, and your reason for applying for the position. The employer's remembrance of a professional conversation and quality follow-up will give you a step up in the resume pile over those who have had no contact other than sending a resume.

4. **Strengthen your resume by using the suggestions in chapter 9.** Those things that improve your education also improve how you look to employers. Consider the resume that includes a candidate's participation and involvement in public speaking, publishing, and research. If you were hiring, might you not consider him or her over those who had only excelled and showed skills academically (e.g., through good grades)? A well-rounded resume shows someone who goes beyond the minimum and is willing to take risks and try new things.

5. **Let the career planning and placement center professionals know what types of jobs you are seeking so they can point you in the right directions.** They often keep files of job placements sent to them, and you might find the listings of counseling positions according to your specialty and locations of interest.

6. **Actively seek employment.** Some individuals are more passive in their job searches and may only send out several resumes with no cover letters, follow-ups, or leg work. Once your resume is complete, invest the money and time in sending out as many as possible and follow them up with phone calls and/or visits. This is your career, not a game. The time and money invested now will pay dividends in the future.

7. **Be willing to relocate to the degree possible and seek opportunities in a variety of agencies** (e.g., schools, agencies, hospitals, shelters,

prisons). You never know what opportunities there may be within the various settings.

8. **Check newspapers for opportunities regularly and act promptly in applying.** The good jobs often disappear quickly.

9. **Talk with faculty members, peers, and coworkers as to who and what they know in the areas and locations in which you are interested.** Many employment opportunities never make it to the paper, so use those contacts made in all of your networking efforts up to this point.

10. **Seek feedback from trusted peers and faculty members as to how they perceive you and how you might best be received in an interview.** Getting an interview means that someone has found you interesting on paper, and now you need to make sure of how you are perceived in person. See what people think about your dress, demeanor, and overall presentation so that you present yourself as well in person as on paper.

11. **Seek feedback after your interview regardless of whether or not you get the job.** Ask how you were perceived, and how you might improve your qualifications, your resume, your presentation. In addition to feedback, these follow-up discussions can sometimes lead to additional opportunities when the employer gets to know you and your determination better.

# 11

# Is a Doctoral Program in Your Future?

*My mother was so proud to see the only one of her four children graduate from college, and I (Richard) was thrilled to finally be done with my education. My BA degree in hand, I was pleased to be looking forward to nothing more than a good elementary school teaching job and raising a family for the next 30 years. But a funny thing happened to spoil this picture. It struck me that I was getting more excitement from talking to my sixth-grade students about their problems than about their science and reading lessons. The school counselor got to do that every day and I was jealous! So it was back to school for a counseling degree, and my mom worried about me giving up a good job for more education, and she never really understood what this counseling stuff was anyway.*

*Now my education really was done for sure. The master's degree in counseling was completed, and I had a great school counseling job in Idaho, a place I loved. I had no idea that only 3 years later two university faculty would show me another world that was exciting enough to leave a job and place that was so comfortable. When I told my mother that I was going back to school to get a doctorate so that I could teach counselors, there was a long pause before she answered, "But didn't you already go to school to be a teacher years ago? Are you ever going to be done with school?"*

*Thankfully, there were no more degrees for me to acquire after the PhD, but the education never seems to stop. There is just so much to learn, so many new research findings to understand, so many new ideas on how to help people more effectively, and constant changes in one's view of life that keep pointing toward new trails to follow. The need for education is never ending.*

❋ ❋ ❋

## Is a Doctoral Degree for You?

Many factors influence a counselor's decision to obtain a doctoral degree. Among the reasons commonly given are

- desire for greater autonomy,
- interest in supervising other practitioners,
- desire to teach counseling and mentor others,
- wish for a job promotion, pay raise, or administrative position,
- search for a higher level of training,
- interest in a doctoral-level license,
- curiosity about a particular research question to investigate,
- desire for greater status and power in the profession, and
- enjoyment of learning.

These reasons revolve around the fact that a master's degree in counseling is considered a professional entry-level degree. It recognizes the ability to practice counseling as a professional under supervision; after sufficient experience, greater autonomy is awarded. However, some experienced practitioners decide that they wish to move on to the doctoral level of credential where the norm is functioning more independently, particularly as a scholar, but also as a consultant, teacher, supervisor, and practitioner.

Getting a doctorate requires money, time, effort, and commitment. Depending on your interests and career aspirations, such a goal either may or may not be worth what is required to obtain it. The critical questions are, How do you know whether a doctorate is right for you? Can you get into a doctoral program? Are you likely to flourish, or at least succeed, in a doctoral program? How do you pick the program that best meets your needs?

There are no simple answers to these questions because much of the critical information for making the best choices lies within you. Only you can decide whether you are willing to do what is necessary to obtain this degree. Such a journey can be very fulfilling, but will certainly also be demanding and stressful. This chapter highlights the issues and information that you most need in order to make an informed decision about whether pursuing advanced training beyond a master's degree is the right decision for you.

In addition, even if you have no interest in a doctoral program at this point in time, it is helpful for you to learn what your professors and supervisors have gone through in their educational journeys. By the time candidates have obtained doctoral degrees, and completed their internships as teachers, supervisors, researchers, and clinicians, they are ready to take leadership positions within the field. They have the skills, the knowledge, and the confidence to function independently as well as to serve as mentors for others.

## Why Might You Want a Doctorate?

This is the best possible starting question for the person who is contemplating doctoral training. The answers vary from person to person and have a direct effect on whether this level of training will meet your needs, whether it is worth the effort, where you should do it, how hard it will be, how valuable it will be for you, and how much you will enjoy it or hate it. Very often people try to make this into a simple question, but it is not. It is as complex as the combined motivations, needs, personal situation, and abilities of each individual, so it should be given considerable attention. Eventually, we find that the answers most often relate to licensing, third-party payments, employment opportunities, status, money, and also learning and growth.

### Licensing

A license offers you sanctioned permission to practice counseling. Depending on the state in which you reside, or wish to practice in, there may be different levels of credentials required in order to be eligible for a license. Most states only license psychologists at the doctoral level, but others offer limited licenses to practice psychology under supervision. Marriage and family therapist licenses or professional counseling licenses are generally offered at the master's degree level, but they may also offer additional privileges if the candidate has a doctoral degree.

You need to check very carefully about the licensing requirements of the states in which you are interested in working. Any program you apply to needs to offer the specific training you require. For instance, some counselor education doctoral programs are not interested in training people for licensure as psychologists. This situation is increasingly the norm as nearly all states have passed separate licensing laws for counselors and psychologists. Sometimes states accept a PsyD (doctorate in psychology) as an option for those who wish to be practicing psychologists but are not interested in preparation as scholars or professors. You need to think long and hard about what you want to do with your degree: practice as an advanced-level counselor or psychologist, supervise other counselors in an organizational setting, develop and administer programs, teach at a university, conduct research, or make consultation your primary business. These roles are not mutually exclusive, but various doctoral programs specialize in providing appropriate training for some of these professional activities over others.

### Third-Party Payments

Related to the issue of licensing is third-party payment of fees, which is another practical reason that may affect the choice to attend a doctoral program. Nearly all states have developed licensing laws that allow counselors to be paid directly by the consumer. However, these laws do not necessarily mean that an insurance company or government agency is obligated to reimburse the counselor or client for services provided. The increasing use of insurance companies to pay for health care means that a counselor in private practice, or working for a profit-making organization, could have trouble getting paid for services rendered. A doctoral degree often qualifies the provider for reimbursement when a master's degree does not. Specific situations vary based on state laws and third-party regulations, but it is still easier for doctoral-level counselors to gain reimbursement than master's-level counselors.

### Employment Opportunities

There is no doubt that there are things you can do with a doctorate that you cannot do without one (besides get better restaurant reservations). The greatest opportunities for doctoral graduates are in the areas of university faculty positions in counselor education, supervision, consultation, and leadership positions in agencies and school systems. For example, those who want to work in a university counseling center, direct a community agency, hold supervisory positions, or be director of guidance in a school system will find that a doctoral degree is more likely to qualify them for these positions.

One employment opportunity where a doctorate is virtually required is a full-time faculty position, training counselors at a university. Some experienced master's-level counselors may be hired to teach a course or two at some institutions, but rarely are they hired on a full-time basis (although they may be at community colleges). Professionals for university positions are hired to do much more than teach. They are expected to add to the profession through research, publication, and becoming well known in the profession. Although the master's degree may make you a quality practitioner, it is the doctoral degree that is designed to prepare you to meet the employment requirements for becoming a faculty member.

The prestige and credibility that goes with having a doctorate can have varying professional and personal effects. It can open doors because it promotes initial confidence in your knowledge and skill, but it has little effect when your actual performance is observed and evaluated. Clients, for example, quickly forget, if they ever cared, whether or not you have a doctorate. After their first session or two, their evaluation of you is based quite simply on whether you have been helpful or not. Businesses, schools, and agencies that have not seen your work are more likely to look to you for assistance if you have a doctorate. But even in these cases, they normally seek someone whose work they have seen as effective over the person with only the advanced degree.

### Status

Prestige and credibility are other factors that can be very important personally to the individual counselor. Some people use success in school to gain a sense of accomplishment or to validate themselves. Whether these needs are healthy or not depends on the degree to which they affect the individual. A healthy view of the degree might have persons see it as a significant accomplishment in their life of which they can be proud. A less healthy need for the degree might see people viewing it as the thing that defines and validates their being. ("If having a master's degree signals to others that I must be intelligent and worthy, just think what a doctorate could do!") The healthy view allows doctoral students to spend time seeking information and skills meaningful and useful in their future careers. The unhealthy view has students doing what they need to do to get the degree rather than to ensure maximum growth and development.

### Money

Increasing income is sometimes a motivating factor for people seeking a doctorate, and the fact is that people with doctorates do make more money in general. However, two important considerations must be evaluated to understand this fact fully. First, people who acquire a doctorate must put money into education and generally also lower their own income for the period of time they work on the degree. Obtaining a doctorate takes time and energy that must come from other portions of your life. Second, people often give up experience-related income in one professional track to start as a beginner in another. For example, there are many experienced master's-level school counselors who might well have to move geographically, make no more money, or perhaps even take an initial pay cut to work as a new faculty member at a university or as a new supervisor in a government agency.

### Learning and Growth

This is the motive that we are most excited about. Assuming you find a program that meets your needs, is respectable, has a high-functioning faculty, and includes like-minded peers who make you feel challenged and understood, there are few life experiences that can be as challenging and growth producing. However, you can also find some doctoral-trained professionals with negative stories about the hoops they had to jump through, the humiliation they suffered, the sleepless nights they experienced, and the constant stress they lived under. Like so many difficult challenges in life, the struggles involved in personal and professional development involve both high and low points. Even most of those who have the worst tales to tell wind up saying that if they could do it all over again, they might do it differently, but they certainly would do it.

A doctoral program, especially one that you attend as a full-time student with others who come from different parts of the country and walks of life, is an ideal setting in which to learn. Typically, you are given some responsibility as a research or teaching assistant and also supervise master's students. Seminars tend to be small and composed of the best and brightest professionals around. In comparison to a master's program, as a doctoral student you are often treated much more as a peer. This increased responsibility also assumes more self-directedness, which demands a higher level of commitment, assertiveness, and maturity than in undergraduate or master's degree programs.

## What Exactly Is a Doctoral Degree?

Everyone has their own unique vision of what the title *doctor* means. Consider the reflections of my daughter (Richard's).

> I had just completed my degree and was quietly celebrating with my wife and two daughters, ages 6 and 3. The celebration was a family affair because everyone had in some way made sacrifices and contributed to the effort. At what seemed like the right moment, I explained to my 6-year-old the basics of what it meant that I was now Dr. Hazler. She listened and then calmly asked, "Can you take my tonsils out?"
>
> "No," I said.
>
> She hesitated before replying, "Then you're not a real doctor, are you, Daddy?"

This perception of the title *doctor* is not unusual or surprising, although it was a little personally deflating. Many people, including doctoral degree holders themselves, have misconceptions about the degree. However, there are some basics that differentiate it from other degrees and titles. The doctoral degree is qualitatively, as well as quantitatively, different from the master's degree. Most master's degree programs have a fairly standard list of courses that must be taken, and a program is generally approved by an adviser. In contrast, the doctoral degree generally has many choices that have to be made among curriculum and internship experiences. The doctorate usually requires a committee of three to five faculty members to develop a program, approve courses, and supervise progress toward the degree. This committee gives much more attention to the design of the program and the student's progress than at the master's level. This additional individual assistance and evaluation is to be expected, and it should be appreciated when faculty take a strong personal interest in doctoral students. Faculty are training doctoral students to be their peers and colleagues, which is very different from most other degrees.

The increased individual attention given to doctoral students can also be seen in the selection process, size of classes, and the amount of paperwork that must be completed. Most programs require more information related to selection criteria for their doctoral applicants and admit fewer students than they do at the master's level. For example, a sample master's program might admit 50 students per year while that same program might accept only 8 to 15 doctoral students. Individual interviews with faculty are almost always required as a part of the selection process to make sure that the individual's needs and style will enable him or her to get the most from the program. Once in the program, students will notice that doctoral classes are traditionally smaller than master's-level classes and that more professional interaction from doctoral students in class is expected. It is safe to say that expectations for performance are considerably higher and competition is more demanding.

All this individual attention requires more formal evaluation of how the student is progressing in the program. After being admitted to a program, students are generally approved or not approved for continuation after they have had a chance to demonstrate their abilities in their first few semesters or quarters. This is also a point at which some programs have students take qualifying exams to determine strengths and weaknesses that must be considered in developing a final program. A program committee is put together when these initial assessments have taken place. Only at this time does a student, and his or her committee, formalize a program.

Later in the program students take written and/or oral comprehensive exams to verify what has been learned. An extensive internship is also required in most counseling doctoral degrees to demonstrate practical use of the knowledge and skills learned. The program is completed with a dissertation in which all the theory, research, and practical aspects learned can be brought together in a way that will add new information to the profession.

The dissertation is a culminating research experience that is very different from anything experienced in most master's degree counseling programs. Master's programs often have only one or two courses on research and/or statistics, and the focus of faculty and students is on how to be an effective practitioner. Research, theory, writing, and statistics play a much larger part in the doctoral program because graduates are expected to be able to advance the development of other professionals in addition to being an effective counselor.

## What Are the Differences in Doctoral Degrees?

You will hear the term *doctorate* used as if it were a universal academic credential that is essentially the same no matter where you are located in time and place. Your experience will show you that this is far from the actual situation. You have probably noted, with some confusion, the different initials that practicing counselors and supervisors list after their names, all denoting the title *doctor*. PhD (doctor of philosophy), EdD (doctor of education), and PsyD (doctor of psychology) may all be commonly found, although each is intended for a slightly different purpose.

The PhD degree is the oldest doctoral-level degree in the field by far. *Doctor of philosophy* signifies more than professional competence in a specific field. It communicates that the individual has a varied education that includes strong skills in the research area as well as a broad knowledge base. An EdD program may look very similar or very different from a PhD program, but the conceptual difference is that the EdD focuses more on the specific field of education rather than on the broader philosophy area of the PhD. The PsyD is organized in somewhat the same way as the EdD in that it focuses on the specific area of psychology, and most specifically on the clinical applications of psychology. It tends to be a more clinically applied program rather than one that is research specialized.

The programmatic differences between PhDs and EdDs have become blurred over the years because either may be offered through a college of education. The fact is that you are likely to see just as many differences between any two PhD programs as you see between a PhD program and an EdD program. The PsyD remains the most different and specialized degree with the least degree of employment flexibility for the graduate.

Employability based on the degree designation of PhD, EdD, or PsyD varies, although there are some general patterns, as described in Table 4. But you must remember that they are patterns and not laws or rules, and demarcations are not as strong as they may appear in the table. Employability is more closely tied to the quality of a program and how much your course work and experience match the needs of the job than to the degree designation.

PhDs in counseling psychology are found in counseling positions as licensed psychologists (sometimes as licensed professional counselors), in supervisory positions, or in teaching positions in counseling psychology programs. PhDs and EdDs in counselor education are also found in counseling positions as licensed professional counselors (sometimes as psychol-

• Table 4 •
### General Emphases Differences
### Among Counseling Doctoral Degrees

| Degree | Specialty Field | Emphasis | Affiliation Professional |
|---|---|---|---|
| PhD or EdD | Counselor Education | Supervision, research, training | ACA |
| PhD | Counseling Psychology | Clinical treatment research, training | APA Division 17 |
| PsyD | Clinical Psychology | Clinical treatment | APA Division 24 |

ogists), in supervisory positions, and in teaching positions that are most often in counselor education programs. There are certainly many PhDs in counseling psychology who also teach in counselor education programs, and some counselor education graduates who work in counseling psychology programs. However, these crossovers are most common where counselor education programs and counseling psychology programs are housed in the same department at a university.

EdDs complete programs in colleges of education that are very similar to PhD programs in the areas of counseling, supervision, and counselor education. They primarily differ in that they may have less extensive research requirements. EdDs may be able to attain licensure as psychologists, marital and family therapists, or licensed professional counselors depending on their specific program and regulations in a given state. They also can be found teaching in counselor education programs.

The PsyD was designed as the clinical degree for psychologists who want to focus on being quality practitioners. It has fewer research and training components and does not generally qualify someone to become a full-time faculty member in most psychology programs. It may also not be looked upon as positively for positions that require extensive leadership, training, or research skills.

As if this is not complex enough, we also want to mention that doctoral programs are structured differently in other parts of the world compared to what we do in North America. Whereas North American doctorates tend to be course-work based, combined with a dissertation, the British model, which is used throughout Great Britain, Australia, New Zealand, and many parts of Asia and Europe, is much more research based. Rather than requiring course work that is then followed by a research study, the British model PhD requires the apprentice to spend 3 to 5 years completing a more significant and substantial research product that may have twice the size and scope of an American dissertation. Students work in highly individualized plans of study, in collaboration with two to three supervisors who mentor the process. In this system, students are expected to show more initiative and independence than what we might be used to in North American universities.

Students make a decision on which doctoral program to attend based on factors that include

- admission requirements of each program;
- geographical convenience (which programs are offered nearby); and
- career aspirations to be
  — an advanced practitioner,
  — a professor of counseling,
  — a supervisor or trainer in corporate or school settings,
  — a professor of psychology, and/or
  — an administrator of an agency.

Because this brief overview may create as many questions as answers for you, we urge you to speak to your adviser and faculty members about which program(s) are most suitable for your needs.

## Who Is Admitted Into Doctoral Programs?

Virtually anyone who has acquired a master's degree in counseling or a closely related field (e.g., marital and family therapy, human services, psychology) from an accredited school and has had quality professional work experience can get accepted into a doctoral program somewhere (some remedial work may be required). The question is not so much whether a person is acceptable but where and under what conditions a person is appropriate for a particular program.

Adding to the confusion are the many different kinds of doctoral programs (e.g., counselor education, counseling psychology, family therapy, community psychology), each of which has different ideas of what it is looking for in prospective students. Some programs emphasize extended work experience (e.g., 5 years or more, several of which are in a supervisory role). Some place high value on performance on standardized tests such as the Graduate Record Examination and/or the Miller Analogies Test. Some place greater emphasis on undergraduate and graduate GPAs, while others are looking for a solid background (and track record) in specific research skills. Then there are programs that look to create a class that is as culturally, ethnically, and geographically diverse as possible. Others place great weight on interviews that are conducted or recommendations made by colleagues from other institutions. Writing samples are another factor emphasized by many programs. Still others wish to evaluate your performance as a counselor during mock sessions or in videos you submit.

Additional factors that may also play a part in the selection process in a given situation include the clarity of your career aspirations, your particular field of specialty, and your relationship with someone on the faculty.

The good news is that no matter what your particular strengths are (GPA, GRE scores, work experience, interpersonal skills, or sheer determination), there is probably a place for you somewhere if you have the persistence to look thoroughly and long.

Ideally, programs prefer to admit a culturally diverse group of people with high test scores, excellent grades, wonderful references, excellent writing skills, maturity, and extensive professional work experience. But this is only a dream that does not reflect reality: most people are much less than perfect. We know that people change and that we cannot go on past record alone to predict future success. The best examples of this point are the number of graduate students who are now excelling academically in their programs, even though their undergraduate records from many years ago were somewhat less than impressive. Consequently, programs wind up looking for people who have many, but not all, strong qualities. They seek students whose qualities best match the nature and makeup of the program and its faculty. For example, a program that stresses research and scholarly inquiry might be especially interested in quantitative skills as measured on the GRE. Another program that is more interested in a high level of altruism and moral integrity in their students will be more focused on character references, a substantial record of good deeds, and an extensive interview process.

Potential students often do not apply for admission because they believe that their poor test scores or grades that do not meet formal requirements mean they cannot get in. This thinking is faulty. One of us (who shall remain unnamed) applied to over 25 doctoral programs before he was finally admitted on probation to one that was willing to give him a chance. All programs make exceptions to their requirements when they see something special enough about an individual to override their other concerns. Not applying eliminates the possibility that a given program will see the unique strengths of the individual.

Those who want to make the best possible case for attending a doctoral program must spend time logging substantial experience in the field, obtaining quality references, creating high-quality written material, preparing systematically for entrance examinations, taking courses to demonstrate current success, doing extensive research on what particular programs are looking for in their students, and making professional contacts with faculty. The more strong qualities an applicant can demonstrate, the better the chances are for being admitted to a given program.

Here are a few other important points to keep in mind as you seek entrance into a program: If you do not, at first, succeed in your efforts, do not give up! Find out what you can do to strengthen your credentials and application. Some students have applied four successive times to the same program before they were finally admitted! Then again, others may have to accept the fact that perhaps a doctoral program is not ideally suited to their life. What is important is to learn from the application process so that you know more about yourself and the programs to which you are applying.

Then use this new information to either get the most out of the program or to reapply more effectively.

## How Do You Find the Program That Best Matches Your Needs?

The most common problem people encounter in finding the right doctoral program (there really is not a right program, but there are those that are best suited to meet your needs and interests) is a tendency to be too selective. A search that is held to a 100-mile radius of home will be lucky to turn up more than one or two viable options. Even these opportunities may prove limited because programs often prefer students who are geographically mobile, and thus more likely to relocate after graduation to a powerful job. It makes much more sense, if at all possible, to be somewhat flexible and expand the area of search well beyond commuting limits, possibly even looking nationwide. It is possible, of course, to find a good program next door, but that is likely to be the result of luck rather than planning. The more potential choices are expanded, the greater the likelihood is of finding the best possible program for you.

Minimizing geography as a limitation allows you to start your search process by consulting several books that describe various details about programs, including the specialties they offer, the number of students they admit, the financial assistance that is available, and the admission requirements. Books such as *Peterson's Guide to Graduate and Professional Programs, 2005* (2004), *Graduate Study in Psychology 2004* (APA, 2003), and *Counselor Preparation 1999–2001: Programs, Faculty, Trends* (Hollis & Dodson, 1999) contain much of the factual material needed, such as types of degrees, faculty, theoretical foundations, assistantships, and costs. They give you the comparative information that will help you recognize differences in programs and how they meet your particular needs.

You should speak to people in the field, including faculty members, supervisors, other students, and anyone who knows more than you do, to help sort out the confusing maze of options available. There are considerable debates in the field, as well as territorial skirmishes, as to whether counselor education or counseling psychology provides the best training. (Each is accredited by different organizations; the former is based in counseling as a professional identity, and the latter is based in psychology.) Frankly, we are somewhat biased and freely admit that our hearts and souls belong to counseling. But talk to as many people as possible to gather sufficient information to make your own decisions. As already mentioned, a lot depends on your career goals, including whether you wish to be primarily an advanced practitioner, a counselor educator, and/or a supervisor.

Deciding whether a particular program is truly right for you requires real personal involvement beyond reading about and writing to schools. Printed materials, brochures, and applications describe programs as the university wants them to be perceived. This is somewhat like describing your job to your parents. The description may be more of what you want to believe rather than the most accurate picture of the way things really are.

The best way to get an accurate feel and understanding of a school and program is to talk directly with graduates, faculty, and current students. Do not wait until you have been admitted and school has already begun to meet people from the program. Get as much information and seek as much involvement in the program as possible before you make this major investment in time, money, and effort. Before you decide to invest tens of thousands of dollars, and commit half a decade of your life, visit prospective schools and find out what things are really like. Attending summer classes or workshops given by a particular program is often a helpful way to get a feel for the actual school and its faculty.

## How Difficult Are Statistics for the Nonstatistician?

The word *statistics* arouses fear in many (if not most) potential counseling doctoral students. You may be relieved to know that most of your apprehensions are worse than the experiences you will actually encounter. There is no getting around the fact that doctoral students in counseling, who have had little background in mathematics, may have to work hard on the statistics and research portions of their program. But the fact is that those who put in the necessary work not only come through just fine but also recognize that they have acquired some quite useful analytic skills along the way.

You should also keep in mind that qualitative research methodologies do not use statistics at all during the data analysis. Research methods such as grounded theory, phenomenology, narrative, critical theory, case study, and feminism rely instead on making sense of interviews, focus groups, naturalistic observations, and other similar structures. Rather than using numbers to describe or analyze phenomena, they may use words and images as the source of data. This is consistent with some of the most influential research conducted by some of the historical leaders in psychology and counseling such as Sigmund Freud, Erik Erikson, and Jean Piaget.

Whether you choose to do a quantitative or qualitative study, you are still likely to have some training in both methodologies because they are both useful tools, depending on what you wish to discover. It is certainly true that, for some, statistics can be a challenging aspect of a doctoral program, but very few people are unsuccessful in doctoral programs because of an inability to do math. In fact, the advent of computers has reduced the calculation aspects of statistics to make it more a study of analytic thinking, which is an ability that all counselors should have. Still, some students will need to work harder, and some will have it easier. Some students will work by themselves, and others will need to work with peers or even get a tutor. The important point to remember is that students who recognize their own ability level and do what it takes to get the job done from that starting place will find success. What keeps people out of doctoral studies is not an actual inability in this area but an unreasonable exaggeration of what is expected.

## What Should I Know About the Dissertation Process?

Writing a dissertation is hard. Now that we have that out of the way, we can start to explore some of the realities. Yes, there are many people who complete all the steps in their doctoral degrees except the dissertation. Many more are scared away from the degree because of the dissertation. The reality is that these people could have done the dissertation! If you can get through the rest of a doctoral program, you ARE prepared to do the research and write a dissertation. The things that stop people from completing or even starting this last step could be summarized as fear, time, and choosing where to put their energy.

The dissertation creates more fear than any aspect of the doctoral program with perhaps the possible exception of statistics. It is probably the largest research and writing project you have attempted, and it probably demands a different style and skills than you have used before. But the fact that it is hard should not be translated into unbearable, impossible, or horrible. *Hard* can also mean challenging, interesting, and even exciting. The problem with the fear of a dissertation is that it keeps people away from working effectively on it by creating myths that can be difficult to dispel. Five doctoral students (Annandale, Downs, Jensen, Mickelson, & Tobler, 2004) from Brigham Young University explained part of their journey in challenging and overcoming some of these myths:

> Most of us started with the following irrational belief—my dissertation needs to be the most important and biggest project of my life. It created so much pressure that the experience was anticipated as ominous, threatening, life defying, and nearly impossible. . . . Listening to faculty directly involved in the process helped dispute our irrational beliefs, even learning that it was OK to submit a draft, expect to make revisions, and recognize that length did not equal quality. We became more open to feedback as we recognized that faculty were more than willing to engage collaboratively with us in the process.
>
> Another frightening myth was that you have to do your dissertation alone. . . . Since only one name appears on the final dissertation project, the implicit message is that no one else helped, no one else should help, and every student walked the grueling path alone. . . . The anxiety helped us make commitments to support each other and not allow anyone to get left behind. . . . Without these experiences, it all would have been far more tedious, lonely, and painful.
>
> It is the myth of the perfect paper. I need to slave endless hours over it until it is polished, flawless, and pristine in every way. These unrealistic expectations do nothing but impede progress and lead to two likely outcomes: procrastination and failure. . . . What we found was that turning in something that was admittedly not our "best" work was met with unexpectedly positive and encouraging feedback. This significantly assisted the process of good rewriting and helped us feel more comfortable with subsequent re-submissions.

> The reality is that a dissertation can be an exciting, enjoyable, and mean-
> ingful experience. . . . Coming to this reality meant finding those aspects of
> the overall dissertation process that we could enjoy. Some of us had disser-
> tation topics that promoted travel and work with other enjoyable people.
> Others set rewards and activities to signify measurable progress. Even the
> reading and writing elements became more enjoyable as we expanded
> ideas, topics, and research questions. We came to a place that we had little
> imagined possible upon entering the program: our thoughts about the
> process were changing from drudgery to discovery. (p. 12)

The second major problem that keeps people from finishing their dissertation is the issue of time. Every program has limits on how long you can
take to complete a doctoral program because there comes a point at which
what you learned in class has become too outdated for practical purposes.
This time frame can range from 6 to 9 years in most cases, which sounds
like a very long time, but it often doesn't work out that way. First you have
years of classes generally followed by a yearlong internship. The people
who will finish relatively quickly will be the ones who find time in
between classes and internship to select, design, and collect data on their
dissertation. What they have left is only to write down the results! The
ones who run out of time are those who cannot find time during their hec-
tic program to develop their dissertation before they return to the work
world where the pressures to select other priorities increase.

Choosing the priorities of where doctoral students will use their time
is the third major factor in whether people finish their dissertation or
not. While actively in the program, students face the demands of classes,
internship, and probably some form of teaching or research assistantship.
Then there are those other pieces of life like family, friends, recreation, and
sleep. There is just not enough time to do it all. Deciding how much time
and energy to put into developing a dissertation becomes a question of
choosing what valuable pieces of school and life you will give less attention to than they probably deserve. The fears surrounding the dissertation
make it a prime choice for putting in the "some other day" category.

Once you leave full-time student status and go back to the work force, life
priorities are confounded again. Moving, learning a new job, giving more
time to family that has been feeling neglected, and trying to remember
what a real life is like all pull you away from that dissertation. You begin to
forget what the topic was or why you chose the topic you did. The papers
you collected are in a pile, but remembering what the pile was about, then
diving in and sorting it into something useful, and finally beginning to do
productive work with it will take days, not the hour or two you can set
aside. It takes a strong will to take the time away from work, family, and
living and dedicate it to that project that looks more challenging now without faculty and peers around than it did while in school.

As much struggle as these issues may cause, they do not stop most people from finishing their dissertations. Most people eventually make the
sacrifices and time commitments to get it done. Sometimes they make
those commitments early, and sometimes they get the job done in the very

last month of the last year before their time runs out. You will have to make your own choices that fit your model for learning and living. The most important thing to remember is that you can do it if you give it the time and energy it takes.

## Focus Activities: Making Personal Use of This Chapter

This chapter addresses issues around obtaining a doctoral degree. Although the master's degree in counseling is a professional degree, and you can easily spend a full career utilizing those skills, most counselors, at one time or another, consider going on to get a PhD, EdD, or PsyD. This chapter and the following exercises should provide you with the information that will enable you to weigh more thoroughly the pros and cons so that you are better prepared to make that decision. Remember to do more than just read and think about these exercises. Make the best use of them by following through and writing your reactions and observations in your journal.

1. **Why do you want a doctoral degree?** List the reasons you can think of in your notebook. Do all of the reasons seem appropriate and healthy? Or do some seem inappropriate (such as getting the degree to outdo your brother)? Talk with someone such as your mentor or adviser about your reasons and their implications for entering a doctoral program.
2. **Know what a doctoral degree is and what completion of a doctoral program entails.** Talk with faculty members at your institution as well as those at institutions that you are considering. Also speak with students from those programs about their experiences because you often find a more realistic picture comes from those who are actually going through the process. Make a list of programs you are considering and what each requires. Refer back to this information regularly as your ideas develop.
3. **Find out what you can do as a professional with a doctoral degree versus a master's degree.** List the specific professional benefits (such as licensing, third-party payments, additional opportunities) of going on for a doctoral degree versus making the best use of your master's degree (such as earning versus paying for school, counseling versus research emphasis).
4. **Look for doctoral programs that best match your needs if you are leaning toward the decision to go on for your doctorate.** The career planning and placement center is a good starting place for listings of programs and their requirements. Also purchase or find copies of such books as *Peterson's Guide to Graduate and Professional Programs, 2005* (2004) or Hollis and Dodson's *Counselor Preparation 1999–2001: Programs, Faculty, Trends* (1999), which contain much of the information you need about various programs. After gathering initial infor-

mation, call the programs and request further information, including graduate catalogs, requirements, and applications for admission.

5. **Try to speak directly with faculty members and students from programs that interest you most.** See how well their expectations match your own.

6. **Compile all of your information along with your subjective reactions to each program.** Be honest with yourself. Remember to look for the program that seems to be the best fit with your personality and needs.

7. **Explore your anxieties about entering a doctoral program** (such as possible rejection, statistics courses, dissertation, comprehensive examinations). List your anxieties in your notebook, and do not be afraid of having them. Everyone has fears about such a big step, but it is only those who make the choice to conquer those fears that wind up with a degree.

8. **Once you have made the decision to obtain a doctorate, you must remember that all fears cannot be conquered at once.** Take things a day at a time, and do not worry about bridges before you must begin to cross them. If you find yourself worrying about statistics, comprehensive examinations, and the dissertation from the beginning of your program, you will be overwhelmed and waste energy that could be better used on the classes and activities here and now. Plan ahead and be organized, but once you have planned (set your program) and have done all you can for the time being (gotten a tutor for statistics), take things a day at a time and focus on those things that really must be done now.

9. **Use creative ways to combat your fears.** Self-talk, support systems, studying in groups, seeking a tutor or relationship with a student who can help you with the task, and speaking with those who had similar fears and still completed the task are among the possibilities. List those ways of dealing with fears and anxiety that you have found to be personally most effective and use the ones that work the best.

# · 12 ·

# The Transition From Student to Employed Professional

The object of graduate education in counseling is to prepare you to be an employed professional. The first part of your mission is to acquire all necessary skills, knowledge, expertise, and experience that qualify you for such a position. The second part, just as crucial, is to make the transition from student to practicing counselor. This involves not only a change in your physical location and financial status but also, most of all, a change in your self-identity.

A main emphasis in this book is encouraging students to take initiative, be assertive, and use creativity in making the most possible out of their counseling education. Such self-directive actions, when used appropriately, make prospective counselors stronger and more confident in their own ability to function as independent professionals. Unfortunately, one of the primary reasons this emphasis is needed is that students often feel, or at least act, like an underclass who only have the ability to take from their program but not to give to the profession until some later time. Students often express that they will develop more of their own professional initiative once they leave the program. Our experience has been that the more professional initiative students take during their program, the more success they have in their professional career following graduation.

## What Are the Differences?

As you make the transition from student to professional, there are a number of changes that will most likely take place. These include being a leader instead of a follower, showing initiative and autonomy instead of seeking approval, cooperating instead of competing, and being an expert instead of a novice.

### Being a Leader Versus Being a Follower

Students must be followers to some degree in their program in order to recognize and experience new information as well as to implement what is learned. However, when this follower model is taken too far, it makes the transition from follower-student to leader-professional much harder. Succeeding as a follower-student can often promote a state of mind that does not value the initiative, assertiveness, and creativity that are so important to success as a professional counselor in the real world.

Consider, for example, the first day of a class when the course syllabus is being distributed. The most frequently asked questions about assignments are often "Does that mean double-spaced?" "What is the minimum number of pages?" "Do we have to use references?" These questions relate to the details of getting work done in a way that will please the instructor (perhaps to get an A). The focus is on how to be a good follower rather than on the exciting possibilities for learning and development through the assignment.

Many students feel even more uncertain, confused, and frustrated by the responses faculty offer: "Take as much space as you need." "Do whatever it takes to get the job done." "I don't know. Depending on what you have to say, and how you communicate, you may need 5 pages or 20." Faculty reluctance to give specific answers is not designed as a devious form of torture. Rather, this ambiguity is meant to simulate more closely what takes place in counseling settings in the real world. A supervisor, for example, might ask you to compile a report describing the range of services your school or agency offers and including all relevant data. You will indeed be expected to ask qualifying questions to clarify your task, but those that are on length and style will get the same general answers as you were given by faculty: "Whatever it takes to get the job done."

The more clearly professional questions will be those that revolve around the purpose, substance, and use of the report: "What needs will this meet?" "How will we make use of it?" "Why are we doing it at this point in time?" "Who will be the audience that uses it and what will their needs be?" "What is the expected impact of the report?" Questions such as these demonstrate that the professional has immediately begun thinking about the value of the report and how to put professional skills and information to best use. Most supervisors will be pleased to see that this professional is ready to go beyond being a follower of the supervisors' orders to being a professional who can add new substance and direction to finding solutions to the problems of the organization.

### Showing Initiative and Autonomy Versus Seeking Approval

Another example of the differences between the role of student and employed professional is that as a student, you may find yourself functioning tentatively with a focus on seeking approval and validation from a superior, but as a trained professional, you are expected to show initiative and autonomy that will move your organization forward. Certainly, there are some supervisors who feel threatened by this type of assertiveness and potential movement into new directions. Just remember that you have been trained as a human relations specialist. You should have the information and skills necessary to work both with information and the psychological circumstances of clients, colleagues, and supervisors.

### Cooperating Versus Competing

Competition with classmates is another common characteristic of many students who judge their success on whether they receive more praise and better grades from faculty. The professional counselor finds a greater emphasis placed on cooperation with other staff members than on competition. The potential for competition is in the workplace just as it is anywhere in our society, but the true professional recognizes that cooperation is the model desired for the overall best functioning of an organization. It is those who work best to promote the overall functioning of an organization that receive the most opportunities for promotion and recognition both within and outside of the organization. It should also be obvious that clients are also best served by professionals and organizations that work harder at cooperation than competition.

## Being an Expert Versus Being a Novice

The term *student* is generally associated with other expressions like *apprentice*, *novice*, and *just learning*. Trust and confidence in the student's ability to perform as a professional are not widely accepted. This can be a benefit for students when it relieves some of the pressure of needing to serve as an expert while not feeling prepared to do so. The student, therefore, has a societally accepted excuse for not making all the best decisions. Once you have that degree in hand, however, people's reactions to you change quickly. Experienced professionals know you still have much to learn, but clients and noncounselors see you as a qualified expert beginning with your first day on the job. You will find that your status has changed from learner to expert almost overnight, even though we all know that no actual transformation ever really took place upon graduation.

In his personal story of transition from medical student to psychiatrist, Viscott (1972) described his first day on the job. The first moment he walked on the hospital ward, he was addressed as *doctor* and expected by staff and patients alike to act like one. The fact of the matter, however, was that until that point the only training he had received in psychiatry was through a 3-week rotation and a few paperback books! "Still, knowing as little as I do, tomorrow I am going to walk onto the psychiatric ward in Union Hospital and be expected to act and talk like a psychiatrist. What the hell do psychiatrists really do?" (p. 15).

Viscott's experience may be an extreme example of an abrupt transition from neophyte to expert, but it nevertheless highlights the differences between what it means to be a student versus an employed professional. The moment you arrive on the job as a professional, you are expected to leave behind the deferential, competitive, and insecure aspects of yourself as a student. You are now a professional, and the expectation is that you will act that way.

Faculty and supervisors in your graduate program will make every effort to help you feel professionally prepared for those first moments on the job. In fact, with your practicum, field experience, and internship placement, you will be far better prepared than most other professionals to begin your responsibilities as an employed helper immediately. Nevertheless, the more preparation you can make before you graduate, the more likely the transition from student to counselor is to be a smooth and successful one. People expect you to change from student to professional overnight, but the reality is that you must work on developing your independence, assertiveness, and professionalism throughout your graduate program by using the faculty, peers, supervisors, and clients you see each day to expand these aspects of yourself.

## Grieving the Loss of Graduate School

Graduate school is not an easy experience, and students look forward to the day when they are graduates and can begin the professional life of a counselor. However, as much as you may anticipate that day, you are also likely to experience a certain amount of ambivalence about leaving school. Even leaving the pressures of grades, late night classes, papers, and exams will not be enough to eliminate feelings of loss about other aspects of your experience.

Graduate school is a structured opportunity for you to study intensely about a subject of great interest to you. The many soul-searching discussions you have with peers lead to relationships that last a lifetime. It is a place where you receive the most intensive supervision and close observation you will ever experience. During your practicum, for instance, you may have as much or more than 1 hour of individual supervision for the clients you see, plus hours of group supervision, plus direct feedback from a partner assigned to observe your sessions, plus much informal discussion of your cases with various faculty members and colleagues. This luxury is unique and short-lived. Many times in your professional life you will look back on this opportunity with wistful memories as you consider how hungry you are for input on your work later in your career.

There is also some degree of grieving associated with leaving behind close relationships with faculty and classmates. Previous experiences remind you that as much as you may intend to keep in touch with people, the fact of the matter is you will stay in contact with relatively few people from the program.

People are inclined to remember the good old days when learning was their primary mission in life. You will quickly realize that the added pressures of work and deciding how to build your new life make the simple "I must learn all I can" approach to graduate school look like a clear, noble, and direct way to exist.

Graduate school, even if it represents just one or two evenings a week and impinges on time that you want to spend with family and friends, still represents a commitment you make to your own growth and development. The money and energy you pay is your therapy, your way of taking care of yourself. In a sense, graduate school is a gift you give yourself to create new opportunities at the same time that you nourish your brain and heart. When school abruptly stops, it is much like the end of therapy. You know you have grown and that it is time to move on, but you miss the relationships and have anxiety over all the unknowns you must again face. Your intellectual growth will no longer be guided by others, and it is now up to you and you alone to make yourself read the journal articles and books necessary to continue your learning and keep you current. It is up to you to find the colleagues who also wish to have those stimulating discussions that inspire and move you to new heights.

We recognize that these predictions may seem farfetched if you are just beginning or are in the middle of a program. Grieve the loss of graduate school? You have got to be kidding. But just think back on other challenging experiences you have had in your life that involved high levels of work and commitment. Once the experience is over, the pain and inconvenience do not seem to have been so great. You may even miss the experience with the accompanying focus, direction, and accomplishment it provided.

## Recruiting a New Mentor

Graduate school is specifically designed to provide you with mentors to act as advisers and guides. Faculty members can play a much larger role in your life than just instructors and supervisors. They can provide you with support, guidance, and direction during critical times when you are making important decisions. At least some faculty members are almost always available in their offices for you to approach about your concerns. There are also any number of other experienced professionals who expect you to go to them for help, particularly when it deals with counseling decisions or concerns about a particular case. Your practicum supervisor, on-site supervisor, previous instructors with whom you have a good relationship, and current instructors all know that part of their job is to assist you when you need help. You may wind up taking these resources for granted in school, but you will need to actively seek and nurture similar ones once you leave school.

There are few opportunities in the work world to find the always available and reliable help that was ever present for you in school. Your colleagues are busy, your assigned superior may not be someone you necessarily trust or respect, or he or she may not even have much time available to meet with you on a regular basis. Many beginners thus experience a certain amount of isolation after making the transition from student to employed professional. Such a situation calls for actions on your part to ensure that personally developed sources of support will be there for you even when the more formal sources of support are not available or appropriate.

Mentors will be just as important to you in your job as they were during graduate school. The principal difference is that you have to be more assertive and self-initiating in your efforts to recruit those who can serve in mentoring roles. The importance of this task cannot be overemphasized. Professional mentors are likely to

- **help you function effectively in the system:** Mentors know the rules inside and out. They also know how to get around the rules when it is in the best interest of your clients. They understand the politics and coalitions of your organization and can guide you as to how to stay out of trouble while still upholding your own beliefs.

- **become your advocates:** Mentors can speak on your behalf. They act as buffers and protectors. They lobby for you during those times when opportunities arise for you to move within the organization or to outside opportunities.
- **provide emotional support:** During stressful periods when you are struggling, a mentor is someone you can trust to be there for you. This person will help you to keep things in perspective.
- **be a source of knowledge:** You are likely to feel overwhelmed by everything that you did not learn in graduate school and now wish you had. Every day you will have a dozen questions about why things work the way they do, what to do with a particular client, how to get around some obstacle, or how to handle a situation for which you are unprepared. You can muddle through as best you can. You can fake it. Or you can reach out to those you trust to provide you with the information needed to do the best possible job.
- **provide a model of what you want to become:** Mentors offer a living example of what is possible if you work long and hard, stay focused and alert, and take on the best parts of those counselors you most admire. Mentors are instrumental in creating directions to head toward in your career and your life. They support and inspire you. They are your lifeline to survival in a profession that can often be confusing, ambiguous, and stressful, and that is ever changing.

## Adjusting to the Realities of Everyday Practice

All the rewards of being a professional counselor are now available to you as you begin your practice. You get to help people, and they appreciate your efforts. Your counseling skills get used every day, and they get better as you gain experience. The relationships you are developing with clients and staff are not only helping them but are also helping you to better understand and promote growth in both others and yourself. We really do love being counseling professionals, but as in any situation, there are also the less desirable aspects of the experience that must be recognized and handled by the professional.

Everyday practice is also a place where many clients do not want, or know they want, what you have to offer. Their relatives may be intentionally or unintentionally working to sabotage any progress that you help them to make. Your working conditions are always less than ideal, and the resources readily available are barely adequate. You may well be overscheduled to the point where you could work 18 hours a day, 7 days a week, and still not catch up to everything there is to do. Some of your colleagues cause you to wonder how they got their jobs or how they manage to keep them. Some seem so worn out; but surely they must have felt as energetic and enthusiastic as you at some time in their career. How did they become so cynical and jaded? Paperwork! Paperwork! You can wind up feeling as if you have no idea what you are doing or whether you are even headed in the right direction. There is no time even to catch your breath.

We hope it comes to you as no surprise that the work of a counselor is often a bit different than what you may have expected when you were a student. This is true of most any professional who first enters a job upon graduation. However, even though most counseling students have had some experience in the field before they begin their formal training, which gives them a limited idea of what to expect, there are a number of areas in which you may struggle when you make your transition into employment. These include single-counseling-theory allegiance, politics and power struggles, and ethical dilemmas for which you are unprepared.

## Single-Counseling-Theory Allegiance

The theories course may have given you the distinct impression that there are a dozen major schools of thought in the field, such as psychoanalytic, existential, Adlerian, cognitive, behavioral, gestalt, humanistic, and systemic. It may have seemed as if your job was to find the one approach that seemed most compatible with your personality, preferences, and interests (usually with some prodding from your instructors who had their own biases), and to learn this well enough to apply it in sessions with your clients. Even though programs are certainly moving in a direction of being more integrative in the way we work, students often feel pressure to affiliate with one theoretical approach to helping. This is particularly true when you are being presented with so much new information, and what you desire most is to become really good at using any part of it.

Then you get a job in which you find that practitioners rarely feel able to adhere to one and only one theoretical approach. Depending on their clients' needs, presenting complaints, and the realities of the time and resources available, they may employ a number of different approaches. Recognizing the trouble you had trying to master the complexities of one theoretical approach emphasizes the difficulties involved in becoming fluent in the application of three or more.

During any given week we are aware of applying principles of existential theory in helping clients and students find meaning for their lives and accept responsibility for their choices; using cognitive interventions (from rational-emotive therapy) to urge people to talk to themselves differently and dispute their irrational beliefs; capitalizing on systemic ideas (structural, strategic, and Bowenian therapies) to provoke changes in the families of those we see; applying psychodynamic principles to generate insights into the origins of how problems developed; using behavioral structures to helping people set specific goals that they can work toward; and harnessing Adlerian concepts, Reality therapy, and a handful of others, all integrated into a personal style that is uniquely our own. How did we learn to do what seems like such a massive task?

The challenge you face is trying to find your own voice and style when confronted with so many competent individuals attempting to convince you that the way they work is the most effective. You will be amazed at how much support exists for each of the dozen or so most prominent schools of thought. Some work better than others in certain situations and with certain clients, but for the most part they all work equally well for those who know how to use them effectively.

The secret to this phenomenon of many successful theories is that all of the different forms of counseling work because they are not as different as they appear. In spite of their apparent differences in language, style, concepts, and underlying philosophy, they all do essentially the same things: create a productive alliance with the client that is based on mutual trust and respect, provide opportunities for catharsis or affective experiencing, provoke alterations in one's consciousness, capitalize on favorable expectations or placebo effects, use rituals to heighten the potential for systematic influence, and facilitate the completion of therapeutic tasks. In addition, most effective counselors are powerful people who others wish to emulate. Regardless of their chosen specialties, or espoused beliefs, they all command others' attention and respect, influence people in positive directions, and provide support and encouragement during difficult times.

The journey to our personal theories is one we will all take. Some, like Greg Janson (1998), have paid more attention to their personal process. Greg found what was most useful to him, and his guidelines seem on target for each of us:

> *Write it down.* . . . Putting your thoughts on paper helps clarify them.
> *Check it out with others.* . . . Ask questions and challenge them. See what they have to say.
> *Test it.* . . . Compare your assumptions to the realities of your experiences as a counselor.
> *Seek out commonalities and connections.* . . . Focus on the underlying commonalities and connections between human beings and the difficulties they face.
> *Be prepared to change.* . . . Keeping up with research and remaining accountable as a professional makes change a constant in our profession.
> *Don't expect certainty.* . . . Theory provides focus, direction, and structure. There is no one theory that provides all the answers, for all of us, all the time.
>
> I am comfortable with my humanist/existentialist approach because that is who I am. . . . I have the notion that therapy is like a journey that my clients and I take together. I don't have all the answers. What I can do is be with them as I remember that the best way to teach courage is to model it and the best way to understand humility is to practice it and the best way to see another is to show myself. I try to remember that not all voyages of discovery lead me to where I want to be. This is my theory and I find it useful, for now. (p. 46)

Not worrying about whether you have chosen the single best approach to helping people will help you in your transition from student to professional. Instead, try to remain open to the possibility that there are many ways to help people find their way in the world. Learn as much as you can from those you admire, and integrate the best of what they do into your own style. Allow your clients to be your teachers as you pay close attention to what you do that proves to be most and least helpful to them.

## Politics and Power Struggles

You probably recognize that within your department coalitions have formed based on friendship, professional positions, and common interests. You have no doubt noticed that certain faculty members do not necessarily get along as well as others. You may have also recognized (or perhaps experienced firsthand) how easy it is to become caught in the middle of certain factions that are vying for influence. Students must do their best to stay out of the middle of political battles and stay on friendly terms with as many people as possible. Yet in spite of best intentions, casualties can result when a student gets in the middle of a confrontation between faculty.

Here is one student relating his experience and the results:

> I didn't have that much problem with the academic requirements of my program, nor did I mind the practicum and other skills courses. The greatest difficulty for me was staying out of trouble with a few of my professors. It was understood in my department that if you were close to one person, it meant that you were on the shit list of another. I tried my best to stay on good terms with everyone, but it was impossible. The political battles were ferocious. And whenever a professor was mad at a colleague, sometimes he or she would take it out on the students who were identified most closely with that person. I couldn't wait to get out of school for that very reason. Little did I realize that the best preparation I had for survival in a job was learning how to navigate through the shark-infested waters of people trying to control one another.

Political intrigue is a part of all organizations whether they are universities, schools, agencies, or partnerships. Many different factions form in organizations based on similar agendas that often directly conflict with the agendas of others. It is important to recognize with whom you are most closely affiliating and how to handle those situations in which the affiliations may bring you into conflicts.

Political survival in an employed position depends on your ability to understand and influence your role in the interpersonal dynamics of your organization. This takes more than a simple assessment of who controls things. You must create a place for yourself in such a way that you offend people only when it is intended. Then you need to employ sufficient relationship development skills so that people will either support you or at least not work to undermine you. These are skills you probably developed quite well in the role of student: being deferential without being obsequious, being assertive without being aggressive, acting decisively without being offensive, and being cooperative without appearing overly compliant. They are not new skills but ones that will likely need to be reemphasized as you enter a new professional environment.

## Ethical Dilemmas for Which You Are Unprepared

You probably memorized major portions of your ethical codes and used that information to make hypothetical ethical decisions. Even your limited experiences seeing clients should have provided opportunities to discuss with supervisors certain ethical conflicts. Yet you will still feel confused when you begin to function as a professional counselor in spite of what you learned. Problems you may face could easily include the following:

1. You become aware of a colleague who is inappropriately seductive with his clients. Although you have no evidence that any sexual improprieties have taken place, you have heard from some of his clients that they feel uncomfortable when he asks for hugs. You know that you are supposed to confront this colleague, and then if you do not receive sufficient reassurance, report this behavior to the ethics committee as a possible violation. This sounds direct and easy, but it never seems to be that simple. What do you do when you realize other colleagues know about this behavior but nobody else has done anything about it? Are you supposed to report them as well? Are you missing something of critical importance? Very often what seems to be a direct and simple decision in theory becomes a complex series of personal and professional issues in practice.

2. You have been working with a family for several weeks. They have made remarkable improvement during this time, and you are working toward closure. During one session, the father shamefully discloses that several years earlier, when he still had a drinking problem (he has been sober for over 3 years), he touched his stepdaughter in an inappropriate way while she was sleeping. He claims this happened only one time, and he has felt remorseful ever since. The stepdaughter remembers the incident, discloses that she did feel uncomfortable about it at the time, but because nothing else had happened since then, she had forgotten about it until this moment.

   You are legally and ethically required to report this incident to child protective services. An investigation will follow that might result in tearing the family apart over an incident that occurred several years before. Yet by not reporting the incident you will be held responsible if this behavior or another more serious one were ever repeated. The decision is never so simple as it was in class. Now real people, undergoing real therapy, are going to have their lives directly influenced by the decision you make, and those circumstances up the stakes tremendously. Getting the right answer to get a good grade seems very trivial at such times.

3. You walk into a restaurant to have lunch by yourself. While you are reading the menu, an ex-client of yours asks if she could join you because you are alone. The counseling relationship ended quite successfully a few months previously. On the one hand, you see no harm in sharing a meal with this person, even catching up on what has

been happening in her life. But on the other hand, you are uncertain if this would qualify as a dual relationship.

4. You have a small private practice in which you see people according to their ability to pay. An older man comes to see you desperately needing help, but he has no money to pay for the service. He does, however, grow his own vegetables and wonders if you might accept a bushel of corn in payment for a few sessions. You offer to see him for just a few dollars, aware of the prohibition against bartering. The man's pride will not allow him to do that as he considers it charity. He insists on paying you with something that he grew himself. What do you do?

Each of these cases, plus a hundred more that we could describe, has what might be considered a correct answer for class. The difference in the field is that what is right no longer seems quite so simple when real people are to be affected. You notice others practicing more loosely than you think appropriate. You do not wish to appear as someone who is sanctimonious and elitist, but it is important to maintain the highest professional standards. There is a balance you will need to strike in the field among theory, reality, and your personal convictions that never truly appears in a classroom.

## The Pressures for More and More Education

It is a wonderful feeling to be finished with your education and ready to begin your career as a professional counselor. There is a sense of completion, ending, and fulfillment. Unfortunately, it only lasts until that first day of work in your new job. That is when you realize how much there is still to learn. Agency procedures, the development of local professional relationships, paperwork tasks, and the unique agency models for counseling and prevention will provide the initial learning pressures. Then come the staff meetings in which people are talking about new prevention goals, treatment models, diagnoses, drugs being used, and additional populations that need attention. You will feel as if you never went to school or that the highly rated program you were in did not have a clue as to what was needed in the real world.

The best that quality degree programs can do is to give you a solid foundation that can be applied in many different situations. They can never give you all you need to know. There are too many specifics about particular agencies, locations, client populations, and ways to combine theories than could ever be presented. Add to that the fact that the profession is continually faced with new problems, innovative techniques, emerging client populations, revised funding initiatives, and biochemical interactions that lead to new drugs and procedures. The result is a never-ending flow of new information that demands our attention and—that's right—more education.

## Meeting Continuing Education Demands

The profession faces the pressure for providing continuous learning in three basic ways: supervision, self-study, and workshop training. These are the models for education that have no end to them and emphasize emerging needs. They are designed to keep you abreast of the latest developments and particularly those that are unique to you and your situation. They do not carry a degree or an ending date, but only the promise of helping you better understand yourself, the field of counseling, and your clients, and how they can interact to make you as up-to-date and effective as possible.

Depending on your state licensing requirements, typically you will be required to attend several workshops each year that are designed to keep you up-to-date on new innovations in therapeutic methods as well as on legal and ethical changes.

## Supervision as Education

Supervision provides the mirror you need to develop the effective self-evaluation essential to an appropriate learning plan. You work 8, 10, 12 hours a day and come home beat. Where is there time to sit back with client files and watch tapes of yourself, and to evaluate what you do, what your client does, and how those match what is in the files? Of course, you also need time to read new journals and books that come out so that you can compare yourself to all that new information. Oh yes, do not forget to invite other professionals to your home in order to compare all your findings to theirs. The bottom line is that there is not the time and energy in any of us to do it all, so we have supervisors who help us condense many of these pieces into a relationship designed to improve and understand our own work and compare it to that of another highly qualified professional.

The common anxiety about supervision is the feeling of being judged and potentially being found lacking by another professional. Get over it! Of course, you will be doing things that are not perfect, and you won't be completely current on the overwhelming literature emerging on clients and techniques. That is the normal situation because there is just plain more information available than is possible to consume. The best counselors jump at any chance for supervision so they can step outside their own view of the world and see their ideas and work from a different viewpoint. The most important learning starts with recognizing what we would not normally see ourselves.

## Self-Study

Once professionals recognize their need for specific information or skills, the most common form of education they seek is self-study. That is why there is a huge market in mental health and counseling books, not to mention the myriad of professional journals available. You can explore issues through reading whenever you have the time. You do not need to match your schedule with anyone else's, so your learning can take place morning, noon, or in the middle of the night when you cannot sleep worrying about your difficulties with a client in serious trouble. Effective supervision often points us in the right direction for learning, and then it is up to us to seek the information that will carry us to where we need to be.

An interesting adaptation of the self-study model is the rapidly growing business of home study training provided by professional organizations and profit-making companies. This is a model that allows you to work at home and at the oddest hours that you might choose while also giving you direction, resources, and guidance—for a fee of course. Advertisements abound for opportunities to study almost any mental health topic, take a test, and receive your continuing education units (CEUs). The Internet is responsible for the most dramatic current expansion of this model by allowing much faster access and response time than the traditional postal correspondence courses.

### Workshop Training

After self-study, the most common form of continuing education has become attending workshops on specific topics. A major industry has sprung up around training workshops because of the bombardment of new problems faced by counselors and legal requirements to keep current. Obtaining continuing education is now a requirement for maintaining your professional position. Gone are the days when you could earn a license or certification and simply pay your fees each year. Now you have to spend 10 to 25 hours of involvement per year acquiring officially sanctioned training.

There are generally two ways to acquire your continuing education training credits. The oldest form is to attend a state or national conference at which many presentations are being made on a variety of topics. These conferences, however, have not been able to meet the expanding demands for specific training, so that half-day to 2-day workshops offered all over the country on specific topics have become the most common model for acquiring the training. Whatever combination of models you choose, you can expect to spend some of your own money acquiring your continuing education.

## Being a Professional Counselor

The emphasis throughout this orientation to the profession is to acquaint you with the realities of what you will face in the developmental process of becoming a successful professional counselor. These realities include the ways of gaining admission to the right program and then surviving and flourishing in training. Success in the period from the end of training to your early professional career involves the critical tasks of finding suitable employment and functioning optimally as a professional. This transition from prospective student, to student, and then to practicing counselor is a gradual process that has already begun for you even if you have done no more than read this book and done some of the suggested exercises. The critical point to remember in this process is that counselor education is not something that happens to you, but rather something that you must create yourself with the able assistance of faculty and supervisors.

One of the most exciting aspects of this field is that as your expertise grows, so does your functioning in a number of personal areas. Training to be a counselor involves much more than mastering a set of skills and a base of knowledge. It involves being a student of the world and everything that dwells within it as well as being a participant. Effective counselor training—with sufficient self-initiative on your part—should expand your abilities both to take information and ideas and to give at the same time. Balancing giving and taking is a key to making the most of graduate school and also to your continuing growth as a professional counselor and human being. Graduate school can give you a foundation, professors can get you started, and your clients can be your best teachers; but these gifts are not free, either humanly or economically. You must give of yourself in each case before you can take the growth that is offered. The more you give of your human self, the more you learn about humans and the more you are able to give back to other human beings and to yourself.

## Focus Activities: Making Personal Use of This Chapter

This chapter addresses concerns and issues surrounding the transition from student to employed professional. These changes may seem exciting in some ways and fear producing in others. You must approach the transition and these feelings with open eyes and realistic expectations in order to better cope with and adjust to the change. The following exercises and suggestions should get you thinking about the implications of this transition so that when you are confronted with problem situations, you will be better prepared to react appropriately. We know you must have a thick journal by now, so consider buying another one for this last set of activities and for all you will be learning as you go on as a professional counselor.

1. **What changes do you foresee for yourself in the transition from student to employed professional?** List them in your notebook, and talk with professionals in the field about your concerns. See how they react to your concerns, and find out whether they had any comparable experiences. How did they handle their own difficult transition experiences and what might they have done differently?

2. **List those things you will miss from your student experience in your notebook** (such as the network of peers and relationships you developed, structure, supervision). Leaving graduate school and the role of student produces a sense of loss related to a number of specific issues.

3. **Now list the actions you might take to replace some of the most critical losses in your new setting.** For example, how might you

develop and maintain a new network of peers? How might you make your new situation more structured? How might you ensure that you are getting the supervision you need? People, places, and actions will never be exactly the same, but you can find ways to replace those that are most important to your continued development.

4. **Seek new supportive professionals.** You do not have to disregard your graduate school mentors, but it is helpful to find one in your new environment to provide the immediate support you need. Follow the suggestions offered in this chapter regarding the importance of a mentor and how best to find one that meets your needs. Make some notations on your progress in your notebook.

5. **Learn the system and how to work within the system.** You have struggled long and hard to understand the politics and personalities within the educational system and how to get along within it. Now it is time to learn and adjust to a new system. Talk with your new supervisor and coworkers about what is expected of you and how you can best work within the system. Because you may not always be told the whole picture as a new employee, be sure to keep your eyes and ears open to see what appears to be appropriate behavior. Refer back to the steps about working through conflict and getting along with people offered at the end of chapter 8. Copy them, post them at your desk, remember them, and live by them. These suggestions will not ensure total success in dealing with people, but they give you a framework within which to work and aid you in being perceived as a good worker and a good person.

6. **Be alert for legal and ethical issues for which you feel unprepared as a new counselor.** Be sure to seek supervision and consult your mentor(s) and coworkers, particularly when you are unsure of how to deal with an issue. Remember that it is always better to consult. It is those who think they do—or believe they should—know everything who do the most damage.

7. **Develop your individualized continuing education plan.** Maintain it in a separate notebook or file on your computer. Use the following guidelines in developing your plan to assure your clients, your agency, your licensing or certification board, and yourself that you are keeping current on the issues critical to your work.

   - *List issues that have arisen on which you could use more information or skill development.* One good way to do this is to write down the one to four key issues at the end of each month as you change your calendar. Refer to this list as you consider buying books, seeking workshops, or attending conferences. It will keep your education focused and help you spend your money wisely.
   - *List continuing education requirements of the agency, licensing boards, and certifying bodies to which you need to periodically report.*

- *List the conferences you normally attend and the number of continuing education units you are likely to require there.*
- *List professional organizations and private companies that regularly offer workshops in which you might have interest.* Check those sources regularly.

# References

American Psychiatric Association. (2000). *Diagnostic and statistical manual of mental disorders* (4th ed., text rev.). Washington, DC: Author.

American Psychological Association. (2001). *Publication manual of the American Psychological Association* (5th ed.). Washington, DC: Author.

American Psychological Association. (2003). *Graduate study in psychology 2004* (37th ed.). Washington, DC: Author.

Annandale, N.O., Downs, P., Jensen, D., Mickelson, B., & Tobler, S. (2004). Overcoming dissertation myths and fears. *Counseling Today, 47*(1), 7, 12.

Arredondo, P., Toporek, R., Brown, S. B., Jones, J., Locke, D. C., Sanchez, J., et al. (1996). Operationalization of the multicultural counseling competencies. *Journal of Multicultural Counseling and Development, 24*, 42–78.

Barletta, J. (1995). Studying abroad: To go or not to go, what is the answer? *Counseling Today, 37*(10), 42.

Baruth, K. E. (2002). Seeking more diversity. *Counseling Today, 44*(10), 26, 29, 31.

Davis, R. (2001). Grad student syndrome: The quiet isolator. *Counseling Today, 44*(4), 28, 31.

Dickman, C. (2003). Assignment B—The client experience. *Counseling Today, 46*(8), 27.

Foss, L. (2002). Becoming a group counseling specialist. *Counseling Today, 45*(4), 30, 40.

Henson, K.T. (1999). *Writing for professional publication: Keys to academic and business success.* Boston: Allyn & Bacon.

Hollis, J. W., & Dodson, T. A. (1999). *Counselor preparation 1999–2001: Programs, faculty, trends.* New York: Taylor & Francis.

Igelman, C. (2000). Helping when hurting. *Counseling Today, 43*(5), 25, 28.

Janson, G. R. (1998). A journey to a theory. *Counseling Today, 41*(3), 46.

Kozlowski, K. (2004). Dressing for Diversity 101. *Counseling Today, 46*(10), 9, 21.

Krause, N. (2000). Being 'good enough.' *Counseling Today, 43*(6), 25.

Paladino, D.E. (2002). Self-integration: A counseling student's biracial development. *Counseling Today, 44*(2), 26, 30.

# References

*Peterson's guide to graduate and professional programs, 2005.* (2004). Princeton, NJ: Peterson's.

Protivnak, J. (2003). Counselor preparation: Becoming yourself in a world of conformity. *Counseling Today, 46*(4), 33–34.

Snow, S. (2002). My clients taught me how to be human. *Counseling Today, 45*(6), 20, 24.

Viscott, D. S. (1972). *The making of a psychiatrist.* Greenwich, CT: Fawcett.

Ziff, K. (2002). Success with statistics. *Counseling Today, 44*(7), 24, 29.

# Appendix A
# Professional Counseling Web Sites

## License and Certification Sources

American Psychological Association—www.apa.org/
Council on Rehabilitation Education—www.core-rehab.org/
National Association of Social Workers—www.naswdc.org/
National Board of Certified Counselors—www.nbcc.org

## Program Accreditation Sources

American Association for Marriage and Family Therapy—
    www.aamft.org/index_nm.asp
American Psychological Association—www.apa.org/
Council for Accreditation of Counseling and Related Educational
    Programs—www.counseling.org/cacrep/default.htm
Council on Rehabilitation Education—www.core-rehab.org/
Council on Social Work Education—www.cswe.org
National Council for Accreditation of Teacher Education—
    www.ncate.org/

## Professional Organizations

American College Counseling Association—www.collegecounseling.org/
American Counseling Association—www.counseling.org
American Mental Health Counselors Association—www.amhca.org/
American Psychological Association—www.apa.org/
American Rehabilitation Counseling Association—
    www.counseling.org/site/PageServer?pagename=no_arca
American School Counselor Association—www.schoolcounselor.org/
Association for Adult Development and Aging—www.aadaweb.org/
Association for Assessment in Counseling and Education—
    www.aac.ncat.edu/
Association for Counselor Education and Supervision—
    www.acesonline.net/
Association for Counselors and Educators in Government—
    www.dantes.doded.mil/dantes_web/organizations/aceg/index.htm

Association for Creativity in Counseling—www.aca-acc.org
Association for Gay, Lesbian, and Bisexual Issues in Counseling—
www.aglbic.org/
Association for Multicultural Counseling and Development—www.amcd-
aca.org/amcd/
Association for Specialists in Group Work—www.asgw.org/
Association for Spiritual, Ethical and Religious Values in Counseling—
www.aservic.org/
Chi Sigma Iota—www.csi-net.org
Counselors for Social Justice—www.counselorsforsocialjustice.org/
International Association of Addictions and Offender Counselors—
www.iaaoc.org
International Association of Marriage and Family Counselors—
www.iamfc.com/
National Association of Social Workers—www.naswdc.org/
National Career Development Association—www.ncda.org/
National Employment Counseling Association—
geocities.com/employmentcounseling/www.neca.html

# Appendix B
# Counseling Employment Search Web Sites

The following Web sites will direct you to potential job opportunities for counselors. Please keep the following points in mind as you make use of these sites:

1. Because counseling and related positions can be listed under any number of headings, these sites were selected to give you the widest variety of opportunities for finding positions that match your interests, needs, and skills.
2. Individual sites offer choices for seeking positions either nationally or statewide, but the numbers and types of choices vary for each site.
3. Some states provide comprehensive sites that offer a variety of employment search and career exploration options, but others have much more limited information available.
4. Web sites continue to change more frequently than searchers would like, so keep in mind that the addresses listed here may well have changed. You may then need to look for the site through a search engine like Yahoo or Google.

## Nationwide Counseling Job Search Resources

Chronicle of Higher Education Chronicle Careers
    www.chronicle.com/jobs/
Health Care Job Store (Case managers )
    www.casemanagementjobs.com
Higher Education Jobs
    www.higheredjobs.com/
Human Services Career Network
    www.hscareers.com/
Monster Jobs for Mental Health Counselors
    www.mental.health.counselor.jobs.monster.com/
Social Services Job Site
    www.socialservice.com/

## Statewide Counseling Job Search Resources

Alabama
    www.alabama.gov/working/index.php
Alaska
    www.jobs.state.ak.us/
Arizona
    www.az.gov/webapp/portal/topic.jsp?id=1162

Arkansas
www.arkansasjobs.net/
California
www.ca.gov/state/portal/myca_homepage.jsp
(Then go to "Labor & Employment")
Colorado
www.co.gov/employment
Connecticut
www.ct.gov
(Then go to "Working")
Delaware
www.state.de.us/dhss/main/career.htm
District of Columbia
www.dcop.dc.gov/dcop/site/default.asp
(Then go to "Employment Opportunities")
Florida
taxonomy.myflorida.com/Taxonomy/Business/Florida%20Workforce
Georgia
thejobsite.org/applicants/ApplicantResourceCenter.asp
Hawaii
www.ehawaiigov.org/working/html/resources.html
Idaho
www.dhr.state.id.us/jobseekers.htm
Illinois
www.illinoisskillsmatch.com/
Indiana
www.in.gov/jobs/stateemployment/jobbank.html
Iowa
www.iowa.gov/state/main/busemploy.html
Kansas
www.accesskansas.org/working/index.html
Kentucky
www.kentucky.gov
Louisiana
http://www.louisiana.gov/wps/portal/.cmd/cs/.ce/155/.s/3500/
_s.155/1089/_me/1089/
Maine
www.maine.gov/portal/working/jobs.html
Maryland
www.maryland.gov
Massachusetts
https://web.detma.org/Jobseeker/CM1.ASP
Michigan
www.michigan.gov/mdcs/o,1607,7-147-6876-57453-.,00.html

Minnesota
www.state.mn.us/cgi-bin/portal/mn/jsp/content.do?contentkey=
Employment_in_Minnesota_111402101151&contenttype=EDITORIAL&
hpage=true&agency=NorthStar
Mississippi
www.mississippi.gov/frameset.jsp?URL=http://www.ajb.org/ms/
Missouri
https://www.greathires.org/cgi-bin/jstab.cgi
Montana
www.discoveringmontana.com/work/emp_opp.asp
Nebraska
nebworks.neded.org/jobseekr.htm
Nevada
www.nv.gov/sitemap.htm#EMPLOYMENT
New Hampshire
nh.gov/hr/employment.html
New Jersey
wnjpin.state.nj.us/jobseeker/joblist.htm
New Mexico
www.state.nm.us/spo/#
New York
www.nysegov.com/citguide.cfm?superCat=36&cat=75&content=main
North Carolina
www.dpi.state.nc.us/employment
North Dakota
discovernd.com/employment/jobseekers.html
Ohio
ohio.gov/index.stm
Oklahoma
www.youroklahoma.com/?c=3&sc=49
Oregon
www.emp.state.or.us/emplsvcs
Pennsylvania
www.state.pa.us/papower/taxonomy/taxonomy.asp?DLN=
30600&papowerPNavCtr=%7C30601%7C#30601
Rhode Island
www.ri.gov/browse.php?choice=showpage&pcat=46&mcat=6
South Carolina
www.state.sc.us/jobs/index.html
South Dakota
https://sdworks.state.sd.us/pls/works/works_ss.main
Tennessee
www.jobsearch.org/TN
Texas
www.state.tx.us/category.jsp?language=eng&categoryId=4.2

Utah
  www.utah.gov/working/employment.html
Vermont
  www.vermont.gov/employment-training/opportunities.html
Virginia
  www.vipnet.org/cmsportal/employment_850/
  employment_979/index.html
Washington
  www.wa.nea.org/joblink/default.htm
West Virginia
  www.wv.gov/sec.aspx?pgID=32
Wisconsin
  www.wisconsin.gov/state/employment/app?COMMAND=
  gov.wi.state.cpp.job.command.LoadSeekerHome
Wyoming
  statejobs.state.wy.us/

## School Counseling Job Search Resources

Alabama
  www.alsde.edu/html/JobVacancies.asp?footer=general
Alaska
  www.jobs.state.ak.us/
Arizona
  www.ade.state.az.us/
Arkansas
  www.aeaonline.org/members/edu_jobs.asp
California
  www.edjoin.org
Colorado
  www.co.gov/employment
Connecticut
  www.state.ct.us/sde/employ/jobs-main.htm
Delaware
  www.teachdelaware.com/DefaultDE.cfm?CFID=
  2260596&CFTOKEN=8685a1-23dfc5bb-a4a2-4711-8f08-9628518ab717
District of Columbia
  www.thereview.com/district_of_columbia_teaching_jobs.phtml
Florida
  www.fldoe.org/employment.asp
Georgia
  www.teachgeorgia.org/
Hawaii
  doe.k12.hi.us/personnel/teachinginhawaii.htm
Idaho
  www.idahoeducationjobs.com/

Illinois
  www.isbe.state.il.us/teachers/
Indiana
  ideanet.doe.state.in.us/peer/welcome.html
Iowa
  www.iowajobs.org/
Kansas
  www.ksbe.state.ks.us/cert/cert.html
Kentucky
  www.kentucky.gov
Louisiana
  www.teachlouisiana.net/index.asp
Maine
  www.state.me.us/education/jobs.htm
Maryland
  www.marylandpublicschools.org/msde
Massachusetts
  www.doe.mass.edu/jobs/
Michigan
  mtn.merit.edu/joblistings.html
Minnesota
  www.mnasa.org/Jobsite/jobsitemain.html
Mississippi
  www.mississippi.gov/frameset.jsp?URL=http://www.ajb.org/ms/
Missouri
  www.moteachingjobs.com
Montana
  jobsforteachers.opi.state.mt.us/
Nebraska
  www.nebraskaeducationjobs.com/
Nevada
  www.doe.nv.gov/hrt/resources/dist.html
New Hampshire
  www.neanh.org/jobs/index.cfm
New Jersey
  www.njhire.com/DefaultNJ.cfm?CFID=2260615&CFTOKEN=51c8c31-
  ba9c8026-b90e-45a8-8281-f91d5aacfdf4
New Mexico
  www.state.nm.us/spo/#
New York
  www.highered.nysed.gov/tcert/career/joblinks.htm
North Carolina
  www.dpi.state.nc.us/employment
North Dakota
  www.jobsnd.com/
Ohio
  www.ode.state.oh.us/jobs/

Oklahoma
  www.sde.state.ok.us/home/defaultns.html
Oregon
  www.ous.edu/aca/tchrjobs.htm
Pennsylvania
  www.teaching.state.pa.us/teaching/cwp/view.asp?a=13&Q=
  32441&teachingNav=%7C93%7C109%7C
Rhode Island
  www.ri.gov/browse.php?choice=showpage&pcat=46&mcat=6
South Carolina
  www.cerra.org/
South Dakota
  www.state.sd.us/deca/jobs.htm
Tennessee
  www.state.tn.us/education/mtjobs.htm
Texas
  www.tasanet.org/EducatorsJobBank/ejb.html
Utah
  www.utaheducationjobs.com/
Vermont
  www.vtreap.net/
Virginia
  www.pen.k12.va.us/cgi-bin/disp.pl
Washington
  www.wa.nea.org/joblink/default.htm
West Virginia
  wvde.state.wv.us/jobs/
Wisconsin
  www.dpi.state.wi.us/dpi/jbsintro.html
Wyoming
  onestop.state.wy.us/appview/wjn_home.asp